THE POOR
YE NEED NOT HAVE WITH YOU
Lessons from the War on Poverty

THE POOR
YE NEED NOT HAVE WITH YOU
Lessons from the War on Poverty

Robert A. Levine

The M.I.T. Press
Cambridge, Massachusetts, and London, England

Contents

Contents

Acknowledgments

Many people have reviewed the material contained here and offered advice. The viewpoints and factual statements, however, are fully my own responsibility and should not be blamed on anyone else. There are people on the following list who would probably like to disown the whole thing, but they helped and are therefore doomed to have their assistance acknowledged.

Three people went through a first draft in exquisite detail and provided many many important and useful comments. These are Thomas Glennan, James Sundquist, and Walter Williams. In addition, my wife Carol went far beyond her conjugal duties and read through the manuscript twice.

The people who read one or another version of the manuscript entirely or in part and provided useful, if sometimes ignored, advice include Donald Baker, Hyman Bookbinder, John Evans, Hans Heymann, William Jacobson, Herbert Kramer, Jonathan Lane, Paul Levine, Sar Levitan, James Lyday, Selma Mushkin, Clifford Parker, Anthony Partridge, Rhona Pavis, Lillian Regelson, Mary Robinson, Ralph Smith, and Prudence Steiner.

Particular thanks are due to Joseph Kershaw of the Ford Foundation, who not only administered in the most helpful manner the grant under which this book was written but also provided comments based on his experience in the Office of Economic Opportunity. Thanks are also due to The Urban Institute of Washington, D.C., which housed me, and to

Acknowledgments

William Gorham, the President, and the members of the Institute, who lived with me during the process.

Finally, I owe real gratitude to Mrs. Mary Jackson, my secretary, who took it all down, typed it all up, and told me when I was wrong.

THE POOR
YE NEED NOT HAVE WITH YOU
Lessons from the War on Poverty

1
Prologue
on Problem Solving

On the night of January 23, 1968, I spoke at a banquet of the Junior Chamber of Commerce of Bethlehem, Pennsylvania, on "Poverty, Provocation, and Problem Solving." My contention then was that the United States was in danger of irreversible political and social polarization because political views were increasingly being based on the desire to *punish* the people held responsible for causing problems rather than on any attempt to *solve* the problems. We were becoming more concerned with political action that made us feel good because "we had gotten even" than we were with political solutions.

On returning to my hotel room that night and flipping on the TV news, I learned, as did most Americans at the same time, of the capture of the U.S.S. *Pueblo* by the North Koreans. At the time there seemed no relationship between the subjects I had spoken about and the incident in the Sea of Japan. More than a year later, it has become obvious that the *Pueblo* incident is very relevant to the differences between problem solving and the politics of punishment and provocation.

For the *Pueblo* incident marks clearly the coming of age of the problem-solving style in the international relations of the United States. The crucial aspect of the *Pueblo* incident is what did not happen. We did *not* try to recapture the *Pueblo;* although the Navy apparently had thoughts in this direction, they were cut off sharply in Washington. We did not send paratroops in to try to get the crew back. We did not bomb anything in retaliation. What we did was to recognize early that once the ship with its intelligence documents and equipment had been captured, the only real objective remaining for U.S. policy was to get the crew back. Through a year of painstaking negotiations we tried to do just that — to solve the real problem — and by the end of the year we had done it, using what must surely be one of the oddest documents in the history of international affairs, an agreed-upon confession repudiated in advance by agreement. But the oddness is not the point; the sticking to the solution of the problem is.

In domestic affairs and in the antipoverty effort in particular, we have not yet reached this stage. Certainly we talk a lot about problem solving — more and more, recently. Certainly the United States made a major and visible move in this direction when President Nixon abandoned the simple "whodunnit" solutions of his campaign (e.g., his acceptance speech at the Republican convention, in which the crime problem was to be solved by getting a new Attorney General) and, having been elected on November 5, set out on November 6 to look hard and afresh at each problem. In some aspects of the War on Poverty in particular the Nixon Administration went rapidly ahead of President Johnson's; in some it retreated. In any case, the dominant style was that of problem solving.

Nonetheless, in domestic affairs, in matters of race and matters of poverty, the "whodunnit" Politics of Provocation still plays too large a role.

The Politics of Provocation is the style of a petulant child who acts the way he feels like acting, without regard to consequences, in order to provoke a parent or a playmate. It is forming opinions on the basis of *whom* we like or dislike rather than *what* might or might not work. It might be called the Politics of Revenge, but this would dignify it more than it deserves. A better description is given by a more childish term. It is the politics of getting even, of having the chip knocked off our shoulders. If we don't like the poor, we get even with them. If we don't like the Pentagon, we get even with it. Then we feel better because we have shown someone how angry we are. Whether the good of the country or even our own personal viewpoints are advanced by an action is irrelevant so long as the action makes us feel good.

The Problem-Solving style is the reverse of this. It measures the rightness of an act by the broader consequences of the act. If all the consequences are good, then the action is unequivocally good, and vice versa. It is the rule of reason in politics. It is the rule that leads us to weigh what we are doing or advocating according to the effects it has rather than how it makes us feel. I am not saying that the end always justifies the means. The nature of the means is part of the effect to be weighed. But I am saying that, if the end doesn't always justify the means, the means *never* justifies the end. And the Politics of Provocation never goes beyond the means.

The Politics of Provocation today is most often directed against "them," the members of another race. In the words of the Kerner Commission on Civil Disorders, "Our nation is moving toward two societies, one black, one white."[1] The Kerner Report discusses this problem mainly in terms of its economic and social roots, but it is also a problem of the Politics of Provocation. They — the Negroes — are moving too fast. Look at the Black Panthers and the militant black students. It sure makes you feel good all over to hate the Panthers and the students. Of course the Panthers and the students have adopted the same style of thought. Whites are "honkies"; there is no difference between any of them and George Wallace. "They" — white society as a whole — murdered Martin Luther King. This is the Politics of Provocation turned back on us — but we started it.

Actually, of course, who started it is at the core of the Politics of Provocation but is completely irrelevant. And yet the stress on punishing those responsible is pervasive. And it is by no means confined to the unsophisticated or those who try to exploit the unsophisticated. Take the Kerner Report itself, a magnificent and necessary document as a whole; its highlighted accusation of "white racism" directed much of the subsequent debate in precisely the wrong direction. That the charge is true — that racism still pervades white America — cannot be doubted. That white racism comes as near as we can get to a *first* first cause for our current racial troubles also cannot be doubted, considering the fact that whites have ruled for our entire history. But only if the racism charge directs

1. National Advisory Commission on Civil Disorders, *Report* (New York: Bantam, 1968), p. 1.

attention to the real obstacles to black equality, will it have served a crucial purpose.

Unfortunately, however, the racism referred to by the Kerner Commission is ill-defined, and the charge has directed attention not to problems and obstacles but to guilt. This has had two unfortunate results. It has provided an emotional and intellectual crutch for black racism, reinforcing those tendencies of all individuals and groups to blame the other guy and ignore the necessary changes in themselves. Thus such phenomena as black student intransigence — "These demands are nonnegotiable" — and black defense of the indefensible — murder of policemen doing their duty — are traceable in part back to the interpretation of the Kerner charge which places guilt. To some blacks, placing guilt on whites seems to imply absolution from guilt, future as well as past, and leads inevitably to a spiral of provocation — Cleaver to Reagan to Chance.

Perhaps even more important, the accusation of white racism in the Kerner Report has led many whites to attack the race problem at the point where change is most difficult and least likely, attitudes rather than behavior. Certainly it is a noble spectacle when many whites examine their consciences for signs of racism. It is slightly less noble when each examines the consciences of others, but in any case, whatever happened to the idea that *behavior* can be changed by law and other forms of social action even when *attitudes* cannot? It is discrimination, discriminatory action, that suppresses Negroes in the United States, and the success of many civil rights laws has indicated that such discrimination can be changed. Fair employment laws, which have worked, voting rights laws, which have worked, antilynching laws, which have worked, even the school desegregation decision, which has worked in many parts of the country, have all changed behavior without (or in advance of) changing attitudes. Indeed, some crucial points of racist behavior stem from nonracist attitudes. Some people really are afraid of falling property values, job displacement, and so forth. Proper social action could calm such fears and bring out latent goodwill.

The point is that by continuing in this direction of solving the problems of discriminatory behavior we can make progress far faster than we can against the attitudes that cause it. Anti-Semitic behavior has long since ceased to be a problem for American Jews in spite of the fact that anti-Semitic attitudes persist.

Prologue on Problem Solving

These observations serve as an introduction to the New York City school dispute. What began as a difference of degree as to the scope of decentralization of a school system obviously too large to be manageable, in time became a confrontation between teachers' union and community and finally became a sharp racial conflict with accusations of anti-Semitism and anti-Negroism being tossed back and forth in a remarkable display of the fruits of the Politics of Provocation. Now both the accusations are accurate; anti-Semitism and anti-Negroism exist, in distressingly large and increasing measure. Furthermore, by the standards of the Politics of Provocation, both are justified. That is, anti-Semitism can be "justified" because Jewish teachers have treated Negro students and parents badly — not most Jewish teachers, but that can be slurred over; anti-Negroism can be "justified" because Negro community school boards have treated Jewish teachers unfairly — not all boards and certainly not all Negroes, but that can be slurred over. Each "justifies" the other, and each justification widens the split. Nor is this split merely an inevitable result of group dynamics; it is exacerbated by people who would certainly subscribe to a paper consensus on problem solving. One recent book made a very convincing case that the Ocean Hill-Brownsville community school board deliberately decided to confront the union and the city Board of Education by "transferring" teachers illegally in the spring of 1968.[2] But an earlier account detailed actions of the union and the city Board over the past ten years that would "justify" the community board action just as surely as that community action "justified" the subsequent illegal strikes of the union.[3] The *first* cause is undoubtedly slavery, but what is the relevance or utility of looking for justifications?

What I am saying, then, is that the common belief that, in order to solve a problem, we must go directly to the root cause is not necessarily so. Although we have no cure for cancer, arresting it is still a very useful activity. Similarly, with social problems, it is frequently annoying symptoms or more tractable intermediate causal factors with which we should deal.

In any case, racial questions in the United States are still pervaded far too much by the Politics of Provocation, and not only in the minds and acts of the benighted. Solutions will be possible only when whites, in-

2. Martin Mayer, *The Teacher's Strike* (New York: Harper & Row, 1968).
3. David Rogers, *110 Livingston Street* (New York: Random House, 1968).

cluding some leading intellectuals, realize that the thrust toward black power and black identity exists and when blacks realize that 10 percent of the population is a minority that is bound to lose without obtaining the support of large elements of the 90 percent majority.

What about the closely related issue that this book is all about? What about the War on Poverty and the role of problem solving for the War on Poverty? Poverty is by no means a black problem. Fewer than a third of the poor are Negroes. But the race problem is to a very great extent a poverty problem, and this is at the heart of what troubles this nation. Let me lay a factual basis for estimating some consequences of antipoverty actions.

The first and the most important point is that even a quick look can convince us that poverty as it is currently defined in the United States is a completely solvable problem. If we were to provide every last poor family and individual in the United States with enough income to bring them above the level of poverty, the required outlay would be less than $10 billion a year. I do not propose that we end poverty this way — money payments are needed, but so are other programs — but I use this $10 billion of additional spending as a measure of the magnitude of the problem. Ten billion dollars is a lot of money in absolute terms, but even so, we are very rich in the United States, and $10 billion is slightly less than 1.5 percent of our Gross National Product. This problem, which causes us so much anguish, is so trivial that its size can be measured as 1.5 percent of GNP, one-third of the normal annual increase of GNP. On the face of it and in hard numbers, this is a problem of a size that can be solved. Poverty in the United States differs from world poverty by the fact that American poverty is a small fraction embedded in a mass of wealth, whereas American wealth is a small fraction embedded in a mass of world poverty. World poverty is not a problem that can be solved as quickly as we want.

So we have a solvable problem, but it is not solvable by the Politics of Provocation. Let's look at one major example — Public Assistance. If there is one point about Public Assistance on which all Americans agree, it is that it is a rotten system. On the one hand, it degrades recipients of welfare payments without providing sufficient support. On the other hand, it is in the aggregate costly, and the cost is growing rapidly and frighteningly.

6

Why? There are many reasons for the rottenness of the current welfare system, but let me concentrate on the single major factor. Welfare as it exists today has built-in incentives for its own perpetuation and acceleration.

Until the passage by Congress of the 1967 Social Security and Public Assistance amendments, welfare recipients were taxed 100 percent on any earnings they might receive. If a recipient family's need level were computed say at $2,500 (and in most states actual welfare payments are less than minimum need computed by the states themselves), then the family's annual welfare payment might be as munificently high as $2,500. If by part-time or low-skilled work family members were to earn $1,000 a year, then that $1,000 would reduce their welfare payments by an equal $1,000, leaving $1,500. The total income of the family would remain at $2,500. In other words, to earn would gain the family nothing — a 100 percent tax.

Under the 1967 law, we graciously reduced this tax rate to 66⅔ percent. In addition to a small fixed dollar sum for work expenses, families on relief may now retain a full one-third of earnings. A 66⅔ percent tax bracket thus now applies to two income categories: those making less than $2,000 or so a year; and those making more than $100,000 a year. Rough justice, perhaps. It seems likely that if we look at welfare as a problem to be solved and we want to end the welfare system, then we ought to provide a little more incentive for people to get off welfare through their own earning power.

Second, the current welfare system is primarily for broken families, for children without a father in the house. What an incentive to break up the family and get the father out of the house. An unemployed man who cannot support his family can support them by leaving home so that his wife can go on "the welfare." And the consequence of such a broken home is a high possibility that the next generation will also be on welfare. The rule of reason would suggest that to end the system, we should try to keep the family together rather than trying to break it up.

Finally, there is the degrading welfare investigation, characterized by looking under the bed and checking the relatives. This is to make sure that nobody slips through the system who might be supported in some other way, that no sinner takes advantage of the system and just goes ahead and lives on the $2,500 or less when he could earn or get income in

7

another way. This is the Politics of Provocation with a vengeance. Who cares that the system required by such investigation is self-perpetuating, degrading, and calculated to create an atmosphere of hopelessness and thus perpetuate itself? What difference does that make so long as we can catch those last two people who might chisel on welfare if we did not spend hundreds of dollars investigating them? We could, of course, let them declare their assets and income by affidavit and attack chiseling through a sampling process, and this is finally being tried experimentally. It is precisely what we do on the income tax, and in spite of the fact that this country loses far far more money by tax chiseling than by welfare chiseling, nobody suggests an income tax investigation like the welfare investigation. Taxes is "us"; welfare is "them."

Now let's face it. Under an affidavit system of welfare someone would inevitably live on the dole while sitting on his porch and fishing; someone would cheat, just as in the tax system. Nonetheless, an affidavit system would be cheaper and far less self-perpetuating than the investigation system. But the Politics of Provocation dictates that it is more important to catch that last sinner than to start doing away with the whole bloody thing.

The Problem-Solving style can cut through this mess. It would dictate a simple system of income support, a national system of income support, a noninvestigatory system of income support, and, most important, a system that would increase the incentive to work rather than trying to force people to work regardless of the consequence, a system that would encourage families to stay together instead of encouraging them to break up.

The so-called Negative Income Tax is one such system, characterized by its preservation of the financial incentive to work by "taxing" away only a part of a poor family's income support payment as total family income increases through increased earnings. The unfortunate name, "Negative Income Tax," stems from the fact that as family incomes *above* poverty levels decrease toward poverty, less and less is paid in "regular" income taxes, until, near the poverty level, no tax is paid. The "Negative Tax" extends this relationship below the poverty level, by having those below the zero tax point pay less than zero, that is, negative taxes, or positive payments. (For a detailed description see Chapter 6, page 204.)

In any case, the crucial position of such a system in an overall anti-poverty strategy is one theme of this book.

It is probably easy for most liberal intellectuals to subscribe to the foregoing description of welfare problems and solutions. Yet many liberal intellectuals have their own hangups that get in the way of problem solving, hangups frequently left over from the attitudes of the 1930s.

For example, many liberal intellectuals still dislike business so much that they would exclude it from the antipoverty effort.[4] Yet it seems doubtful that the program can work without business. Business is essential for two reasons: The marketplace can substitute a workable form of decentralization for immense and unworkable centralization, and in one central field, job training, business is where the expertise is.

Let me make clear that I do not think business is more moral than government bureaucracy or less moral. I don't even think that business is more efficient, man-for-man, than government bureaucracy. As a matter of fact, I am not even sure that business is less bureaucratic or less political than government. But business does have one thing going for it. It has the price and market system.

Government works by setting and enforcing rules and doing so in vast and intricate detail. That is the trouble with the welfare system. The federal welfare law sets some rules, the state welfare systems set some subrules, county welfare interprets these, and then they are left for final interpretation by social workers. Rules on top of rules within rules — how could it possibly work? A recent book about the Vietnam War gives an example of the transmission of orders from high echelons to lower ones:

> "Stop burning down those houses!" [the Lieutenant-Colonel] told his captains by radio. "There's no VC in those houses!" The captains told their lieutenants don't burn those houses if there's no VC in them — the lieutenants told their sergeants if you burn those houses there had better be VC in them — the sergeants told their men go and burn those houses, there may be VC in them — and Morton kept striking his C-ration matches. Or something or other — anyhow,

4. See, for example, Michael Harrington, "The Social Industrial Complex," *Harper's Magazine,* November 1967, pp. 55–60.

soon there wasn't a Vietnamese farmhouse that wasn't just a layer of smoldering black dust.[5]

That is the story of the hand-me-down rules that government must live by.

Business is no better morally and no more efficient man-for-man, but the market system allows business to decentralize effectively. Instead of setting and enforcing rules, business can work by setting incentives to achieve the proper results and letting the incentives enforce the rules through the self-interest of the participants in the system. In an over-simplified model, Junior Executive X does what the business wants to do because there is a Christmas bonus in it. The A Corporation does what the economy expects it to do because there is a profit in it. Thousands of Junior Executives and thousands of businesses follow their interest instead of following a detailed set of rules, and it works — not perfectly, but it works. It works well enough, in fact, that after 50 years of bureaucratic enforcement of the rules even the Soviet Union is beginning to follow the price system. There is no substitute for incentives motivating decentralized decision making.

Left to itself, business will not necessarily move in socially desirable directions. But government can adjust incentives through subsidies, tax credits, and similar devices to induce such movement and take advantage of the power of decentralization. In the antipoverty field, this has just begun. Chapter 5 discusses the Job Opportunities in the Business Sector (JOBS) program, in which government subsidy payments are provided to business to train the poor. The program is not working perfectly — business incentives are complex — but it is working and on a large scale. Of course, some of the subsidy payments to business for training will be "wasted" in the same sense that some payments under a rational welfare system will be "wasted" by going to people sitting on their porches and fishing. Some part of the dollars spent under *any* simple system will inevitably be classed as that sort of waste. And such waste will certainly irritate the Politicians of Provocation. The provokable Politicians of the right will be appalled by paying some money to some person who could go and earn money himself if he would just get off his rocking chair. The

5. John Sack, *M* (New York: New American Library, 1967), p. 159.

provokable Politicians of the left will be irritated by paying some money
to some business that is carrying on sham training. But that is part of the
system, and waste of this sort may be necessary to make the system work
at all, for the alternative to the shady business practice is the impossibly
bureaucratic job program. A simple comparison of alternative consequences dictates that getting rid of the unworkable systems is far more
important than catching all the sinners.

That is what this book is about: not the horrors of poverty or the
nobility of the poor, or on the other hand the unconscionable ingratitude
of the poor or overreaction of the blacks that makes it so difficult for *us*
to help *them*. Rather, it is poverty as a problem that, at least if it is defined in narrow economic terms, is obviously solvable. The next few chapters question these narrow economic terms, but nonetheless the problem
is tractable as compared with many others (e.g., world population control, death).

But poverty is tractable only if treated as a problem. The phraseol-
ogy of the War on Poverty has been occasionally criticized because of
the military implications of words like war, strategy, battle, and weapons.
At least it is better to think of the antipoverty effort as a war than as a
crusade, in which any setback is a victory for evil, and the moral im-
perative is to defeat the perpetrators of evil rather than to solve the
problem.

2
Who Are the Poor?
The Unimportance of Precise Definition

Who *should* be helped by antipoverty programs and indeed what the precise objectives of these programs should be are not matters for analytical determination. Programs are set up in law for purposes intended by lawmakers, and in theory at least these legislative objectives are the "proper" ones by definition. The role of analysis should then be relegated to finding the best means for achieving the objectives.

The difficulty of keeping to such pure theory, however, is illustrated by Section 2 of the Economic Opportunity Act of 1964, "Findings and Declaration of Purpose."

> Although the economic well-being and prosperity of the United States have progressed to a level surpassing any achieved in world history, and although these benefits are widely shared throughout the Nation, poverty continues to be the lot of a substantial number of our people. The United States can achieve its full economic and social potential as a nation only if every individual has the opportunity to contribute to the full extent of his capabilities and to participate in the workings of our society. It is therefore, the policy of the United States to eliminate the paradox of poverty in the midst of plenty in this Nation by opening to everyone the opportunity for education and training, the opportunity to work, and the opportunity to live in decency and dignity. It is the purpose of this Act to

strengthen, supplement, and coordinate efforts in furtherance of that policy.

Although for the most part this statement specifies the objective as the elimination of poverty, neither this preamble nor any other part of the law defines poverty. And, what may be even more important, the antipoverty objective is intertwined throughout with the objective of creating equal opportunity for all. The distinction between antipoverty and equal opportunity is not a trivial one. Most definitions of *poverty* have to do with low income, but unequal *opportunity* for racial and other minorities exists all along the income distribution, including portions far above any conventional definition of poverty. An educated and relatively well-off Negro, for example, typically earns much less than an equally educated white. The tension between the antipoverty and the equal opportunity objectives provides one of the themes of this chapter and the next.

Nonetheless, the official interpretation of the Economic Opportunity Act as the programs have been run thus far has clearly put the primary emphasis on the attack on low-income poverty. Who then are the poor to be helped by this War? In 1964 at the time of the passage of the Economic Opportunity Act and through the beginning of 1965, the conventional definition of poverty, as used by the President's Council of Economic Advisers for statistical measurement of the extent of poverty included all those in families with annual incomes below $3,000 a year. This definition presented two difficulties. First, because it had no explicit rationale, it was completely arbitrary and therefore led to some difficulties for statistical measurement, and to far greater difficulties when the poverty line began to be used as a guide to program eligibility. Second, the $3,000 line did not allow for variations in the needs of a family consequent upon variations in the size of the family. Primarily for the latter reason the Council of Economic Advisers itself and OEO superseded the $3,000 line in 1965 with the poverty definition that has been in use since then, the definition designed by Mollie Orshansky of the Social Security Administration,[1] based on minimum food budgets for families of different sizes as determined by the Department of Agriculture. The food

1. Mollie Orshansky, "Counting the Poor: Another Look at the Poverty Profile," *Social Security Bulletin,* January 1965, pp. 3–29.

budgets, repriced annually, are multiplied by three in order to get poverty lines for families of different sizes. The rationale behind the factor of three is that for lower-income families, food ordinarily takes up about one-third of family expenditures.

The poverty lines so designed are obviously austere, based as they are on an allowance for food per family member of 75 cents a day (1966 prices). In 1966, the poverty line thus estimated came to $3,335 for a nonfarm family of four with a $500–$600 adjustment for fewer or for more family members. Until 1969, poverty lines for farm families were drawn at 70 percent of those for similar-sized nonfarm families because it was assumed, perhaps questionably, that farm families can grow some of their own food. In 1969, the farm/nonfarm ratio was raised to 85 percent.

The Orshansky line corrected one difficulty with a simple $3,000 line; it allowed for variation in needs with variation of family size. The other difficulty remained; in spite of being anchored to an externally created concept — food needs — the new line was as arbitrary as the old. Neither the exact food budgets nor the factor of three can be applied across the board with any precision. Nor, obviously, can we say that at $3,334 a family of four is poor and at $3,336 it is not. (This arbitrariness is well recognized by Miss Orshansky as well as others. She regularly protests the misuse of her poverty line as a doctrine and program guide, instead of the statistical convenience she intended.)

Nonetheless, because an arbitrary convenience for measurement has been needed, the Orshansky line has been used. From the very beginning the line has been criticized by many people from many viewpoints. Perhaps the first sharp criticism was made by Rose Friedman,[2] who argued that in fact food and other needs were substantially less than estimated by Orshansky. Since the argument was essentially for one arbitrary concept against another, it was difficult to answer (that is, arbitrary definitions come fairly close to being matters of taste, which are not to be disputed) but easy to ignore. It was ignored. Another early criticism came from the Department of Agriculture, which objected to the presumed lower food budgets for farmers being multiplied by the same factor of

2. Rose Friedman, *Poverty: Definitions and Perspectives* (Washington, D.C.: American Enterprise Institute for Public Policy Research, 1965).

three as the higher budgets for nonfarmers, since this assumed that farmers could produce 30 percent of their own housing and other needs, as well as food. Since neither side in this argument had any data to speak of on nonfood costs, the argument raged heavily without conclusion.

Perhaps more important than the arguments that accepted the single income-poverty line concept but argued over the specific numbers were those which challenged the concept. Some of these accepted the economic "command over resources" basis of the dollar concept but asked for a greater degree of sophistication in using it; others challenged the economic basis itself. In the first category came suggestions for supplementing the count of the numbers of poor people below the poverty line with a dollar figure measuring the total amount of money it would take to bring all these up to the poverty line. Later, others, notably Professor Harold Watts of the University of Wisconsin, suggested a weighted concept whereby dollar gaps below the poverty line and dollar surpluses over the poverty line were both measured but were weighted differently, so that incomes far below the poverty line were counted most heavily but even incomes moderately above the poverty line counted somewhat in measurement although not very heavily.[3]

A different sort of economic criticism of current poverty lines stems from the argument that poverty is a relative concept rather than an absolute one and that the poverty line should increase with increases in median family incomes. At the limit this argument becomes nonsense, that in order to abolish poverty we must get rid of the lower fifth of the income distribution. More realistic is the contention that, since the concept of poverty has changed over the years, the advent of an antipoverty program should not freeze the poverty line at the level of the time of initiation of the program while average incomes continue to rise.

One point should be made immediately about this contention. Although it is sometimes claimed that the relative poverty concept implies

3. Harold Watts, *An Economic Definition of Poverty*, University of Wisconsin Institute for Research on Poverty, Discussion Paper No. 5–67. This is probably the best discussion of the issues involved in various sorts of income poverty lines. A number of publications including Watts's tabulate the incidence of poverty according to different concepts; see, for example, Resources Management Corporation Paper UR-062, *Economics of Poverty: Methods and Measurements*, February 19, 1969. These tabulations are not repeated here because I feel that problems of measurement have been overstressed already and that the differences are not crucially important or relevant.

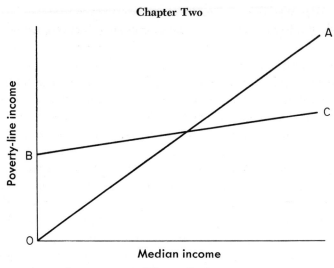

Figure 1
Relationship of Poverty Threshold and Median Income

that poverty thresholds should rise at the *same* rate as median income, it does not necessarily do so. Figure 1 illustrates why. In order to have the poverty line rise as fast as median incomes, the relationship between the two must be represented by a line through the origin, *OA* in the figure. But *some* relativity between median income and the conventional poverty line might as easily be represented by *BC*, in which the poverty line is a combination of a "true" minimum needs bundle represented by *OB* and some relationship to median income represented by the slope of *BC*. In fact, some sketchy evidence exists that something like *BC* has represented the conventional definition of poverty in the United States over a long period of time. That is, the standard has risen as median income has increased but has risen less fast and has had a minimum-needs component as well as a relative component.

Even *BC*, however, would indicate a year-to-year change in the conventional standard of poverty (other than the year-to-year price adjustment already included), and such a change has not been built into the current definition. It might be, but then another arbitrary factor, the rate of increase, would have to be added to the already arbitrary level of poverty. For this reason, it seems preferable to use a level standard, realizing that this may present certain problems in interpreting year-to-year poverty numbers. That is, poverty will decrease more rapidly over time as measured by the level standard than it would by the rising standard. In any case, which is the "true" rate is not the crucial question. The crucial question is whether poverty would have changed at a *different* rate than it did, given different public policies. And this question can be answered as easily using the level standard as it can using the rising standard.

More fundamental than suggestions for changes in the economic measure of poverty are the criticisms that argue that poverty is not an economic concept at all and should be measured by the number of people in families possessing a bundle of economic, social, and psychological attributes sometimes summarized as "the culture of poverty." That there is in this alternative definition of poverty some validity — that is, some relation to what is conventionally and legislatively meant by poverty — is undeniable. But because nobody has been able to get any useful measures of the number of people possessing the bundle of "poverty attributes," the concept has not been made operational. It should be clear in any case, however, that sticking to an economic definition of poverty does not by itself emphasize economic programs as against noneconomic ones; the economic definition is just a definition, and once the causes of economically defined poverty are analyzed, the bases for poverty and suggested program solutions turn out to be only slightly less sociopsychological than they would be under the culture definition.

What we finally come to is that the decisions about how to define poverty and the lines of definition are arbitrary; none is correct, but some are more convenient for various uses. And because of their arbitrary nature a good deal of care should be taken with the uses to which they are put. Specifically, to the extent that these definitions are used for measurement — of general scope, intergroup distribution, and changes of the poverty population — and so long as we stick to the antipoverty rather than the equal opportunity objectives of the program, the current measures are about as good as any alternatives. The kinds of modest changes in the poverty line that have been suggested would make little difference in the relative distribution or the changes over time of poverty. It seems to me to be futile to spend major efforts in redesigning what is essentially an accepted but arbitrary concept. The Orshansky line annually adjusted for price change has served adequately since 1965 to measure change and to estimate the incidence of poverty in various groups, and there seems little reason to create and backdate a new series.

There is one problem, however, that is all too frequently swept under the rug. These poverty lines, although designed initially for statistical counting are in fact used also for program guides; OEO in particular has directed that, for most programs, recipients be below the designated poverty lines. Even though in some cases these directives have been ignored, for many programs they are honored, and they certainly do tend to deify an arbitrary set of numbers intended for other purposes. Yet, so long as the primary objective of the War on Poverty is the conquest of poverty rather than the equalization of opportunity all along the line, some arbitrary ceiling on what is meant by poverty is needed in order to keep programs from drifting upward toward a clientele that is easier to reach than the truly poor but is less in need. The difficulty of keeping antipoverty programs focused on the truly poor can be illustrated by the fact that the farm price support program was generally accepted by the public in the 1930s as, in large measure, an antipoverty program; now it is generally acknowledged to be a program almost entirely for the well-off farmer. Similarly, the Farm Security Administration, which was a strong antipoverty agent in the 1930s, has become the Farmers Home Administration, administering primarily to lower-middle-class farmers. Slum clearance programs, sold on an antipoverty basis, have done much for luxury and middle-income housing but little for the poor. The focus moves off poverty very easily, and some limit is needed to keep antipoverty programs targeted on the poor.

An analogy to this need for an arbitrary lid on the operational as well as the statistical definition of poverty can be taken from the history of the nonuse of tactical nuclear weapons in warfare. In the early 1960s, a stone thrown into the proper areas of the Pentagon could stir up half a dozen or more Air Force and Army Generals to argue that tactical nuclear weapons were being made that were much less powerful than many nonnuclear weapons and the distinction between nonnuclear and nuclear weapons should thus be abolished.

Nuclear weapons, it was argued, should be used in warfare simply because they were more efficient than their conventional counterparts — more power for a pound. The argument that won out, however, was that the admittedly arbitrary line between nuclear and conventional weapons was a distinction that already existed in the minds of political and military decision makers; once this line was broken, all differences would become differences of degree, and there would be no other accepted line at which escalation could be stopped on the way to the megaton. Similarly, the arbitrary Orshansky distinction between the poor and nonpoor is one that exists in the minds of decision makers, and if programs are allowed to break this line, they can soon be targeted far above any true poverty levels as the farm programs of the New Deal have been. Thus, although the existing poverty lines are arbitrary both for statistical measurement and for operational purposes, some arbitrary lines are needed, and these serve well simply because they already exist as a convention. To reopen an argument as to whether they are "correct" seems a fruitless exercise.

Who then are the poor as measured by these arbitrary lines? To begin with, they constituted some 25.9 million Americans in 1967, a figure down sharply from 34.3 million in 1964, when the explicitly named War on Poverty began, and from some 40 million when John F. Kennedy became President. Because of the arbitrary nature of the poverty lines, these numbers have no meaning in themselves, but the year-to-year changes are meaningful because they would have occurred and been visible under *any* system of measurement, even (to a lesser degree) the annually increasing one.

Similarly, it is meaningful to use poverty lines to measure the relative distribution of the poor. Tabulations of poverty typically recognize the racial factor, and Tables 1 to 3 categorize by race as well as by other characteristics. A striking fact brought out by these tables is that poverty among whites declined at a faster rate than among nonwhites from 1964 to 1965, but the situation was reversed sharply beginning in 1965. In fact, although the data are not shown in these tables, this marked a change in a much longer trend; from 1959 to 1965 poverty consistently decreased more rapidly among whites, but from 1966 to 1967 the differential in favor of nonwhites that had begun the previous year accelerated.

Table 1 adds to the racial categorization, groupings by age. The

Table 1
Poverty by Age and Race 1964–1966
(thousands of persons)

Age	Total				White				Nonwhite			
	1964	1965	1966	% Incidence 1966	1964	1965	1966	% Incidence 1966	1964	1965	1966	% Incidence 1966
0–5	5,758	5,337	4,508	19.0	3,486	3,128	2,629	13.2	2,272	2,209	1,879	49.3
6–15	8,215	7,915	7,367	18.5	5,067	4,733	4,496	13.2	3,148	3,182	2,871	51.0
16–21	2,982	2,947	2,746	14.5	1,988	1,914	1,766	10.7	994	1,033	980	39.4
22–54	9,237	8,261	7,415	9.7	6,360	5,500	5,012	7.4	2,877	2,761	2,403	29.1
55–65	2,696	2,620	2,536	14.7	2,098	2,055	1,925	12.3	598	565	611	38.1
65+	5,364	5,144	5,396	29.9	4,615	4,370	4,639	28.0	749	774	757	52.0
Total	34,252	32,224	29,968	15.5	23,614	21,700	20,467	12.0	10,638	10,524	9,501	40.9

Source: Office of Economic Opportunity

table indicates that a disproportionate number of the poor are aged, over 65; the incidence of poverty (proportion of a given group that is poor) among the aged is almost double the overall average. In the sharp drop of poverty between 1964 and 1966, all age groups were involved except for the old, among whom the number of poor actually increased slightly. But the table also brings out one other interesting fact—a much larger portion of the white poor are aged (23 percent) than the nonwhite poor (only 8 percent). Among whites, people who have lived above the poverty line decline into poverty with lost jobs and inadequate pensions as they age; among nonwhites, poverty is a lifetime problem.

Table 2 looks at poverty in another way, by location. It shows that the bulk of poverty, more than one-half in 1966, is in Standard Metropolitan Statistical Areas (SMSAs); this figure rose above the 50 percent mark in that year. It shows that rural poverty, farm and nonfarm, has been going down sharply, and although this has been due in part to migration of the poor from rural areas, this migration has not been enough to increase big city poverty, in central cities of SMSAs. Poverty in the very small cities outside SMSAs, however, has increased against the trend. Table 2 also shows that the incidence of rural poverty remains heavier proportionately than urban poverty, 23 percent for both farm and rural nonfarm as compared with 16 to 18 percent in the cities.

The table also shows that the poverty that fits most people's mind's eye picture of what poverty really is — urban slum poverty — is relatively small as measured by the figures (available only for 1966) on poverty areas in central cities and fringe areas. In 1966 of the roughly 30 million poor in the United States only about one-seventh were central city slum poor. Indeed, as shown by the table, fewer than one-half of the poor in the central cities of Standard Metropolitan Statistical Areas were in these designated poverty areas. Again the picture is different for nonwhites: Almost a third of *all* nonwhite poor were in central city slums, and almost three-quarters of central city nonwhite poor were slum dwellers. Even so, the table clearly brings out that nonwhites are better off, at least with respect to income, in these slums than outside of large cities. The incidence of nonwhite poverty in these slums is only 40 percent as compared to 70 percent on farms and nearly 60 percent among nonfarm rural and small city dwellers.

Table 2
Poverty by Location and Race 1964–1966
(thousands of persons)

Location	Total				White				Nonwhite			
	1964	1965	1966	% Incidence 1966	1964	1965	1966	% Incidence 1966	1964	1965	1966	% Incidence 1966
Farm	4,375	3,294	2,458	22.5	3,046	2,093	1,566	16.2	1,329	1,201	892	70.4
Nonfarm	29,877	28,935	27,511	15.0	20,568	19,606	18,903	11.7	9,309	9,329	8,608	39.2
Outside SMSA	13,531	12,911	12,261	21.0	9,799	9,468	8,726	16.7	3,732	3,443	3,535	56.9
Rural Nonfarm	9,000	8,202	7,443	22.9	6,725	6,284	5,443	18.8	2,275	1,918	2,000	56.2
Urban	4,531	4,709	4,818	18.5	3,074	3,184	3,283	14.0	1,457	1,525	1,535	57.9
Inside SMSA	16,024	16,024	15,250	12.3	10,769	10,138	10,177	9.4	5,577	5,886	5,073	32.2
Central City	10,056	10,355	9,501	16.2	5,625	5,431	5,392	11.7	4,431	4,924	4,109	33.1
Poverty Areas	—	—	4,461	32.4	—	—	1,559	23.7	—	—	2,902	40.3
Fringe	6,290	5,669	5,749	8.7	5,144	4,707	4,785	7.7	1,146	962	964	28.7
Poverty Areas	—	—	1,041	21.8	—	—	690	18.5	—	—	351	33.8
Total	34,252	32,229	29,969	15.4	23,614	21,699	20,469	12.0	10,638	10,530	9,500	40.9

Source: Office of Economic Opportunity

Table 3
Poverty by Family Head Characteristic and Race 1964–1966
(thousands of persons)

Family Head Characteristic	Total			White			Nonwhite		
	1964	1965	1966	1964	1965	1966	1964	1965	1966
Aged Head	6,890	6,337	6,424	5,596	5,178	5,265	1,294	1,159	1,159
Nonaged Head	26,151	23,996	21,919	17,455	15,865	14,333	8,696	8,131	1,586
Female Head	7,595	7,394	7,762	4,415	4,357	4,491	3,180	3,037	3,271
Male Head	18,556	16,602	14,157	13,040	11,508	9,842	5,516	5,094	4,315
Disabled	1,159	1,256	1,282	858	896	899	301	360	383
Able	17,397	15,346	12,875	12,182	10,612	8,943	5,215	4,734	3,932
Worked 40 or more weeks	12,518	11,030	9,201	8,776	7,599	6,186	3,742	3,431	3,015
Less than 40 weeks	4,879	4,316	3,674	3,406	3,013	2,757	1,473	1,303	917
Total	33,041	30,333	28,343	23,051	21,043	19,598	9,990	9,290	8,745

Source: Department of Health, Education and Welfare

The first two tables showed who the poor were by age and where they lived. (For policy purposes the implications of these tables might relate to the distribution of funds, say, among old-age programs, youth training programs, and Head Start for the first table; and between rural and urban areas for the second.) Table 3 throws additional light on the economic cause of poverty.[4] By tabulating the poor according to the age and labor force characteristics of the family head, it indicates, for example, that in 1966 almost one-third of the poor were in families headed by relatively fully employed (40 weeks or more), nonaged men, another eighth were in families headed by nondisabled men who were unemployed for a substantial portion of the year, and the remaining 55 percent were in families headed by people for whom it is very difficult to see that work, or other earnings opportunity programs, have much meaning. The primary need of the aged, the disabled, and most of the female family heads in poverty is simply direct income support — money. Allowing for the fact that some female family heads want to and should work, but also allowing for the fact that with the low unemployment rates of recent years many of the poor unemployed male family heads are close to unemployable, roughly half the income-defined poor just need income.

Indeed, Table 3 shows that it is *only* against poverty in families with heads in the labor force that progress was made from 1964 to 1966 (and this again is consistent with a much longer-run trend). Poverty among families with male heads in the labor force went down by a quarter in these two years. It is quite clear that this relatively "easy" target is shrinking and that much more will have to be done soon for those to whom earning opportunity is meaningless. This does not mean that all opportunity programs are meaningless. Table 3 data are based on family heads, and opportunity programs for their children are necessary to prevent the recurrence of poverty.

For the purpose of computing program needs, data such as those in Tables 1 to 3 can be cut up much more finely. It is important to know, for example, how many of the nonaged unemployed male poor are urban (most), how many of the nonaged *fully employed* male poor are Southern

4. Tables 1 to 3 illustrate the difficulty of the shifting numbers estimated in poverty. The total numbers in poverty in Table 3 differ from those in Tables 1 and 2 for the same years because Table 3 was produced later and takes account of some statistical errors discovered late in the game by the Census Bureau.

(most), and so on. Two-dimensional tables are limited in what they can bring out, but in fact these three tables have brought out a good deal about poverty. As one might have guessed, the poor are disproportionately nonwhite, aged, rural, and in families headed by females. As one might also have guessed, poverty has dropped sharply in the last few years, and this drop has been concentrated primarily among those who could benefit from opportunity programs in a hot economy. One might not have guessed, however, that it is only recently that nonwhite poverty began to decline as sharply as white poverty, that the poverty of the aged is primarily a phenomenon of whites (but anyone who has felt the political pressure of the aged might have guessed this), or that poverty is now more than half a metropolitan problem.

One guess that very few people might have made is that such a small portion of poverty as defined is in urban slums. The typical mind's eye picture of poverty in the United States is the black urban slum, the Appalachian Hollow, perhaps the genteel home of the aged, and among a few other groups, particularly Indians and migrant workers. But if we add together all nonwhite poor in 1966 (9.5 million) plus all white aged poor (4.6 million) plus, arbitrarily, half of rural nonfarm white poor to represent Appalachia (2.7 million), we end up with 16.8 million poor, barely half of the total, in the categories and locations the word "poverty" conjures up. Of course one can add or subtract different groups or fractions of groups according to one's own mind's eye picture of poverty, but in fact this 16.8 million estimate is generous if anything. And nonwhite central city slum poverty alone — Hough, Bedford-Stuyvesant, Southside Chicago, Cardozo, Watts and all the rest — is only 2.9 million.

This kind of reasoning has led some to contend that the picture of poverty in the United States has been vastly exaggerated, by a factor of two or more. But because the poverty line *is* arbitrary, this contention does not stand up very well. Were we to take just the group whose membership under the current definition added up to this 16.8 million and adjust the poverty line upward to reach again the 29.8 million poverty estimate for 1966, we would still include under this new poverty line (perhaps $4,500 for a family of four) only people who by any income-related definition are still pretty damn poor.

If this computation of data on "mind's eye" poverty categories does not indicate that the current poverty concept and numbers are a vast fraud, however, it does imply that we should not discard the additional *equal opportunity* objective too easily. In fact, the black poverty, other minority group poverty, and Appalachian poverty that we picture in our minds does not include merely those with very low income now included under the poverty line. It includes also the Negro woman domestic with two children who nonetheless earns more than the $2,500 poverty line for such a family; it includes the unattached black male who picks up $3,000 a year at casual labor; it includes the Appalachian scratch-miner who makes $4,000 a year but as long as he stays in Appalachia has no opportunity for much more. Indeed it includes very many people who in terms of a single year's income are over the arbitrary lines but in terms of opportunity to advance themselves and their families are nonetheless stuck — the maid, the janitor, the scratch-farmer, the part-time miner, and so on.

Suppose instead of calculating poverty by counting all the people below the arbitrary poverty lines we make equally arbitrary estimates of the proportions of the people in the high-risk poverty and low-opportunity groups who are clearly below the level where they "have it made" as individuals or families. Table 4 does this for six groups: Negroes, reservation Indians, Puerto Ricans whom the census taker identified as white rather than Negro, Mexican Americans, who are defined by the Census as being white, Appalachian whites, and non-Appalachian Southern white poor.

Table 4
Groups in Need of Opportunity

Groups	Population (thousands)	Arbitrary Factor to Estimate Those Needing Help with Opportunity	Estimated "Opportunity Needs"
Negroes	20,700	.75	15,525
Reservation Indians	400	.90	360
White Puerto Ricans	2,934	.75	2,201
Mexican Americans	3,200	.75	2,400
Appalachian Whites	17,500	.50	8,750
Southern White Poor Outside Appalachia	7,500	1.00	7,500
Total			36,736

The total of the numbers in the table does not add up to much more than the numbers of the poor by the standard definition. This is not an argument about whether we count the right number of people as poor; as suggested, this is arbitrary anyhow, and the factors in Table 4 could easily be lowered to make the total come out 29.8 million or anything else. Instead the table suggests a completely different way to look at poverty as it is thought of by Americans and as it may have been explicitly thought of by those who passed the Economic Opportunity Act.

It would be possible to categorize these low-opportunity groups in much the same way as Tables 1 to 3 did with the conventionally defined poor, and it would be possible to direct economic opportunity programs toward them. Some programs, in fact, might be much more effective if directed toward the "opportunity" groups rather than the overlapping "poverty" category.

It is difficult to see, for example, why a job-training program should be directed primarily toward people with low incomes, regardless of their needs for jobs and their capabilities of absorbing additional skills. We might do more in the long run to equalize opportunity and to end poverty if we were to aim high-quality job programs at the worker who has reached a ceiling slightly above the poverty line with his current training but is clamoring for the kind of training that will bring him into the mainstream of the American labor force. To do this would violate the *caveat* discussed earlier about not letting poverty programs float upward as did the farm programs of the thirties. Nonetheless there are those (Albert Wohlstetter and Sinclair Coleman of the Rand Corporation, for example) who argue that, in fact, the real social problems lie in unequal racial opportunity at the top of the scale even more than at the bottom.[5] It is to the conflict between these two objectives that the next chapter turns.

5. Albert Wohlstetter and Sinclair Coleman, *An Analysis of Racial Disparities in Income: A Summary*, RM 6125-RC-OEO (Santa Monica: The Rand Corporation, 1970).

3
The War on Poverty:
Objectives

The relative stress on the two objectives — antipoverty and equal opportunity — is not a sterile intellectual question, it is crucial for future program direction, for the United States is gripped by both these closely related social problems. The problems of poverty are those of low incomes at the bottom end of the income distribution, those families and individuals whose income is so low that they cannot live a minimally decent life by American standards. The problems range from literal starvation, as has been adequately demonstrated a number of times, up through the misery of trying to exist on the welfare minimum. The programs to attack these problems are those programs designed to establish a floor under the American standard of living.

The problems of unequal opportunity are problems of the ceiling rather than the floor, and ceilings exist on the opportunities of those members of minority groups who are above the poverty line as well as on those below. With the possible exceptions of American Indians and migrant farm laborers, no identifiable group of Americans has a majority or anywhere near a majority of its members in the kind of income poverty defined by the Orshansky line. Yet, for several groups, of which Negroes are by far the largest and most obvious, a disproportionately large number of people are in poverty and a disproportionately small, even tiny, number have reached a level where their opportunities are close to equal with those open to the majority group.

The problems of poverty and unequal opportunity overlap. They are so closely related that it is difficult to see either how the floor can be raised without considerable upward movement for the ceiling or how the ceiling can be raised without also raising the floor. The factors that restrict opportunity for the low-income poor (largely present discrimination and the legacy of past discrimination) restrict it all along the line, for the near-poor as well and even for the better-off. It is difficult to see how discriminatory patterns can be broken or programs to compensate for the results of previous discrimination can be instituted for the poor alone. Indeed, attempts to do this have hurt OEO programs.

But even if it were possible to set up compensatory programs restricted to the poor, it seems very likely that antipoverty and equal opportunity programs will be more successful if each is backed up by the other. On the one hand, "inferiority" (both the *feeling* of group failure and the real lack of anybody on the top to give a helping hand) means that the poor individual has a double burden if he is a member of a poor group. Typically, the less capable members of more successful groups, be they WASPs, Jews, or Japanese Americans, have been helped by those at the top. But for blacks, Indians, and other less successful groups, there are few at the top to help. On the other hand, the welfare population at the bottom end of the poor group exerts an inevitable drag on those in the middle and at the top who might as individuals be on their way up. It does not help a black businessman if the bank looks at him as a member of a bad-risk "welfare class."

Since its start, the ambivalence between the antipoverty and equal opportunity objectives has affected the programs of the War on Poverty. The low-income-raising objective has been dominant, but it has been substantially modified by the other. Some of the antipoverty programs under the Office of Economic Opportunity have been directed almost exclusively at the low-income objective; the Out-of-School Neighborhood Youth Corps, for example, has provided work experience under the guise of training and income transfer under the guise of work experience, and has done both almost entirely for youth from families whose incomes were below the poverty line. Since income transfer has been such an important component, low-income targeting seems proper. But many of the programs collected under the title of Community Action, on the other hand, have been aimed at group problems, primarily those of Negroes and other minorities in urban ghettos and underprivileged groups in rural areas. Few of these group or target-area-oriented programs have drawn sharp distinctions by income levels of beneficiaries, nor should they have. A neighborhood center cannot install a turnstile to keep out those above the poverty line, although some Community Action programs that aid specific individuals or families (health and legal services, for example) do use standards of medical or legal indigence. These are typically well above the Orshansky lines.

Thus the blending of antipoverty and equal opportunity objectives has existed, and undoubtedly it will continue to exist. The operating question of what the program mixture should be — what programs exclusively for those with low incomes, what programs to equalize opportunities for the nonpoor as well as the poor — depends, however, on the answers to three underlying questions:

1. What was the legislative intent — the objective of those who designed and passed the antipoverty legislation?
2. What were the underlying conditions that brought about a War on Poverty in this country at this time?
3. In what sequential priority order does it make most sense to attack the two related problems of low-income poverty and unequal opportunity?

The obvious answer to the question of intentions of the designers is that of course they intended to attack poverty; otherwise they would not have oriented the programs around the word "poverty." In fact, this is not clear; a pretty good case can be made that the War on Poverty is the War on Poverty only by semantic accident, that the word "poverty" happened to be the single word that came closest to a description, but that the intentions of the designers were at least as close to the objective of equal opportunity. The sequence went from the *idea* of equal opportunity, which is relatively difficult to summarize in a single word or paragraph, to the *word* "poverty," to programs that were oriented around the antipoverty objective because the word had been used. That they were mixing two objectives was not clear to the designers at the time. Practical men, they started with programs not with carefully defined problems or objectives. They were politicians, not semanticists, and they knew that precision in objectives can lead to loss of political support. But in retrospect, it seems clear that neither low-income poverty nor equal opportunity all along the line was their sole objective.

According to James L. Sundquist, who has done the most careful study of the origins of the War on Poverty, "Until 1964 the word 'poverty' did not appear as a heading in the index of either the Congressional Record or the Public Papers of the Presidents."[1] Sundquist goes on to say that "By the Spring of 1963" President Kennedy, according to Arthur Schlesinger, Jr., " 'was reaching the conclusion that tax reduction required a comprehensive structural counterpart, taking the form, not of piecemeal programs, but of a broad war against poverty itself. Here perhaps was the unifying theme which would pull a host of social programs together and rally the nation behind a generous cause.' "[2]

In other words, Kennedy and his advisers started with the "host of social programs" and came up with poverty as the problem they were to solve rather than the reverse. According to Sundquist,

> The measures enacted, and those proposed, were dealing separately with such problems as slum housing, juvenile delinquency, dependency, unemployment, illiteracy, but they were separately inadequate because they were striking only at surface aspects of what seemed to be some kind of bedrock problem, and it was the bedrock problem that had to be identified so that it could be attacked in a concerted, unified, and innovative way. Perhaps it was Harrington's book that defined the target for Kennedy and supplied the coordinating concept — the bedrock problem, in a word was "poverty." Words and concepts determine programs; once the target was reduced to a single word, the timing became right for a unified program.[3]

It becomes pretty clear from this account that the set of programs Kennedy was interested in were those attacking the social problems that kept people from equal opportunity all along the line. His intentions were

1. James L. Sundquist, *Politics and Policy* (Washington, D.C.: The Brookings Institution, 1968), pp. 111–112.
2. Ibid., p. 113.
3. Ibid., pp. 113–114.

not confined to the problems of the lowest ends of the income distribution although there was certainly a special stress on low incomes. Most slum dwellers are not poor, nor are most delinquents, unemployed persons, or illiterates; they are, however, disproportionately members of ethnic and other groups in which the incidence of poverty is also disproportionately high — the unequal opportunity groups.

Nothing is ever simple, of course. Poverty and unequal opportunity at the bottom end of the income distribution were the most visible manifestations of the overall problem, and there was, all along, a definite concern with antipoverty in this collection of ideas. Professor Robert Lampman of the University of Wisconsin who, as a member of the staff of the Council of Economic Advisers, provided the major economic ideas for the War on Poverty planning in 1963–64, had done a study on the lower end of the income distribution as early as 1959 for the congressional Joint Economic Committee.[4] Nonetheless, it seems to have been as much the obstacles to equal opportunity as the existence of very low incomes that impelled first President Kennedy and then President Johnson and their advisers. Their ambivalence is illustrated by the fact that they began a War on *Poverty* centered on an Economic *Opportunity* Act.

Indeed, if we look behind the statements made at the time to the underlying motives impelling the prime movers, we discover from a number of sources that what initially moved Kennedy in this direction was his experience of seeing endemic poverty in West Virginia when campaigning in the 1960 primary election.[5] Surely, he had seen many individual cases of poverty when he campaigned for Congress in the wooden tenements of Charlestown, Massachusetts, in the late 1940s and when he campaigned for the Senate in the 1950s. But in West Virginia he confronted the inequality of an entire group of Americans, deprived by their location and by the decline in coal mining of any chance for economic progress. The difference was misery and poverty located in the midst of misery and poverty, together with the blockages that prevented the members of an American group from moving up to an American standard of living. It is

4. Robert L. Lampman, *The Low Income Population and Economic Growth* (Nos. 12–13 of the study papers on "Employment, Growth and Price Levels," Joint Economic Committee of the 86th Congress, 1st Session, December 16, 1959).
5. Sundquist, *Politics and Policy,* p. 113, for example.

interesting to note that although unequal *racial* opportunity also played a major and parallel role — the 1963 civil rights march on Washington made clear that black demands were shifting from equal political rights toward equal economic opportunities — the initial public image of the War on Poverty was disproportionately that of white Appalachia. In the early days of the War on Poverty, the striking photographs were those of President and Mrs. Johnson visiting Appalachian shacks. This was in large measure a political strategy designed to obtain Southern votes in Congress. Later, when the combination of the greater ease of organizing programs in city ghettos and the urban riots of 1964 through 1966 shifted the image of the anti-group-poverty portions of the program (largely Community Action) much more toward a Negro as compared to an Appalachian white emphasis, the program suffered politically.

The stress on group poverty and unequal opportunity distinguished the program from earlier efforts. During the days of the New Deal, low-income poverty was a problem of people who were indistinguishable from the majority by race or other characteristics. The New Deal ethos called for improving the economy so that the vast majority of the majority groups could make it on their own, for using Social Security so that those who were left behind because of age, accident, or economic fluctuation could continue the standard of living to which they were accustomed, and for mopping up the presumed random remainder with Public Assistance. It was not until the 1960s, when it was discovered that this remainder was not random at all but concentrated very highly in groups characterized by unequal opportunity, that poverty as a specific separable problem became a concern of the United States.

The point of this historical review is to suggest strongly that neither the conscious nor the subconscious impetus to the War on Poverty was solely low-income misery but the concentration of this misery in groups within which the individual opportunity to rise was very limited. The case here has been slightly one-sided because it is necessary to demonstrate that poverty isn't entirely a matter of low income. I do not mean to suggest that the elimination of low-income misery was not relevant but rather that the intended objectives were very mixed and were never explicitly separated out.

Next, in deciding which of the dual objectives the existing programs are best designed for, it is useful to look at four kinds of programs, based on the program-budgeting categories used by OEO. (These are described more fully in Chapter 5.) The four categories are Manpower programs, Education, Community Action, and Income Maintenance.

Among the Manpower programs, it is quite clear that the implicit opportunity objective has been central and that even though the programs have for the most part been limited to individuals and families below the Orshansky poverty line, the program benefits have been of a type needed by individuals in low-opportunity groups whether or not they came from families below the Orshansky line. The primary function of the Job Corps, for example, is the education and training of youth so that they may be capable of living an economic life above that of casual labor, to which so many untrained Negroes, Mexican Americans, Puerto Ricans, and rural Southern whites have been doomed. Although low income has been one criterion for youth entering Job Corps, it was one among a set that was designed to distinguish those most liable to a casual low-opportunity, low-income future: poor school performance, broken homes, and so forth. Similarly, the JOBS Program for on-the-job training of adults by private industry has aimed at placing these adults in entry level jobs from which they could progress toward opportunities calling for more and more skill. Most adults, certainly most men, are capable without training of earning incomes above the poverty line in casual or dead-end jobs (unless the poverty line for the particular family is quite high because the family is large). But future opportunities for janitors and dishwashers are limited, and the objective of the JOBS Program is to bring adults into the blue- and white-collar mainstream of American industry with all the opportunity for advancement implied. This is an objective for the Orshansky poor, but it is an objective shared by many members of low-opportunity groups who are nonetheless above the Orshansky line.

Alone among the current Manpower programs of the War on Poverty, the Neighborhood Youth Corps Out-of-School and summer programs, although euphemized as training, are really cover operations for putting some money into the jeans of poor kids, and this is an objective that seems dependent upon the low income of the kids and their families.

The difficulties with attempting to associate Manpower programs too

closely with low-income antipoverty goals are indicated by the fate of the
Work Experience Program designed under the original Economic Opportunity Act as a work and training program for adults in categories eligible
for Public Assistance. The intended beneficiaries of this program, those
eligible for Public Assistance, were among the poorest of the poor and
thus the neediest from the low-income standpoint. But need and ability
to benefit from training and job opportunities are measured on different
scales; some very low-income people are trainable, some not; some people
needing training to grasp opportunity are poor, some not. Being on Public Assistance did not make Work Experience enrollees trainable, and, in
fact, the program failed rather miserably because it tried to use the technique of training for job opportunity on individuals whose sole common
characteristic was low income rather than ability to succeed in training.

What is true of Manpower programs is also true of Education. The
objective of antipoverty education programs is obviously not any immediate change in the income of children in the programs. It is to get them
enough education so that they will be able to extend their future education and training to the point where they can hold down decent jobs
when they reach working age. This is an opportunity objective par excel-
lence, and it is thus not easy to justify providing Head Start and similar
education programs only to children whose family incomes are below the
poverty line. The liability to failure in education extends to most of the
children in slum areas, and with this liability goes unequal opportunity
and disproportionate likelihood of future poverty. Although it seems
likely that those at the upper end of the income distribution in the ghetto
areas are more likely to make it through the education system, the existing poverty line is too low a cutoff to distinguish those with greatest likelihood of failure. Unlike the OEO programs such as Head Start, Title I
of the Elementary and Secondary Education Act recognizes this distinction between poverty and opportunity by providing aid to *schools* with
large numbers of low-income children rather than providing the aid to
the children themselves. There are many other problems with Title I, but
at least it does seem to make the proper distinctions among the objectives of educational programs and their recipients.

Community Action programs are for the most part group-oriented,
and as such they tend to conform fairly closely to the group opportunity

objectives rather than the low-income poverty objectives. Community Action brings services and organizational help to the geographical and ethnic groups among whom the programs are located. And the help is typically help not for the poor alone but for the black, the Spanish-speaking, the mountain people, and so on.

Some of the services delivered by Community Action, however, are directly related to income, and for these services income lines have a reasonable rationale. That is, health services and legal services are to a great extent the equivalent of income transfer payments except that they are transfers in kind rather than in cash. For this reason, it makes a good deal of sense to deliver them only to those who need the transfer because their incomes are too low to purchase the services directly on the open market. It should be noted that in practice the guidelines for eligibility under OEO health programs in particular are not the Orshansky lines but are locally determined guidelines for medical indigence.

Leaving Income Maintenance aside for the moment, it would thus seem that the bulk of the programs in the other three categories of the War on Poverty are of a type that can aid those with low opportunity for the future whether or not their current incomes are low. Given this situation, it becomes an easy step to say that income eligibility standards ought to be lifted completely from opportunity programs in OEO and in other government agencies. Yet that would still be premature. The lessons of the farm programs of the 1930s and the housing programs of the 1950s must still be heeded. If the new programs cease being programs exclusively for the poor and become instead programs for Negroes, Mexican Americans, and various groups of whites, it seems very likely that the chief beneficiaries may not be those somewhat above the poverty line who lack opportunity but those a good deal above it who need help far less than their more deprived brethren.

Some recent examples illustrate this danger. One early OEO program, for example, set up Small Business Development Centers to provide technical advice and facilitate loans from the Small Business Administration for potential entrepreneurs among the poor. Initially the guidelines for qualifying recipients of this program were the Orshansky poverty lines, but it was discovered that, unfortunately, virtually nobody at these low-income levels had the entrepreneurial ability to profit from the SBA program.

The eligibility guidelines were then raised by successive increments until they were substantially above the Orshansky poverty lines, just so somebody would use the program. Those who did, although primarily members of minority groups, were not badly off at all; they were well into the middle class. Initially, also, the guidelines stressed not only entrepreneurship but the need to hire the poor into the small businesses set up under the program. Unfortunately, again, the requirement to hire from the bottom of the barrel was an additional burden on already shaky enterprises, and this requirement had to be lifted. So what was left was a program that had nothing to do with low-income poverty although it did affect equal opportunity objectives.

Nor are these conditions peculiar to an entreprenurial program. In the first year of OEO the Neighborhood Youth Corps (NYC) did not enforce its guidelines rigorously and was well on its way to becoming a summer and after-school job program for the middle class before the Department of Labor realized the political quicksand it had stepped into and began to enforce the Orshansky lines somewhat more effectively. In this case it was not merely those slightly above the poverty line who were benefiting but those well into the middle class and not all those were in minority groups either. At least one child of a United States Senator ended up in the program before the Senator realized his own political liability.

The small business program has gone out of existence, at least in this form, and the NYC now tries to enforce its poverty guidelines rigorously. In fact, however, NYC and other programs like Head Start as well have not been entirely successful in enforcing the poverty guidelines. Inspection reports of OEO as well as the General Accounting Office show that as much as 25 percent of the people in some Head Start and NYC programs have been above the poverty guidelines. But it should be stressed that because of the attempted enforcement of the guidelines the ineligibles who have been in the program were mostly not *very* ineligible. They were from families near the poverty line. And if the poverty line were abolished as a standard of program eligibility, past experience indicates that the beneficiaries of the program would have been the most well-off among minority and other poverty groups. In other words, the analogy drawn in the last chapter between the poverty line as an arbitrary boundary and the nuclear/nonnuclear distinction in weaponry is not a bad one. The poverty line is recognized and performs the function of the ceiling that keeps programs somewhere around their initial objective. Without some use of the poverty line or something like it, it is likely not only that the poverty objective of the program would disappear entirely but that the opportunity beneficiaries would not even be that near-poverty group also in need of opportunity.

Indeed, this reasoning is reinforced by the increasing evidence that the black population of the United States is itself dividing into two societies. One — an increasing portion but still a minority of all Negroes — is beginning to make it economically in American middle-class terms; the proportion of Negro families with incomes over $7,500 and over $10,000 has gone up sharply in recent years. The other — the black "underclass" — is perhaps becoming smaller in size as indicated by poverty and other statistics, but is increasingly being left behind in the worst cores of the black urban ghettos. Walter Williams, in a study of changes in Cleveland between 1959 and 1966, for example, points out that more of the black population is substantially better off, that the population of what he calls "the crisis ghetto" centered on Hough is smaller in 1966, but that the 1966 population in the crisis ghetto is worse off in every way than the 1959 population.[6] The Census Bureau has come up with similar statistical results on most of the metropolitan areas of the United States.[7] In these circumstances, it would be far too easy to concentrate opportunity programs above the poverty line, ignore the real misery of the 40 percent of the central city poverty area black population still below the line (1966 data, see Table 2 in Chapter 2), and accelerate the creation of a permanent black underclass.

What we end up with is not a simple situation. Many of the existing OEO programs and the opportunity programs of allied agencies such as the Departments of Labor and Health, Education and Welfare are more effective in opening up opportunity for those above and below the pov-

6. Walter Williams, "Cleveland's Crisis Ghetto," *TRANS-action*, September 1967, pp. 33–42.
7. U.S. Bureau of the Census, *Current Population Reports*, Series P-23, Special Studies (formerly Technical Studies), No. 27, "Trends in Social and Economic Conditions in Metropolitan Areas" (Washington, D.C.: U.S. Government Printing Office, 1969).

erty line who suffer from unequal opportunity than they are in concentrating solely on the income inequities suffered by those at the bottom of the income distribution. Yet were these programs not aimed at the low-income poor, they would be likely to miss even the near-poor targets most able to benefit from opportunity. Furthermore, were the programs not aimed at the low-income poor, it is difficult to see what help would be available to these truly poor people under current programs, and considerations of equity do argue that these are still the priority people in need. Indeed, the political pressures have been strong all along to put members of groups like the aged poor into programs that are quite inappropriate — simply because these are the only programs around.

Add to these difficulties the fact that the designers of the War on Poverty were not at all clear, either implicitly or explicitly, in distinguishing between the opportunity and antipoverty objectives of the programs and add further into this witches' brew the difficulty of solving either problem, poverty or unequal opportunity, without solving the other first; and the question of what our immediate objective should be becomes a very difficult one indeed. Some quick solutions are possible. It would seem a reasonable idea, for instance, to charge those above the poverty line a fee for high-cost services, with the fee being higher for those with incomes further above the line. This solution meliorates some situations while still leaving the basic question unanswered.

The question of what our immediate objective should be cannot be answered on the basis of "what is right" because both objectives are noble ones. It is not a question that can be answered on the basis of the intentions of the framers because they did not sort out their own intentions. Perhaps there is a key, however, in the fact that although we really do not yet know how finally to solve the unequal opportunity problem, we do know how to end low-income poverty.

Try as we may, we cannot quickly end unequal opportunity because we cannot abolish discrimination overnight, and discrimination, racial and otherwise, underlies most of the inequality under discussion. Even if we could abolish existing discrimination, it would take a generation to abolish the effects of past discrimination — starting with unequal education and going through all the other restrictions that make people today what they are today with the past irretrievable. Creating a situation in which every child born in the United States really has an equal chance at life, liberty, and the pursuit of happiness (or at least where unequal chances are randomized racially) is still not within reach of our action possibilities or even our knowledge.

A solution to low-income poverty, however, is. Separating low-income poverty from the opportunity objectives, we could quite easily end poverty at any time simply by providing those who are poor with enough money so that they are no longer poor, whatever the current poverty line is. Income maintenance is not conceptually difficult, and although which particular program is best is still subject to considerable debate, the feasibility of providing enough income to the poor to end low-income poverty is beyond debate. The aggregate amount of money that would have to be given to the now poor in order to bring them above the poverty line is less than $10 billion. If the income maintenance device adopted were a Negative Income Tax that, in order to fill entirely the poverty income gap, would have to provide substantial income to the near-poor (which is not a bad idea anyhow), the total cost would be on the order of $20 billion a year.[8] Adding in the cost to national production consequent upon the disincentive effects of such a large program, the total cost might be $30 billion a year. I am not proposing such a large program immediately, and if done gradually it would never need to reach these levels. But it should be noted that even $30 billion is about 3 percent of Gross National Product, it is less than a year's growth of GNP, and it is only about two years' growth of federal income taxes at present rates.

For this price, we could take care of the more than 50 percent of the poor who have virtually no earnings opportunities anyhow — those in families with aged, disabled, and female heads[9] — and we could solve the low-income problem in the United States. And we could make the opportunity programs in manpower, education, and Community Action fields far more effective because we could direct them at those most likely to benefit, both poor and nonpoor, having satisfied the equity requirements of the antipoverty objective through income maintenance. It seems to me that this is the only way to solve the problem of priority between the

8. If it were a Family Allowance, with equal sums going to the poor, near-poor, middle class, and well-off, the cost would be more than $70 billion.
9. See Chapter 2, p. 24.

antipoverty and equal opportunity objectives. Talmudic arguments about which "ought" to go first are very sterile indeed.

There is one more set of considerations. Once we have admitted another program objective aside from ending low-income poverty, we may have opened the door for a whole host of more or less related objectives; the temptation to use the antipoverty rubric to cover *all* the social ills of the United States has never been completely absent. For example, both the antipoverty and the equal opportunity objectives concern the inequities imposed on *people*, but some tendency exists to confuse poor people with poor areas. That is, the confusion is frequently made between antipoverty programs and the set of economic development programs, primarily rural, that attempt to distribute the economic growth of the United States a little more equally geographically than it would otherwise be. These are not primarily programs to end poverty among people as it is meant here. Nor are they necessarily very closely related. There are some areas of the United States in which there are a lot of poor people. Appalachia immediately comes to mind and so does much of the rural South along with other rural areas. It is frequently argued that programs intended to raise the overall economic level of such areas will inevitably help the poor in these areas. Occasionally they have, but more often than not they have not. Typically, the major effect of such programs has been to prevent middle-class high school graduates from moving out in search of jobs, and frequently even to bring into the area trained and educated people not at all poor.

This is not to argue that rural economic development programs *cannot* be tied closely to antipoverty objectives. Even this may be very difficult, however, and the rural economic development effort is better off if it sticks to its own legitimate objective of maintaining the infrastructure of communities and regions in order to keep up the quality of life for the middle-class Americans remaining there and does not concern itself too much with poverty. In any event, unlike the relationship between the equal opportunity and the antipoverty objectives, the relationship of the area economic development objective to antipoverty efforts must be proved case by case.

Similarly, some other programs with objectives sometimes thought to be similar to the antipoverty objectives really turn out in practice not to

41

be very closely related. Programs that attempt to raise the incomes of all members of a particular group frequently fall into this category. They follow this syllogism:

A lot of old folk (children) are poor.
We want to help the poor.
Therefore we ought to give money to old folk (children).

The logic here is less than rigorous. It has been demonstrated time and time again, for example, that raising overall levels of Social Security is a very ineffective way of helping the aged poor; 80 percent of Social Security increases now go to the nonpoor.[10] Indeed even programs that raise the *minimum* payment levels under Social Security are inefficient in helping the income of the poor because many of those at the minimum payment level would be poor if Social Security were the only pension they received, but in fact they receive other pensions such as Civil Service.

Another program sometimes recommended as an antipoverty program is the Children's Allowance, which would give between $100 and $500 or some other sum to all children in the United States by right. There is a higher incidence of poverty among children than among any other age group except for those over 65. Table 1 in Chapter 2 shows, for example, that in 1966 approximately 19 percent of the children below 16 in the United States were poor, whereas only 15.5 percent of the total population was poor and only 10 to 15 percent of those between 16 and 65 were poor. Even so, more than 80 percent of the children in the United States in 1966 were not poor, and it somehow seems inefficient to provide money to all in order to reach the 20 percent who were poor. Indeed, this would seem almost obvious, but it is not too obvious for some to argue that a Children's Allowance is an antipoverty program.[11]

Nonetheless, unlike poor areas, nonpoor old folks, and well-off kids, the problem of unequal opportunity is inextricably intertwined with the

10. The more you give to Social Security, the less would go to the poor. A 50 percent across-the-board increase in Social Security would net the poor about 12 cents on the dollar. A small increase now would benefit the poor about 20 percent. The larger the increase, the less the poor will benefit. See *Income and Benefit Programs*, Report of the Program Analysis Group on Income and Benefit Programs (U.S. Department of Health, Education and Welfare 1966–2), Table III-4, p. 25.

11. Eveline M. Burns (ed.), *Children's Allowances in the Economic Welfare of Children* (published by Citizens' Committee for Children of New York, Inc., 1968).

problem of low-income poverty in the United States. It is intertwined in concept, it is intertwined in current practice, it is intertwined in political and intellectual history. It is only by understanding this connection that the antipoverty efforts of the last few years can be understood. I believe that it is only by breaking the connection and solving the poverty problem once and for all through income maintenance that the other equally deep problem can begin to be solved.

4
A Biased History of the
War on Poverty

This chapter is not intended to be a definitive history of the Office of Economic Opportunity, nor is it an exposé. Rather, it is an analytical and somewhat personal view of how the War on Poverty got to where it is, as a prelude to the next chapters, which discuss where the War is and where it might be going.

The history of the War on Poverty falls naturally into seven periods since 1961:

1. The period of the Kennedy Administration, which ended abruptly on November 22, 1963. Various programs later included in the War on Poverty were begun during these three years.

2. November 1963 to November 1964, the period in which the explicitly named War on Poverty was created, from formulation through legislation to the beginning of operations by OEO. This is the era sometimes known by its participants as the good old task force days.

3. From the first operations of OEO in November 1964 to September 1965, when the initial period of growth, excitement, and chaos in the War on Poverty hit the doubly reinforced stone wall of Vietnam and established political positions. This was the "Let a thousand flowers bloom" period of OEO.

4. From September 1965 through November 1966, the period of program consolidation and troubles with retreat from some of the

further-out positions of the earlier period. The period ended with the election of 1966, in which the Democratic majority in Congress was sharply reduced.

5. November 1966 to December 1967, OEO's year of the political miracle, the year in which Sargent Shriver and his crew coaxed a better bill with a stronger majority out of a Congress that was markedly more conservative than that of the previous year. This took almost until Christmas of 1967.
6. December 1967 to November 1968, a period of suspense as the old guard changed, many of the programs shook down, and almost everybody waited around for the election.
7. November 1968 and thereafter, the beginning of the Nixon years.

The first six of these periods are treated in this chapter, the seventh in Chapter 8, the Epilogue.

BEFORE NOVEMBER 22, 1963: THE PREHISTORIC DAYS

As Sundquist points out and as discussed in the previous chapter, many of the programs and the ideas for new programs that ultimately came together to form the War on Poverty existed before they were drawn together under this explicit phrase. However, the *idea* of a War on Poverty as such did not exist, and a few key programs existed only as pilots. Community Action existed only in germ in the President's Committee on Juvenile Delinquency and the Ford Foundation's Gray Areas projects, Robert Sargent Shriver existed only in the Peace Corps.

The majority of the basic components of the War on Poverty (although not of the OEO) were already in being before November 1963. In many ways, the most important was the active fiscal policy of the Kennedy Administration, which by the end of 1963 had begun to create the climate of prosperity necessary for the success of any antipoverty programs. The big fiscal boost to the economy came only after the assassination with the passage of the Kennedy-proposed tax reduction, but by late 1963 the movement was well under way toward the less than 4 percent unemployment rates that supported the War on Poverty after its first year.

Parallel to the active fiscal policy was the growth of the civil rights movement — not government created, but certainly government supported. Like prosperity, this activity, highlighted by the 1963 March on Washington, was a necessary support for the War on Poverty throughout its history.

In addition, at least two major statutes passed in the early 1960s were important ingredients in the later War on Poverty. The Manpower Development and Training Act (MDTA) passed in 1962 set up training programs in the Department of Labor. Initially these devoted most of their efforts to retraining the technologically dispossessed, a task that was rather different from the entry level and basic vocational training needed by poverty and low opportunity groups. But the later operations of the War on Poverty shifted the focus of these efforts to antipoverty and opportunity programs, and the programs under MDTA thus later became key portions of the War on Poverty.

The second area of pre-1963 legislation that later became crucial to the War on Poverty was in the 1962 amendments to federal welfare laws. These marked the first coordinated attempt to get people off the welfare rolls through special job training for those on these rolls and through delivery of social (primarily family-related) services to people in need. The former effort (job training) was the direct basis for one of the initial programs of OEO, Work Experience. The social services portion of the welfare amendments were equally crucial to the course of the War on Poverty, albeit in a negative way. By 1965, it was so clear that social services were not effective in getting very many people out of poverty that the intellectual/political effort was to *separate* income maintenance from social services, a thrust that led to the growing interest in the Negative Income Tax and related forms of income maintenance.

The MDTA and the welfare amendments formed bases for the future War on Poverty without necessarily having been intended that way. Conversely, one early piece of legislation that had very explicitly been thought of as some sort of antipoverty measure turned out in later years not to be totally relevant. This was the Area Redevelopment Act of 1961 amended in 1965 to create the Economic Development Administration. As suggested in the preceding chapter, the distinction between aiding poor areas and aiding poor people has become a fairly clear one, but it was less clear before some of these matters had been thought through.

Finally, outside of the legislative precursors of the War on Poverty lay a number of the intellectual springs of what later came into being. Most of these have been thoroughly discussed elsewhere, notably by Sundquist[1] and Moynihan.[2] They included Michael Harrington's book, *The Other America*,[3] and Dwight Macdonald's long article, in *The New Yorker*, which reviewed Harrington and other more technical works on poverty.[4] Both Harrington and Macdonald dramatized the impact and the extent of poverty. The intellectual basis of the War on Poverty also included Sargent Shriver's Peace Corps experience in bringing the knowledge of the economically successful to the aid of the poor.

Equally important were the efforts of the President's Committee on Juvenile Delinquency and the Ford Foundation's Gray Areas projects, which together were the pilots for the Community Action Program. Of particular note are two specific programs from the Juvenile Delinquency–Gray Areas womb: Mobilization for Youth on the lower East Side of New York and Community Progress, Inc., in New Haven. These initiated the dual and sometimes conflicting themes that formed Community Action: Mobilization for Youth in a real sense marked the beginning of Community Action as participation and organization of the poor; Community Progress, Inc., was a first step in Community Action as delivery of well-organized services to the poor with far less emphasis on participation.

NOVEMBER 1963 TO NOVEMBER 1964: THE GOOD OLD TASK FORCE DAYS

The story of the creation of the War on Poverty has already been told in a number of places by a number of participants in the Task Force that brought OEO to birth, notably Sundquist,[5] Moynihan,[6] and Christopher

1. James L. Sundquist, *Politics and Policy* (Washington, D.C.: The Brookings Institution, 1968).
2. Daniel P. Moynihan, *Maximum Feasible Misunderstanding* (New York: The Free Press, 1969).
3. Michael Harrington, *The Other America: Poverty in the United States* (New York: Macmillan, 1962).
4. Dwight Macdonald, "Our Invisible Poor," *The New Yorker*, January 19, 1963, pp. 82 ff.
5. Sundquist, *Politics and Policy*.
6. Moynihan, *Maximum Feasible Misunderstanding*.

Weeks.[7] It most certainly will be told again and again, perhaps until all the participants have had their say; it was apparently one of those rare exciting processes that is complete for those lucky enough to have participated only when they have made their own statements about it. I did not participate in the Task Force, and this section is merely a retelling from primary sources of certain matters that have been frequently discussed but that must be set forth again as an introduction to the story of OEO after it came into being.

The political history of the War on Poverty can be picked up on the day after President Kennedy's assassination, when Walter Heller, the Chairman of the Council of Economic Advisers, reported to President Johnson on Kennedy's interest in beginning a coordinated antipoverty effort and received Johnson's enthusiastic go-ahead. The task was taken up in the Council and the Bureau of the Budget by Robert Lampman, William Capron, William Cannon, and others, and in his January 1964 State of the Union Message, President Johnson declared "unconditional War on Poverty." In February, the President appointed Sargent Shriver, Director of the Peace Corps, as the Chairman of a Task Force to design the program Johnson had already announced. And Shriver in turn obtained Adam Yarmolinsky, Defense Secretary McNamara's Special Assistant, as his Deputy. Shriver immediately began to meet with men of varied ideas and interests and over a period of weeks designed a bill that was presented to the Congress the next month.

The bill has been characterized by Sundquist as "a composite of one central new idea — community action — and long-discussed ideas, like the Youth Conservation Corps."[8] Outside of Community Action the primary emphasis was on job and education programs for youth. Labor Secretary Willard Wirtz had suggested more of a manpower emphasis, but in the final analysis he and his task force representative Moynihan lost the battle over relative emphasis to the advocates of Community Action. Wirtz and other cabinet members also lost the day on their efforts either to put the new operating programs into the Department of Health, Education

7. Christopher Weeks, *Job Corps: Dollars and Dropouts* (Boston: Little, Brown and Company, 1967).
8. Sundquist, *Politics and Policy,* p. 144.

48

and Welfare or to distribute them among various departments with an individual or committee in the Office of the President to coordinate them. Shriver insisted on a separate agency, and Shriver obtained the President's backing. Three major programs, Job Corps, Community Action, and VISTA, were put under the direct management of the Director of OEO, and the others were included in the OEO budget but delegated to other agencies that were to be responsible to the Director for their management.

Shriver also won on the key decision that finally made Community Action central to the OEO program, the decision to drop the suggestion that had been made in December by the Budget Bureau's Cannon and others that Community Action should be a demonstration program in no more than 10 (later 50) areas. Shriver intended that Community Action become a nationwide program, and this was what it was going to be.

Shriver having convinced the Administration, the Administration managed to get Congress to pass the bill in August of 1964. One concession felt necessary by the Administration was the decision to sacrifice Adam Yarmolinsky to the North Carolina congressional delegation and other Southern Democrats who, for obscure reasons of their own having to do with Defense Department programs for civil rights, were out to get him.

Much of the output of the task force has been severely criticized, notably by Moynihan,[9] who had pretty much dropped out of the proceedings after he and Wirtz lost the battles over manpower emphasis and old-line agency control. But the major directions of the task force seem in retrospect to have been close to inevitable, given only President Johnson's decision to push hard for a War on Poverty and given the disjointed activities of the Kennedy period that had begun to formulate programs and ideas that awaited only the gathering together under a single heading.

The lack of emphasis on job creation through federal hiring of the poor or major federal subsidy to private industry was based on economic prognoses that jobs would take care of themselves. The unemployment rate was going down, and it was hoped that the tax cut would make it go down much more sharply, thus demonstrating that unemployment was

9. Moynihan, *Maximum Feasible Misunderstanding.*

cyclical rather than structural. Moynihan argues that a key and faulty decision on the part of the task force and the President was the rejection of a proposal for a five-cent cigarette tax, the proceeds to be earmarked for job creation programs among the poor.[10] In fact, although the rejection of this program was a conscious decision, the decision was foreordained by the fact that taxes were being reduced at the time. The weight of informed economic opinion was that the *major* cause of unemployment was cyclical and could be cured by further economic growth, rather than being a structural imbalance that would require special creation of new jobs for the poor. Even most of those who did put weight on the structuralist hypothesis argued not for direct job creation by government hiring but rather for training of the unemployed so that they could get jobs in the existing private economy. Indeed, although Secretary Wirtz had favored the proposed cigarette tax/job creation program in 1964, by 1965 the Labor Department strongly opposed Public Employment proposals presented by OEO.

And if the deemphasis of job creation came as much out of the general perceptions of the time as out of a decision that could have gone one way or the other, the same can be said of the Community Action Program and its emphasis on participation of the poor. Many — again notably Moynihan — have implied that this was a decision that was made without much attention to its implications and indeed was an accidental decision in which the famous phrase "maximum feasible participation of the residents of the areas and members of the groups served" was intended only to prevent segregated poverty programs in the South.[11] However, if we look not at the decisions as they were made on the basis of various current political factors and forces but rather at the overall environment as it existed, it seems very, very likely that the underlying forces surrounding the creation of the Community Action Program — the Ford theorists and Juvenile Delinquency theorists, yes, but also the militant civil rights movement — would have demanded participation with or without the explicit phrase in the law.

Indeed, had Community Action been set up merely as a coordinating principle for local activities with no separate new action programs, it

10. Ibid., p. 99.
11. Ibid., pp. 87–91.

seems very likely that at this stage of American history, program participants, those who represented program participants, and those who claimed they represented program participants would have demanded in. Had the controversial participation phrase been absent from the legislation and had OEO tried to run the program exclusively from the top down, the militant pressure might have been *on* the Community Action Program rather than *within* the Community Action Program, but the effect on the communities would have been the same. For just as it was the declaration of War on Poverty, rather than the subsequent sales pitches, that raised expectations to unfulfillable levels, it was the notion of community and the notion of participation — both of which preceded the passage of the Economic Opportunity Act of 1964 — that caused many of the political problems of Community Action.

Of course, none of this *had* to happen. President Johnson did not have to declare War on Poverty. He could have decided to continue proposing individual programs, and such a decision might have at least postponed much of the controversy surrounding the poverty program. It also would have postponed much of the effectiveness of the program. Similar results — with both less controversy and less effectiveness — might have been obtained from following the proposal to put the programs in old-line agencies. Certainly, in the light of subsequent history, the programs would have been much less effective in the old-line agencies; precisely because of this lesser effectiveness they would also have been much less controversial.

Paradoxically, however, the decision to sacrifice Yarmolinsky, taken to avoid controversy, may have prompted more future controversy than it prevented. Even though the basic forces causing later trouble were inexorable in their general courses, had Yarmolinsky stayed, he and Shriver might have been able to keep these forces under far better control than they were in the first operating year, 1965, and this might have made very substantial differences in the workings and the politics of the War on Poverty. (But Shriver points out that his hopes for Jack Conway, who ultimately did become his first Deputy, were as high as his hopes for Yarmolinsky. Conway did not work out well, and there were no guarantees on Yarmolinsky. It is a pity history is run only once.)

In any case what eventuated from the complex political process was the Economic Opportunity Act of 1964. This contained three programs administered directly by OEO — Job Corps, CAP, and VISTA — and six delegated to other agencies. The programs were, by Title of the Act:

Title I

Job Corps (OEC-managed), a residential training program for young men and women between the ages of 16 and 21

In-School and Out-of-School Neighborhood Youth Corps (delegated to the Department of Labor), an at-home training and work experience program for young men and women between the ages of 16 and 21

College Work-Study Program (delegated to the Office of Education in the Department of Health, Education and Welfare)

Title II

Community Action Program (OEO-managed), a set of comprehensive locally initiated and planned programs

Adult Basic Education (delegated to the Office of Education in the Department of Health, Education and Welfare)

Title III

Rural Loan Program (delegated to the Farmers Home Administration in the Department of Agriculture), a program of small farm and nonfarm operating loans to rural individuals and cooperatives

Migrant Farm Workers Program (managed by CAP within OEO)

Title IV

Small Business Development Centers (delegated to the Small Business Administration), a program of loans and technical aid to small businessmen who were either to be poor themselves or hire the poor

Title V

Work Experience Program (Delegated to the Welfare Administration in the Department of Health, Education and Welfare), a program of work and training for welfare recipients and those — particularly unemployed fathers — whom the administration hoped to make eligible for welfare, via state action

Title VI

VISTA (OEO-managed), the Volunteers in Service to America, the domestic analogue of the Peace Corps.

NOVEMBER 1964 THROUGH SEPTEMBER 1965: LET A THOUSAND
FLOWERS BLOOM

The Economic Opportunity Act was passed on August 20, 1964, but the funds to make it operative were not appropriated by the Congress until the closing days of the preelection session in October 1964. In order to avoid charges of playing politics, President Johnson postponed the making of the first grants until after the election.

In November 1964, the OEO began to do business, headquartered in a soon-to-be-torn-down hotel near downtown Washington. The first year of OEO operations was an era of very rapid growth, as a budget of $750 million had been appropriated to be spent in half a year by an as yet almost nonexistent organization. It was an era of high spirit and excitement, as all things looked possible. It was an era that attracted some of the brightest social thinkers in the country but perhaps not those with the most well-organized minds. It was an era of great administrative confusion.

Perhaps the most basic problem was that of personnel at the top. Sargent Shriver, the Director of the OEO, remained the Director of the Peace Corps, and although he devoted to the poverty program more than half of what would have been for an ordinary man far more than full time, OEO could have used all of Shriver's seven-day-a-week efforts. This was particularly so because the loss of Yarmolinsky meant that for the first crucial six months he had no deputy; the only central decision point was Shriver himself. In June of 1965, Yarmolinsky was replaced by Jack Conway, the Director of Walter Reuther's AFL-CIO Industrial Union Department, who had been slated to head the Community Action Program. But the Shriver-Conway chemistry just did not work out very well, and in October, Conway resigned. Thus a new program with a big budget and an immense mission was begun essentially by a half-time Director rather than a full-time Director and Deputy.

The problem of control was accentuated by a basic Shriver decision and by his mode of operation. The decision was to go big fast, not merely to get the three-quarter-billion dollars obligated but to get it obligated in highly visible ways that would begin nationwide operations and show effects quickly. This is not to say that Shriver was wrong; an airplane has to move fast to take off at all, and this was the Shriver theory. Further-

53

more, a slow response to strong community demands might have been intolerable, politically and otherwise. But the rapid buildup added greatly to the other problems of control. Also adding to them was Shriver's personal style of operations. He wanted to be in control not only of policy but also of those details that caught his attention. He signed off every grant to a Community Action Agency or demonstration program personally, and the typical occasion of the first year was the meeting in his office where an almost formal debate was carried on by proponents and opponents of a grant with Shriver sitting in judgment. If the proponents won, which they mostly did, he signed. This meant that he knew in detail what was going on, but it also meant that no general policies were laid down, and that not enough time was spent on the individual grant to flag the ones that would be likely to cause future troubles.

Because this was a time for real competition of ideas and a chance for idea men actually to put their ideas into practice, Shriver attracted many brilliant and deeply concerned intellectuals: people like the young lawyer Edgar Cahn and the young journalist Edgar May, who were special assistants to the director, Richard Boone, who had been on the Task Force and was put in charge of planning and policy for the Community Action Program, and Sanford Kravitz, who became the Director of CAP's demonstration efforts. The demonstration programs were particularly significant because they could be set up directly out of headquarters without first getting the approval of the locally established Community Action authorities, and demonstration was potentially a fertile field for new ideas.

One additional member of this cast was William Haddad, a journalist whom Shriver made into his Inspector General, in charge of a department that Haddad used to find out what all the other departments were doing wrong. This was a difficult function, and Haddad added to the difficulties by using his powers ferociously and in favor of his own theories, which were along the lines of organizing communities against the "local establishments."

In belief, although not in method, Haddad was typical of many of Shriver's young theorists, and indeed one unimpressed OEO observer has characterized this group as "the footnote crew," after a footnote in an article Haddad wrote for *Harper's Magazine* in December 1965 after he had left the poverty program.[12] The footnote listed those whom Haddad thought were the good guys. These good guys, together with some less brilliant but equally committed ideologues, characterized and to some extent dominated major parts of the Community Action Program (particularly demonstrations) in the absence of firm control from the top of OEO or CAP. Conway had been replaced as Director of CAP by Theodore Berry, who proved to be a weak administrator, and the less theoretically inclined bureaucrats were preoccupied with just getting the money out.

The theoreticians and ideologues were interested primarily in the set of problems I have called the opportunity and group poverty problems and particularly the problems of urban minorities, particularly the problems of blacks, particularly the problems of political powerlessness. Their primary solution was political and quasi-political organization of the poor (and the near-poor and those who represented the poor) through vigorous use of the "participation" language in order to change various political balances. A typical product was the Shriver speech at the social workers' convention in Atlantic City,[13] in which he told the social workers that they had been fouling up the poor and their problems for too long by paternalism.

Some of the demonstration programs that were begun during that time period were those that later (or in some cases sooner) caused the OEO great grief. The Syracuse demonstration program, which competed with the official Syracuse Community Action Program, and which Moynihan has characterized not unjustly as "systematic agitation,"[14] was a 1965 product. So was LeRoi Jones's Black Arts Theatre, a summer theater program in Harlem, in which antiwhite plays were put on that Shriver himself later called "scurrilous" and "obscene." The program of the Child Development Group of Mississippi (CDGM), which was OEO's political sensation of the following summer, was also started in 1965. This was a Head Start program designed to aid poor preschool children, which was in fact used partially for employment and community organization of

12. William F. Haddad, "Mr. Shriver and the Savage Politics of Poverty," *Harper's Magazine*, December 1965, pp. 43–50.
13. Address by Sargent Shriver at the National Conference on Social Welfare, Atlantic City, New Jersey, May 26, 1965.
14. Moynihan, *Maximum Feasible Misunderstanding*, p. 132.

Negroes in Mississippi; nothing seems to be as justified as employment and community organization of Negroes in Mississippi in 1965, but doing it in a Head Start program for little kids was tough to defend against the onslaught of Mississippi Senator John Stennis. (Some 1966 experiences concerning this problem and others born in 1965 will be discussed later.)

The summer of 1965 was also the time Shriver held out against the blatant attempt of Mayor Sam Yorty of Los Angeles to make the local Community Action Program part of his patronage, with the result that there was no Los Angeles program until the Watts riot of that summer, and that after the riot, program monies were poured in by OEO and other organizations on a not very organized basis. Moynihan discusses Los Angeles in connection with Syracuse.[15] The comparison is certainly unjustified because Syracuse *was* a deliberate attempt by local theorists to use federal funds to undermine a local government, whereas in Los Angeles the effort was to achieve a compromise among Yorty and various other political powers including the completely separate government of the County of Los Angeles. Nonetheless, the effects of program confusion in the first summer were similar. Perhaps the whole effort can be summarized not too unfairly by reporting the fact that things went so fast that virtually no records or reports were kept, particularly in the Community Action demonstration program. Four years later, CAP was still trying to reconstruct what had happened and what had been learned from some of the programs.

But the first year was also the year of nativity of some of the best programs that characterized Community Action later. Not only did 1965 begin the routine locally based Community Action programs that emerged in what ultimately became a thousand communities to both work and quarrel with the establishment without breaking out into open warfare; the year also saw the beginnings of such important programs as comprehensive Health Centers and Legal Services.

Head Start began then too, and the early history of Head Start was perhaps more characteristic of both the virtues and faults of the first year of OEO than were the organize-the-poor spectaculars, although the latter seem to dominate the memory of many historians and journalists. Head Start was born of the marriage of some well-founded theories of

15. Ibid., p. 134.

child development that held that the twig was already irrevocably bent by the time a child entered kindergarten or first grade, with Shriver's desire to get the money out fast. Backed by the President and Mrs. Johnson's concern for poor kids, the decision was made in the spring of 1965 to mount a large-scale summer Head Start program. The program was intellectually compelling and popular enough in local communities to make moving out fast feasible, and without Head Start, OEO might have been left with nothing but small-scale beginnings to show for the first year, perhaps might even have had to turn money back to the Treasury. The program was organized fast and the money was shoveled out fast; that summer 561,000 kids were in pretty well organized Head Start programs. The thing was not done neatly administratively, but the fantastic fact is that it was done at all although it looked impossible, that it was done virtually without scandal or political pork, and that most of the local Head Start programs looked pretty much like what they were supposed to look like, although perhaps the resemblance was not as close as the early-childhood theorists would have liked.

The Head Start effort had another happy effect. It brought volunteers into the poverty program en masse. These were volunteers to do the administrative work 24 hours a day in Washington headquarters, to do similar local work in setting up programs, and finally to help with programs and children. This was the first fruit of a major effort, pushed hard by Shriver and headed by Hyman Bookbinder, Director of a unique organization within OEO called the Office for Private Groups, to generate community support, local and national, programmatic and political. The effort manifested itself in a proliferation of advisory councils: Business Leaders, Labor, Public Officials, Women, Poor People, Head Start, Head Start Researchers. It was in large part responsible for the ability to expand programs fast; in large part too it was to provide vital political support in 1967 (see later).

A less fortunate effect of the Head Start effort, however, was that it sopped up a good deal of high-quality bureaucratic talent — using bureaucratic in the best sense of the word, having the ability to organize and operate in an organization — in OEO Headquarters. In addition to the "footnote crew," the early headquarters staff of OEO had a disproportionate number of the best Washington bureaucrats, but the concentration of so much of their time on Head Start left many other programs substantially in control of the theorists.

Jobs Corps, necessarily a much more highly organized and less volunteer-aided effort than Head Start, showed many more pains of trying to grow fast. Shriver had made the decision early to contract out to private business the so-called men's urban centers of Job Corps, those centers that concentrated on vocational training in large centers near cities for young men who had a little bit of educational achievement. These contrasted with conservation centers, which were farther out in the country and designed to do conservation work for the Departments of Interior and Agriculture while providing basic learning to boys with virtually no educational achievement.

The decision to go private was probably all that made Job Corps possible on any scale at all, but it did not solve the problems. Setting up Job Corps centers on inactive Army bases was necessarily a slow process. And designing proper education curricula and other training programs was also slow, or at least it would have been had it been tried at all in the first year. In fact, what happened was that the Job Corps kept on reducing its size to meet with reality. Shriver, who had once thought in terms of 100,000 young Job Corpsmen by the close of fiscal 1965 on June 30, reduced the 1965 target to 40,000 in the task force days, to 25,000 by Christmas of 1964, and finally to 10,000 in March of 1965. This target was met, but it was met only in the waning minutes of the fiscal year, and it was met at high cost by pouring unready and rapidly selected kids into unready camps with unready staffs. And it was further complicated by the fact that a Job Corps recruitment campaign in the winter had produced 300,000 inquiries that nobody knew what to do with. Job Corps in the first year was thus a chaotic nightmare eventuating not only in a program of lower quality than it should have been for kids whose needs were not as carefully matched with programs as they should have been but also in the violence, sex, and other scandals that hurt Job Corps so badly in its first two years. These troubles in turn also led to a defensiveness on the part of Job Corps administration that for many years turned the corps into something of a closed corporation, largely inaccessible for purposes of planning, control, and evaluation to the management of OEO.

The programs delegated to the Departments of Labor, HEW, and

Agriculture were somewhat inaccessible to OEO control from the beginning. This was particularly true of the Neighborhood Youth Corps, delegated to the Department of Labor. The task force disagreements between Shriver and Wirtz over focus and control of the War on Poverty led to less than mutual confidence. Shriver had his hands full with his "own" problems — Job Corps, Community Action, and VISTA — and had substantially less interest in the delegated programs. And Wirtz and his designated NYC (Neighborhood Youth Corps) program head Jack Howard wanted only to run "their" program their way. Administratively, they did not run it badly; the antipoverty effectiveness of the NYC program, however, is more questionable and is discussed in the next chapter. In any case, NYC was a program subject to little control from OEO, a situation that was exacerbated by the fact that OEO's Assistant Director for Interagency Relations, Lisle Carter, who had this responsibility, spent much of his time the first six months as Acting Deputy Director of OEO in Conway's absence and occasionally as Acting Director. One of my own first memories, having come into the planning end of OEO in early 1965, was having to obtain NYC data through a spy network because NYC was completely unwilling to supply numbers of any kind to OEO.

In spite of the chaotic surroundings — perhaps because of the surroundings, because chaos can be fun — 1965 was an exciting and optimistic year, particularly for the antipoverty planners in OEO. Shriver had hired the Provost of Williams College, Joseph Kershaw, as Director of an office called Research, Plans, Programs and Evaluation (RPP&E), patterned very deliberately after Secretary McNamara's and Assistant Secretary Charles Hitch's Systems Analysis Office in the Department of Defense. Systems analysis had the reputation at the time of being *the* solution to all planning and some administrative ills, and Shriver wanted some of that; realizing himself the inevitability of administrative chaos, he had serious hopes that straight paths toward the goals could be designed simultaneously. (Whether this is possible and whether it happened even in the Department of Defense is the subject of a subsequent book.)

Because of his obligations to Williams College, Kershaw did not come on board until June and he came on to find a skeleton staff of planners that was not filled out until July. Nonetheless, Kershaw and the staff, anticipating the Bureau of the Budget Directive of 1965, which instituted Program Budgeting within the government, produced that summer a five-year antipoverty plan projecting programs that a mixture of analysis and gut indicated were needed for a maximum effort against poverty. This later became known as the Kershaw Report. Although its relationship to the immediate programs and problems of OEO was slender — the $3.5 billion worth of OEO programs being requested in the first year being embedded in about $30 billion of program requests for all War on Poverty programs — Shriver and the top staff were fascinated by the five-year plan and indeed interest was fairly high throughout the government. In command performances, Kershaw briefed Vice President Hubert Humphrey, Budget Director Charles Schultze, and newly appointed Presidential Assistant Joseph Califano.

The plan emphasized three major thrusts. It stressed the need for a major income maintenance program to reach the 26 million out of the then 34 million total poor who were not receiving any support under the Public Assistance Programs. (For 1964, the latest figures available at that time, slightly less than half of the poverty population was in "nonopportunity" categories of families headed by the aged, the disabled, and females.) The major emphasis within income maintenance was on the Negative Income Tax, although considerable interest was also shown in the Family Allowance alternative, in large part because the leading advocate of Family Allowances, Alvin Schorr, had joined the staff that summer.

Negative Income Tax and Family Allowances were substantially different programs, but they came together in agreement that a few years of experience with the 1962 Public Assistance Amendments had demonstrated conclusively that income maintenance should be *separated* from social services, not tied together.

In addition to income maintenance, the need for a public employment program was stressed. Although unemployment had been dropping, it had just crossed the 5 percent mark that summer and was obviously still far too high to sustain an economic opportunity program. Analysis indicated that although further drops in unemployment would help a great deal, even they would not be sufficient for the poor. Another analysis was contracted out to estimate the need of the public sector for workers, and the startling number of 4.5 million came up. This number has served for the last four years as a conventional estimate of this public need. The estimate may be too high (see Chapter 7), but it does indicate that the work is there to be done, if the funds and the trainable workers were but available.

The OEO public employment proposal was the subject of some debate during the summer and fall of 1965, with the negative side of the debate being taken by the Council of Economic Advisers, who believed that the need for such a program was not demonstrable, at least until cyclical unemployment had been reduced as far as possible, which it had not been at the time. Also on the negative side was the Labor Department, which didn't believe in cyclical unemployment but felt training programs could get rid of structural unemployment by better matching the needs of the economy with the capabilities of the unemployed, and that no new net job creation was needed. It is not clear how this fits with Secretary Wirtz's reported earlier support for a massive employment program financed by a cigarette tax.

The third leg of this structure was a Community Action Program that was massive even though it was to be reduced below its maximum potential by being targeted in areas of concentrated poverty such as urban slums and rural depressed areas — a concentration that by 1965 was already the practice in Community Action although it seemed unacceptable in theory to some who were unwilling to give up the vision of Community Action as a universal program in every census tract in the United States. The role of Community Action in this first five-year plan was notable in two ways. First, the economists of the planning division did not argue against the political power and community organization dicta of Shriver's social theorists; they didn't understand the concepts and ignored them. Community Action was to be a deliverer and coordinator of services; organization of the poor was not readily assimilable into the model. Second, Community Action was thought of as federal manager, coordinator, and deliverer of most of the services to the poor. Those causes of poverty that could be solved by delivery of such services were to be solved through direct programs funded by Community Action and managed by local Community Action authorities. Community Action was to be *big*, and indeed the whole poverty program was to be big. The OEO budget request contained in this antipoverty plan was approxi-

61

mately $3.5 billion for fiscal year 1967 as compared with the billion and a half the Administration had asked and Congress had granted with a minimum of trouble in 1965 for fiscal 1966. This $3.5 billion was just the first installment on larger numbers, and it was embedded in a $30 billion recommendation for the overall War on Poverty, $10 billion more than was already being spent. In retrospect, the fascinating thing about these figures were that we really thought they were possible. In the summer of 1965, President Johnson had invited Shriver to a cabinet meeting at which he is reported to have said to each member of the cabinet, "You save money on your programs" and "You save money on your programs" and, pointing at Shriver, "You-all give it to him."

In September 1965 all this changed — it changed sharply, abruptly and very traumatically — it changed because of the rapidly increasing fiscal demands of the Vietnam War, but it also changed because the political fruits had fallen off the tree of administrative chaos and program excess with dull squashy thuds. The mayors of the United States had descended upon Vice President Humphrey, Mr. Johnson's envoy to the cities, and had given him the word as to what had been happening in their cities and what they thought of it. Their thoughts were pretty pungent. The poor were being organized against the establishments, and, not surprisingly, the establishments didn't like it a bit. The theorists and lesser ideologues hadn't allowed for their theories to come home to roost this way, but roost they did, and in the White House and the Vice President's office.

The President and Vice President didn't like it either. Together with the war, it had its effect. The OEO budget, far from $3.5 billion was to be $1.75 billion, a very modest increase over the $1.5 billion for the previous fiscal year. There is no way to separate out the fiscal/military causes for this setback from the political causes. The Vietnam War was of course outside the ken of OEO, but it is tempting to wonder whether stronger control of programs from the top by Shriver and a full-time Deputy might have minimized the multiplier effect that domestic political trouble had on war-induced financial stringency. It may be that Shriver wanted the radical experimentation and was willing to take the risks. But it may also be that, spread too thin, he either did not recognize the risks or was unable to control events within OEO well enough to minimize them.

SEPTEMBER 1965 THROUGH NOVEMBER 1966: CONSOLIDATION
AND RETREAT

The fiscal constraints and political pressures of the fall of 1965 led to a drastic change of attitude not only on the part of the Administration but also on the part of the Congress. Congressional relations had been easy in 1965: hearings relatively perfunctory; Shriver friendly with Chairman Adam Clayton Powell of the House Education and Labor Committee; a budget of $1.5 billion voted as requested, the only major change to the Economic Opportunity Act being the provision to the OEO Director of the right to override a governor's veto on a CAP project in his state (a gesture generated in the Congress itself by an attempted veto by Governor George Wallace of Alabama). But congressional hostility increased very rapidly in 1966, the beginning of OEO's time of troubles.

And in response to the pressures and hostilities from the Congress, the Administration, and the public, the period starting in the fall of 1965 was one of OEO consolidation. The management of OEO was beefed up, and a more conventional bureaucratic cadre began to replace some of the dreamers and zealots. In January 1966, Shriver was finally relieved of his Peace Corps directorship and was able to devote full time to OEO. Before that, however, the political problems raised by the first year of OEO had led the President to provide Shriver with a Deputy, Bernard Boutin, who had come from the directorship of the most solidly business-like of government organizations, the General Services Administration. As it turned out, the difference between the imaginations of Shriver and Boutin was a gap that could not be bridged, and Boutin departed before the summer of 1966.

In the fall of 1965 also, the President appointed a team to investigate and straighten out the administration of OEO. The team was headed by Bertrand Harding, the Deputy Director of the Internal Revenue Service, who had a reputation for being one of the top managers in the federal government. The Harding committee produced a series of administrative recommendations in the spring of 1966. And Harding himself was rewarded, a verb that may not be well chosen, with the deputyship to Shriver in June 1966. Administratively the Harding appointment marked a turning point. Harding was a Deputy in whom Shriver began to put confidence, and this growing confidence was matched with Harding's growing responsibility for administering the program and carrying out the recommendations of his own committee.

At the levels below those of Director and Deputy, personnel changes also moved consistently away from theorizing and toward performance. By the end of 1966, most of Shriver's brightest young theorists had departed, but the second rank of ideologues stayed much longer. The bright young men were replaced as Special Assistants by a continual flow of young businessmen, lawyers, and others whose chief talents lay much more in public relations and interpretation of OEO to various groups of American society than it did in ability to think about the forward frontiers of the War on Poverty. William Haddad departed the inspector generalship and was replaced by Edgar May, who changed the title to Assistant Director for Inspection and operated the troubleshooting job in a correspondingly low-key way, albeit without losing his personal dedication to the initial idealistic goals. The Director of the Community Action Program, Theodore Berry, became ill in the fall of 1965 and was temporarily replaced for a period of three months by William Kelly, Shriver's Assistant Director for Administration, a hard-nosed bureaucrat whose chief boast was that he had worked his way up through the government starting with the lowest grade GS-1. Kelly made substantial progress in straightening out and weeding out various hotbeds of fierce dedication in CAP but had by no means finished the job by the time that Berry came back and retook his old position after a certain amount of bureaucratic infighting.

Richard Boone, who was in many ways the within-OEO leader of the devotees of community power organization departed in 1965 to do his thing as Executive Director of an outside pressure group. He was replaced temporarily by Jule Sugarman, a professional civil servant, who soon became full-time administrator of Head Start; in 1966 his place was taken by Donald Hess, whose previous position was Chief Administrative Officer of the Advance Research Projects Agency in the Department of Defense, a managerial background rather different from Boone's. Sanford Kravitz, the first CAP research and demonstration man, also departed, leaving behind many friends but few records. Two summer 1966 personnel shifts that marked continuation rather than change of direction were the promotion of William Bozman to the Deputy Directorship of CAP as

Frederick O'R. Hayes departed to become Mayor Lindsay's Budget Director in New York, and my filling in behind Joseph Kershaw as Director of Research, Plans, Programs and Evaluation when he returned on schedule to Williams College.

As the personnel shook down, so did the concepts, theories, and operations. Thus CAP began the changeover from its 1965 role of the advance guard for the overthrow of local establishments. Indeed, CAP was dominated through 1966 not by anybody's theories but by the job of creating and funding a thousand Community Action agencies throughout the country. This job was done too fast, and with haste came waste, but the waste was of the routine sort associated with ill-trained and ill-supervised personnel working 12-hour days under undefined guidelines not with somebody's pet political theory gone sour. At the same time, the national emphasis programs of Community Action — the autonomous efforts designed to provide the poor with certain innovative kinds of services on a professional basis: Head Start, Legal Services, Health Centers, and the Upward Bound Program for college entrance of poor kids — all these shook down and began to achieve a permanent stability and status. This movement was aided by the fact, discussed later, that the Congress, scared and angered by the first-year excesses of CAP, did everything to encourage these specific service delivery programs they understood at the expense of the more amorphous locally planned Community Action programs.

This shaking down of CAP operations also led through the year to a changing understanding of what Community Action could accomplish. One result of the trauma of the fall of 1965 was that OEO began to realize that whatever had been the initial intention, CAP was not destined to become a massive deliverer of services to the poor in its target areas. Perhaps it could still fill the role of coordinator of services delivered by itself and other agencies (federal, state, local, and private) and certainly CAP had a role as catalyst in stimulating programs for the poor in target areas. But it was not going to be the manager or commander. This was made crystal clear by the Administration when it put into the legislative hopper and obtained passage of a bill that provided to the mayors and official establishments of selected cities, monies to plan, coordinate, and do other things that looked suspiciously like a lot of the things many people had thought CAP was supposed to do. This bill, in large part a reaction to local and national political fears of federal funding of politically nonresponsible local power centers, was first called Demonstration Cities; but when someone thought that this might be construed as a bill to promote demonstrations in cities, the name was changed to Model Cities.

The difficulties of CAP and, for that matter, of OEO coordination, were further brought out by the increased assertions of independence by the Labor Department and other managers of delegated programs. The Department of Labor continued to refuse to let OEO interfere with "its" business. And over a period of a year, Labor fought within the bureaucracy to be given complete control over all manpower programs both at national and local levels. It took direct pressure from the Budget Bureau for Labor to agree to give OEO (and for that matter HEW) some responsibilities for the manpower coordinating teams which were beginning to be set up in major cities. These teams were tripartite, but Labor was clearly more equal than the others.

Indeed, as the OEO bill ran into troubles on the Hill, the Labor Department lobbyists made no bones about lobbying for their portions of the bill only (NYC and other manpower programs), at the expense of OEO-managed programs and OEO coordination. Since the relevant congressional committees (House Education and Labor and Senate Labor and Public Welfare) had long worked with the Labor Department, Labor's inside track together with its major concern with its own interest had substantial effects on the way the legislation finally came out. The 1966 session marked the beginning of OEO's time of troubles on Capitol Hill. In the House, Chairman Adam Clayton Powell held brief hearings that were notable mainly for the virtual collapse of Job Corps as its statistics were thrown into question and its management seemed unable to follow, never mind control, what was going on. These hearings, together with Job Corps's continued disciplinary and cost troubles led the powerful Congresswoman Edith Green, who had never been very friendly, to confirm her suspicions and become a dedicated enemy both of Job Corps and of Shriver.

After the hearings, however, Powell virtually abdicated and failed to show up at the crucial executive (closed) sessions of his committee. The committee was dominated by liberal Democrats — indeed, it was probably the most liberal in the House — but the liberal Democrats turned out not to be great friends of OEO. To some extent, they reflected the fears of their more conservative House colleagues, by whom the bill would have to be passed. But beyond this, the liberals represented the big cities and felt more than anyone on the Hill the pressures of the mayors in response to the CAP excesses of 1965. In some cases they were frightened that the local Community Action programs in their districts were building up potential rivals for their seats. And in addition to their political fears, they had sincere doubts about the basic ethical questions of federal funding of political challenges to local government and setting up of politically nonresponsive units. All this they blamed on Community Action — on the locally planned and initiated programs of Community Action together with centrally controlled demonstration programs — and they were determined to do something about it.

The resulting bill came out of the House committee in the summer of 1966 with a low dollar authorization (they too were feeling the budget pressures of the Vietnam War), $1.5 billion as compared with the Administration request of $1.75 billion, but more important, OEO's ability to spend the budget was severely hemmed in. The House committee gave the lion's share of the pared-down budget to the Labor Department for the NYC and a few smaller manpower programs to the cost of the Community Action authorization. The committee's bill severely constrained the ability of CAP headquarters and local authorities to spend the money the way they wanted, by earmarking specific amounts for Head Start, Health Centers, Legal Services, and for a new program put in by Congressman James Scheuer, New Careers for the Poor, a quasi-public employment program. In addition, the House cut the Community Action research and demonstration monies back from $100 million to $30 million, thus severely constraining what they felt, for the most part accurately, had been at the root of their troubles. Unfortunately, this constrained the good with the bad. Finally, the House put a statutory limit on the man-year cost of the Corps.

A bit of money and OEO freedom was restored by the Senate Labor and Public Welfare subcommittee chaired by Joseph Clark of Pennsylvania. The committee members, not elected locally and mostly not up for election in 1966, felt the local pressures much less than the House members and were friendlier to CAP and the rest of the program. The authorization coming out of the Senate committee was raised to $2 billion (but it was cut back to the Administration-requested $1.75 billion on the Senate floor, and the ultimate authorization was finally cut down to $1.625 billion in the appropriation process), and the Senate also eased the constraints slightly. But the Senate, like the House, had pet projects and private objectives; Senator Gaylord Nelson of Wisconsin beefed up the language behind a small public employment program he had inserted in the bill the previous year, and the two senators from New York, Robert Kennedy and Jacob Javits, wrote a new manpower provision intended to have special impact on the high-unemployment areas of central cities. Both the Senate and House felt that OEO and the War on Poverty would be better off concentrating money on good hard job programs and getting away from the esoterica of Community Action. Senators Kennedy and Javits, Senator Nelson, and Congressman Scheuer thus inserted three new and separate manpower provisions in the law in addition to the existing NYC. And finally, the Senate, unhappy at the paucity of opportunity programs for elderly folk, added an Assistant Directorship for the Aged to look after their interests.

What came out then as a result of this process, which incidentally did not provide until October appropriations for activities that had already begun the previous July, was a chopped-up bill with many many special provisions and far less freedom on the part of headquarters or localities to plan and operate. This was the intention the Congress had started out with, and the cutbacks in locally planned Community Action operations necessitated by the bill brought this signal of Congressional intent sharply down to local communities.

Congress was not the only locus of external trouble for OEO in 1966. Although not directly connected with OEO, the urban riots of the summer of 1966 were closely enough associated with poverty that they affected OEO politically and otherwise. These disturbances were smaller than those of the previous summer and far smaller than those of the next summer: the biggest 1966 affairs were in the Hough area in Cleveland and in Chicago, where it was primarily a case of whites rioting against Negroes rather than Negroes rioting against their environment — nonetheless, they hurt.

Nineteen sixty-six was also a year when OEO began to be badly hurt by its friends. Perhaps the biggest public event of the year was the CDGM affair. The Child Development Group of Mississippi, as noted previously, was established in 1965 as a Head Start program, but its staff carried it beyond the mission of Head Start into general organization of the black poor and general employment of many people not qualified to provide children with the skilled help the program was designed for. Furthermore, various of CDGM's accounting and administrative practices were questionable at best. Motivated no doubt by his opposition to the very idea of *any* organization of Negroes in Mississippi, Senator Stennis attacked the program. The OEO found enough truth in the accusations that it was difficult to defend the program against them, particularly since CDGM had repeatedly rejected OEO advice and warnings. Even though in other places the accounting difficulties might have been straightened out more quietly and the organization of the poor might have been winked at, a determined attack by a key member of a Senate committee considering OEO appropriations presented grave problems when most of the events alleged were in fact pretty much as described.

As a result, OEO began to back off from CDGM, setting up instead a rival organization to run Head Start in Mississippi, Mississippi Action for Progress (MAP). The degree of change that had taken place by the summer of 1966 in the orientation of OEO in relation to the radical theorists of community organization was illustrated by subsequent events. Once it was known that CDGM was being disestablished, much of the left liberal intellectual movement rose up in wrath against OEO in general and Shriver in particular. Americans for Democratic Action, the Citizens Crusade Against Poverty, of which Boone had become Executive Director, and *The New Republic* all began to accuse OEO of deserting the poor and abandoning its objectives. The culmination of the attack was a full-page *New York Times* advertisement headed "Say it isn't so, Sarge." And, of course, the attackers had some justice on their side. It is a bit difficult to establish any basic compatibility between the goal of ending poverty in the poorest state of the union and the preservation of the establishment represented by Senator Stennis. If poverty in Mississippi were to go, the establishment would have to be attacked. But Shriver's defense was political reality, CDGM had been stupid enough to step outside of the rules of the game in a very unsubtle way, and having been picked up on this, OEO could do little but enforce the rules. The upshot was a compromise and a parallel continuation of CDGM and MAP.

Among those whose main objection to OEO was its stirring up of controversy, controversy stirred up by the left attack on OEO was almost as bad as controversy stirred up by the right. Here was a new version of an old joke. Policeman to demonstrator in Union Square: I'm taking you in. Demonstrator: But Officer, I'm an anti-Communist. Policeman: I don't care what kind of Communist you are, I am taking you in. And the damage to OEO was done.

Self-styled friends of Community Action within OEO, the ideologues who stayed when the top theorists left, did similar damage by leaking to the newspapers the inside story of anything going on within OEO that they disliked. Joseph Loftus of *The New York Times* and Eve Edstrom of *The Washington Post* were the beneficiaries of these leaks, but to those who were suspicious of OEO, here was one more demonstration of irresponsibility, and it hurt.

The War on Poverty planning operation also consolidated during the year and began its retreat toward the reality represented by the more than 50 percent cutback of the budget request in the first five-year plan. The five-year plan itself made two major changes. Income Maintenance was still considered crucial, and little change was made in the ideas here. But the overall employment situation had shifted drastically in the year between the first two plans. Whereas the unemployment rate had been crossing the 5 percent mark at the time of the initiation of the first five-year plan in the summer of 1965, it crossed the 4 percent mark in the summer of 1966, when the second plan was being developed. The Vietnam War, which had been instrumental in reducing the funds available to OEO, had also had a major beneficial effect in reducing unemployment. On balance, the war's favorable effects on the poor seemed clearly to outweigh the unfavorable ones, and, because of the rapid increase of private employment, the second five-year plan dropped the stress on public employment and instead emphasized training for the private market. (This led to some problems with Congressmen who were beginning to buy the Public Employment idea based on the previous year's thinking.) The training concepts in the five-year plan emphasized the tying together and coordination of the array of training programs, which was already large and was due to be increased by the manpower provisions newly introduced into the Economic Opportunity Act by the Congress.

The other change in the plan was the redefinition of the role of the Community Action Program. The new plan set CAP forth as coordinator and as catalyst but no longer as manager and major deliverer of services. But the new emphasis on training and coordination and the rethinking of CAP's role marked what was perhaps a major change in the role of planning. Whereas the planning of the first year had been done in a vacuum, in the second year the operation was beginning to come to grips with reality, particularly the reality introduced by the trauma of budget cutbacks of the fall of 1965. Planning was beginning to relate to operations and to the rest of the program. The product of the planning efforts played a major part both in the formal presentation to the congressional committees and in the executive session negotiations with the committees. Policy as recommended by planning began to affect day-to-day operations: the poverty line was increasingly applied to programs as an operating standard, and at least one program that planners had indicated seemed to have little to do with poverty, the Small Business Program, was beginning to be phased out.

The planning staff also worked hard at maintaining the tenuous OEO foothold in the programs delegated to Labor as well as other antipoverty programs run by Labor. Outside of OEO, the OEO planning staff continued to push the idea of income maintenance and partly because of these efforts it began to be taken more seriously throughout the government.

Like the rest of OEO, however, RPP&E consolidated its grandiose ideas and began to live in the real world rather than the exciting dream world of 1965. As a token of this shift, Joseph Kershaw, before leaving, again briefed the Vice President though he was not invited to brief Joseph Califano, who had become a major White House monitor of OEO.

In other words from the fall of 1965 to the fall of 1966, OEO became

71

a troubled agency. The bill that was finally passed was a restrictive one, cutting back the freedom of the Community Action Program and the budgets of the Community Action agencies, cutting far back on the R&D funds that had been used for so much freewheeling in 1965 and also constraining Job Corps. The congressional actions in turn confirmed to the Administration that its new-found fears of the effects of OEO operations were well founded.

This period in the history of OEO culminated in two significant events. One was the election of 1966, in which the Democratic majorities on the Hill, particularly in the House, were cut back sharply, leading to predictions that OEO, which had done so badly in the outgoing Congress, was likely to be killed in the incoming one since 47 House votes had shifted to the Republicans. The other event was the appointment by President Johnson of a then-secret task force on the organization of the executive branch, headed by a friend of the President's, Ben Heineman, president of the Chicago and Northwestern Railroad. One of the charges to the Commission was to figure out what to do with OEO. The recommendation was widely reported to be that Community Action, the guts of OEO, should be transferred to HUD. Ultimately, near the end of 1966, it was decided to reject this recommendation, but the fact that it was made was a strong sign of the times.

NOVEMBER 1966 THROUGH DECEMBER 1967: SARGENT SHRIVER— KING OF THE HILL

Nineteen sixty-seven was the political year of OEO. Leaving Harding to do most of the running of the agency, Sargent Shriver devoted full time (and full time for Shriver was a lot of time indeed) to the political problem. The political problem was that of getting an agency that had squeaked by the previous Congress in rather battered shape past the new Congress in which in the House, 47 Democrats, mostly liberal, had been replaced by 47 Republicans, mostly conservative. As noted in the previous section, liberal Democrats in the House of Representatives were not necessarily very good friends of OEO, but at least they could be counted on to vote "aye" on final passage. In any case, to anticipate the end of the story, Shriver and OEO completed the political year with a bill which was a substantial improvement over the previous one and an appropriation higher than the previous year's, both of these by increased margins in both Houses. The complete story of this political miracle will have to be told elsewhere, but the fact that it did take place, and the effects on the War on Poverty of both the result and the efforts made to achieve it form part of this story.

The Shriver operation in OEO was typified by the nine o'clock meeting every weekday morning. Starting in January 1967, Shriver met with the chiefs of a three-pronged staff devoted to the solution of the political problem. One prong consisted of his political assistants for the Congress itself, primarily Donald Baker, the General Counsel, and George McCarthy, the Assistant Director for Congressional Affairs. The second group, headed by Herbert Kramer, the Assistant Director for Public Affairs, was devoted to the press and public image of OEO. Finally a number of people worked on generating support among the volunteer and pressure groups, from charity to business, which had been giving OEO consistent backing throughout; the leader here was Hyman Bookbinder, Director of the Office of Private Groups.

The Shriver strategy stressed the individual programs of OEO, particularly the national emphasis programs of CAP, which he felt had far better popular images than the amorphous and controversial operation which was CAP itself. The litany of Head Start, Health Centers, Legal Services, Upward Bound, and sometimes a few others like manpower programs and neighborhood centers was chanted through the corridors of Capitol Hill and the halls of OEO itself. A prototypical Shriver operation was his trip through the mountain poverty areas of North Carolina with the Reverend Billy Graham, a trip the extensive films of which were shown on the Hill to help bring around the moderate Southern conservatives, whom Shriver believed to be the shift group he had to obtain.

The behind-closed-doors events on the Hill in 1967 comprise a story yet to be told or perhaps never to be told. The open events themselves were interesting enough, however. The House began its long hearings in May 1967 after many many postponements. Postponements were due in part to the fact that Congressman Carl Perkins of Kentucky, the new Chairman of the Education and Labor committee who had succeeded Adam Powell after the latter had been ousted from the House, had a good deal of difficulty getting the committee organized to work on poverty at all. In addition, given the sourness of the political events of the previous year, delay may have been part of the strategy worked out by Shriver and Perkins. Let things simmer down a bit. The hearings themselves lasted weeks in contrast to the perfunctory hearings of the previous year. They were characterized by swapping of accusations between Shriver and Republican Congressmen Charles Goodell of New York and Albert Quie of Minnesota, the designers of an alternative bill entitled "Crusade for Opportunity" intended as a "constructive alternative" to OEO. (The substance of the Quie-Goodell Bill makes little difference; it was never a serious factor anyhow.) Other Republican congressmen, from the prehistoric right wing made little attempt to be constructive at all.

In the Senate, Chairman Joseph Clark of the Senate Subcommittee on Labor and Public Welfare began early in the year to conduct a comprehensive series of hearings and studies of OEO. In charge of the studies was Howard Hallman, who in pre-OEO days had been the Deputy Director of New Haven's Community Progress, Inc., the prototype of the service-delivering (as compared with community-organizing) Community Action Program. The Senate study, nationwide hearings, and also long hearings with OEO officials produced a workmanlike and basically friendly set of documents from a basically friendly committee. In the Senate also, the issue during the summer of 1967 got mixed up with the issue of hunger, which became very important as a result in part of the same committee's visit to Mississippi and the testimony taken during this trip by Senators Clark, Robert Kennedy, and Javits among others.

In part because the Senate committee *was* friendly, however, most of the problems and strategy were concentrated in the House. Stemming in part from the long hot summer of 1967 and embittered by large-scale and widespread riots in Newark, Detroit, and elsewhere, the House entered its autumnal session in a mood of acid sourness with no recent precedent. The ability of OEO to demonstrate adequately and realistically that its major effects on the riots had been to help cool them and ameliorate some of the results helped a good deal. It was shown, for example, that virtually no OEO or Community Action employees who worked in the thick of the riot area jungles had been arrested and that CAP neighborhood centers were treated as refuges and sanctuaries. On the other hand, a ten-foot-pole treatment by the White House (or so it has been reported by many OEO participants in the day-to-day battle) did not help at all. The extremity of the bitterness in the House was indicated by the fact that in the fall the House omitted OEO from the continuing resolution that provided operating funds to agencies whose appropriations had not yet been passed. Local OEO programs in many cases went unfunded, Head Start children were thrown out of closed classrooms, and OEO benefited politically from the press and public distaste for this behavior. Also OEO benefited from the widespread sympathy extended to the OEO employees, who had been excluded from a federal pay raise bill by a rump session amendment in the House.

In November and December the worm turned, and, it turned out to be a snake. The public reaction to the petty nastiness of the House in the matters of the continuing resolution and the pay raise worked to build sympathy for the program. Chairman Perkins, facing a refusal of Republican members to come to his executive session to write the bill, took the unprecedented step of writing the bill in public session from which the Republicans could not afford to be absent, and the public session undoubtedly prevented many political tricks that would have been possible in private.

The Shriver public relations operation ground on to a climax. Not only did the liberal papers of the United States produce editorials attacking the House, but so did many of the backwoods papers and many of the conservative big city papers such as the *Dallas Morning News*. Particularly noteworthy was the fact that the mayors, who had a mere two years before descended on Hubert Humphrey to ask him to turn off CAP, now besieged the Hill and demanded that CAP be kept turned on. The establishment-confronters no longer ran CAP, and when the 1966 year of consolidation had ended with a bill that cut back funds going to the cities, the mayors did not like that at all. This set the stage for Shriver's conciliations, which brought the political powers of municipal government down on OEO's side. This was done, incidentally, without any drastic "sellout" to the "local establishments." Most local Community Action programs remained hostile to or at least competitive with the city governments, but the hostility and competition were kept within the limits that made political coalition feasible. It again becomes fascinating to speculate whether, had Shriver and a Deputy worked full time in the first year, it might have been possible to assert control at that time and change much of the subsequent history.

The final ingredient in bringing the city governments around was Congresswoman Green's amendment, which gave them the right to take over the private nonprofit Community Action agencies that ran the program in most cities. It was the Southern and marginal big city votes brought in by this amendment that finally seemed to make the difference. Again as in the CDGM case there were cries of sellout from the zealots, but the Green amendment probably saved the program and in retrospect does not seem to have made much difference in subsequent operations; ultimately very few city governments took advantage of it. Finally, when Congressman Goodell, knowing he had already lost the battle because the majority Republican right wing wouldn't go along with his constructive alternative (in their sourness that fall, they wanted to vote no on everything) called the Green amendment "the bosses and boll weevils" amendment, much of the moderate South came around to OEO's side. This phrase was as mellifluous as "Rum, Romanism, and Rebellion" and on a smaller scale had the same effect in uniting the targets of the neatly turned phrase.

What came out of all this action and reaction was a surprise and a happy one. The new bill was less restrictive than the previous year's, it authorized the expenditure of more money than the previous year, it contained — *mirabile dictu* — a two-year authorization, thus giving OEO a year's vacation from major congressional activity, a vacation that was very welcome indeed after the year's operations on the Hill. It also contained some new provisions. In response to the feeling in the Congress that OEO had not been devoting enough funds and energy to rural areas, it established the new Assistant Directorship for Rural Affairs, a token appointment like the previous year's Assistant Directorship for the Aged. Perhaps more significant, Senators Kennedy and Javits of New York, deeply dissatisfied with the OEO's use of their previous year's Special Urban Impact program as mainly another manpower program, wrote into the legislation a more carefully worded section directing a program of urban impact through general economic and community development. Fortunately for OEO's flexibility, the fixed-dollar authorizations for this and other new programs that were written into the Senate version of the bill were softened considerably by the efforts of Perkins and later by Chairman George Mahon of the House Appropriations committee. And to put the icing on the cake, the bill that provided all these concessions was passed by the biggest margin OEO had ever received in both Houses. Merry Christmas, Sarge.

Although OEO's public image in 1967 was dominated by the Shriver campaign, operations continued on a basis that began to shake down to more of a level and routine than had been possible previously. Thus CAP devoted itself primarily to ministering to the thousand Community Action agencies it had set up too rapidly in the previous years, ministering to them with a budget cut back from 1966, which certainly did not help. But at least they were running and they became integral parts of what was happening in many cities, integral and helpful parts as indicated by their growing help in the riots and the willingness of the mayors to help them when the crunch came. Indeed, Community Action had become so nonirritating to city establishments that at the opening of the Clark Senate committee hearings it was criticized for tameness by Richard Boone of earlier CAP fame and by Kenneth Clark, the Negro psychologist who had been supervising a comprehensive evalution of Community Action programs.

In fact, however, CAP and OEO started at least two strikingly innovative programs in the summer of 1967. One of these, the Southwest Alabama Farmers Cooperative Association (SWAFCA), set up a vegetable producing and marketing cooperative for black farmers in an area near Selma, Alabama, in order that they might get out of the dying cotton-farming culture into a more modern operation on a scale large enough to be profitable. The other innovation, of even more long-run significance, was started by the OEO planning office using CAP funds. This was the "Graduated Work Incentives Program" in New Jersey, a carefully designed social experiment in Negative Income Tax. Rather than being a demonstration of how a Negative Income Tax might work, Graduated Work Incentives was an experimental model designed to get specific data to answer specific questions, primarily about the effects of income maintenance on the incentives to work of the recipients, but also about effects on family stability and related matters. As such, it was not only the first tentative federal feeler in the area of comprehensive income maintenance, but it was the first precisely designed information-gathering social experiment of its kind.

It should be noted that in agreeing to the inception of SWAFCA and the Graduated Work Incentives project, Shriver overrode the strong advice of some of his advisers. Since he was visited by the entire Alabama congressional delegation together with a scattering of mayors in opposition to SWAFCA, it is remarkable that Shriver, who is sometimes painted as a cynical razzle-dazzle supersalesman, agreed to go ahead with the Alabama program. And one of his advisers said of the Graduated Work Incentives Program, "This is not a demonstration in income maintenance; it is a demonstration in how to kill a program on the Hill," but Shriver insisted on going ahead. Not only was his decision courageous, but it also showed what in retrospect has turned out to be remarkable political judgment. Not only did the Graduated Work Incentives experiment hurt little on the Hill in 1967 but by 1969 it became the chief case in point of a willingness and ability to experiment that helped see OEO through the beginning of the Nixon Administration.

On the other hand, the third new departure begun that summer (again with Shriver's explicit okay) came home to hurt OEO badly the following year. This was the Blackstone Rangers program, the funding of a Chicago youth gang to train themselves and do other good things. There are those who claim that this funding averted a major Chicago riot in the year of the Newark and Detroit riots, but in any case a failure to monitor the program adequately led to programmatic and political grief within a year.

Job Corps, too, settled down in 1967. At the beginning of that year, William Kelly, who in his brief previous experience as Acting Director of CAP had begun to untangle the strings, became Director of the Job Corps. Proceeding with a new broom, he managed to straighten out the Corps's data and do a sales job as part of Shriver's team that left the Corps in excellent political shape at the end of the legislative session. Whether Job Corps operations were changed — for the better, as the political advocates of the "New Job Corps" claimed, or for the worse, as some critics of increased Corps discipline feared — is open to debate. It may be, for better or for worse, that the real changes were only to the visible surface.

The big operational change in OEO came when Shriver effectively turned the administration of the program over to Harding so that he could devote full time to the Hill. After two years, Shriver finally had a Deputy in whom he had confidence and who had had extensive experience in running programs. Although Harding had a standing invitation to the nine o'clock political meetings, he seldom went, and he tended to utilize a different set of subordinates from those who helped Shriver with *his* problems. Inevitably there was some choosing up of sides between Shriver's and Harding's boys but remarkably little, and the goodwill between the two men and between those who worked most directly with each of them was by and large maintained.

The kinds of questions with which Harding dealt were less dramatic than Shriver's, but some were nearly as important to the operations of the War on Poverty. The best example is the success of Harding's effort to bring OEO back into the federal government and to bring the programs delegated to other agencies, over which OEO control had become no more than nominal, back under effective OEO suzerainty.

The major example of this success was the manpower programs. The 1966 congressional session had, in its infinite generosity, provided OEO with a four-part manpower program: Neighborhood Youth Corps; the Nelson amendment for Public Employment primarily in rural areas, primarily for the aged, primarily for beautification purposes; the Kennedy-Javits amendments for Special Urban Impact (this was the first Kennedy-Javits amendment that OEO treated as a manpower program); and the Scheuer New Careers Program. None of these parts had much funding except for NYC, which also had sufficient programs to sop up the funds. Harding's advisers suggested to him that this mélange could be operational only if the pieces were tied together into something approaching a comprehensive manpower program. It was obvious, however, that such a comprehensive program would have to be delegated to the Labor Department, which already had NYC, the biggest chunk. There was pressure from the White House to delegate, but the pressure was not overwhelming. A possible alternative was to keep the new programs within OEO and under CAP administration, where they would have added up to a relatively small total of new funding. The administrators of CAP wanted it this way; they pointed out that the other delegations to the Labor Department had been almost completely independent of OEO control, and they felt that turning the manpower mission completely over to Labor would be the beginning of the end of community action and of the CAP concept of local control and participation of the poor. The Labor Department, on the other hand, wanted the delegation very badly; they wanted it with no strings attached.

In this situation Harding decided that a comprehensive delegated manpower program was the answer, but in order to preserve the values of CAP and utilize CAP's ability to reach the poor, indeed to preserve CAP itself, it was necessary to write a strongly worded delegation in which the new programs would be tied closely to local Community Action. To summarize a long story, both Labor and CAP objected — CAP to the point where Director Ted Berry came into an off-the-record background press conference and put his opposition on the record — but over CAP's objections, Harding convinced Labor, Shriver, the Budget Bureau, and the White House. The delegated program was completed in the late winter of 1967, and the rest of the year was devoted to making it work in the face of sabotage at the local level and by some people at the Washington level in both Labor and CAP.

It finally did work — imperfectly, but it worked. And by working, it achieved two objectives. First of all, it set a pattern by which OEO could keep some strings on poverty programs by real as compared with nominal delegation without ever becoming too big itself; this is a pattern that seems likely to be repeated fruitfully as other programs beginning in OEO mature and can be tied more loosely to the apron strings.

Second of all, the delegation agreement made a real difference in the operation of the manpower programs. The Department of Labor is an odd sort of organization. Its federal civil servants work within a highly centralized organization with decisions flowing down from Washington, a substantial contrast to OEO regionalization, in which many decisions are effectively decentralized. At the same time the major local operative arms of the Labor Department are the State Employment Service offices, which are fully funded by the federal government and almost fully controlled by the state governments. Not tied to a strong OEO delegation agreement, Labor would have had the new programs run by the local offices of the State Employment Service, and the programs would have been at the mercy of these local and state agencies. In many states, primarily in the South but by no means only in the South, State Employment agencies have not been well attuned to the poor, and turning the programs over to their complete control would have been a mortal wound to their antipoverty effectiveness. But the tie to OEO with its compulsory tie at the local level to Community Action meant that the Department of Labor was forced to make the comprehensive manpower program into a true antipoverty program because OEO in Washington and Community Action authorities at the local level were always looking over Labor's shoulder. To put it another way, Labor was thus *enabled*, rather than being forced, to do what Secretary Wirtz and others had always wanted but had been unable to push through their own subordinate and state bureaucracies. One can take his choice, but the operative fact was that the stewardship, challenge, and indeed threat of OEO local Community Action made the delegated programs into far different animals than they otherwise would have been.

The comprehensive manpower program was what came to be known as CEP, the Concentrated Employment Program. Its formal structure was set up at a meeting at the Budget Bureau before the delegation agreement had been completed. At this meeting OEO was represented by a member of the planning staff who approved of the program in general but insisted on putting in an OEO footnote that the whole thing would not work because it required business participation without any payoff to business. A year later this prediction had obviously proved correct and something was done about it.

Planning by OEO not only was involved in the Budget Bureau meeting but was intimately involved in the entire set of delegation negotiations; indeed it had done the staff work for Harding. This was one example of the changing role of the Office of RPP&E in OEO during 1967. At the end of 1966, the planning operation had absorbed the agency budget operation, which had previously been under the Office of Administration. Although this would have been a crucial decision in many agencies, it was not important to OEO. As a new agency, OEO never had the vested interest of an old-line budget division, and the budget accountants had always been dominated in the decision process by the new-style program budgeters of the planning staff. But the bringing of budget operations

into RPP&E did signify the greater tie of RPP&E to day-to-day operations. And indeed, as Harding rationalized the administration of OEO,
RPP&E became an important staff arm to him. This did not mean the
abandonment of the five-year plan and long-range thinking; it did mean
the attempt to put into operation the short-range and more realistic portions of the plan. The plan itself needed little changing from the previous
year. Some emphasis was put back on public employment as it became
clearer that even the high level of national employment left out too many
poor people, but otherwise the manpower section concentrated on formal-
izing, rationalizing, and conceptualizing what had been done with the
comprehensive manpower program and making a strong case for tying
into this a new program of subsidies to private business for on-the-job
training of the poor.

In Income Maintenance, most of the theoretical and mathematical
work that could be done had been done; the exciting new departure was
the New Jersey Graduated Work Incentives Project. In its concern with
income maintenance, the Council of Economic Advisers, encouraged by
OEO and others in task force meetings, had persuaded President Johnson
to announce in his January 1967 Economic Report that he would appoint
a Commission to look into all the questions related to income maintenance
and come up with recommendations to him. The President must have
immediately regretted this moment of weakness, for he did not get
around to appointing the commission until a year later, in January 1968.
When it was appointed, it was headed by Ben Heineman, who had previously headed the Commission on the Organization of the Executive
Branch.

JANUARY 1968 TO NOVEMBER 1968: SUSPENSE AND ROUTINE

Nineteen sixty-eight was the year of continued consolidation and straightening out of OEO operations, of improvement of administration, and of
suspense as OEO and the War on Poverty awaited first the election and
then after the election the onset of the Republican victors.

It was quite clear at the beginning of the year that Shriver was
ready to leave now that he could do so in victory. He had achieved the
political triumph of his career, and for him everything else in OEO had
to be downhill. He began turning elsewhere, first to Illinois, where Mayor

Richard Daley of Chicago began his 1968 political operations, which culminated in the debacle of the Chicago convention, by turning Shriver down for the gubernatorial nomination. (The hit of the show at Shriver's vast going away party in May of 1968 was a parody of the song "Bill Bailey, Won't You Please Come Home," in which Shriver sang to a pinochle-playing Mayor "Dick Daley, Can't I Please Come Home?" The answer was no.) Shriver finally went as President Johnson's Ambassador to President de Gaulle, a post for which his 1967 dealings with Congress had qualified him.

By the beginning of 1968, Bertrand Harding had effectively become Director of OEO, and when Shriver left, he was appointed Acting Director. By the time Johnson got around to appointing him Director that summer, however, it was too late for his appointment to be confirmed by the Senate. The combination of Harding, a nonpolitical administrator, with a two-year authorization, which made 1968 a nonpolitical year for OEO on the Hill, made an immense difference in the program. Harding's Deputy Robert Perrin had a background on the Hill, but his style was far lower key than that of Shriver. Where the program had been dominated in 1967 by Shriver's political operations, in 1968 Harding's effort was just to run it.

Virtually all the Shriver nine o'clock meeting group departed, in continued friendship to the program and to Harding. They left out of exhaustion. Kramer left the Public Affairs directorship for a more comfortable consultancy, Bookbinder went, McCarthy went, May left for Paris with Shriver, and many of their subordinates also departed. Even before the 1968 election there was a continuous drift-off of other personnel too as the program settled down to day-to-day operations and individuals left in quest of new opportunities. Jule Sugarman, who had been the administrator of Head Start from the beginning, left for the Department of Health, Education and Welfare, where he was widely expected to be waiting for his program to come home to him again. William Crook, a close friend of President Johnson's, who had first become Southwestern Regional Director and then Director of VISTA and had been mentioned as one strong possibility to succeed Shriver, became instead Ambassador to Australia. Added to such departures was the difficulty of new recruiting after President Johnson created an aura of political uncertainty by his March 31 announcement that he would not run for reelection, and the personnel at OEO ran down a bit, both quantitatively and qualitatively. Many effective people remained, but they were fewer than before.

The discussion of the future turned to the inevitable spin-off or delegation of programs from OEO to old-line agencies. Head Start was expected to move to Jule Sugarman at HEW, the Job Corps was widely considered a candidate to spin off either to Labor or HEW, and the Health Center Program was considered sure to move to HEW eventually. Unlike the discussions of breaking up OEO as a result of the report of the first Heineman Commission and of the political troubles on the Hill in the fall of 1966, these new projected spin-offs were considered the result of OEO successes rather than OEO failures. As the programs matured, there was some question of whether they should be retained under OEO management. The decision not to make OEO the overall manager of the bulk of the poverty program had been made long before 1968; it was made in the fall of 1965, after the first year.

Community Action continued to consolidate its operations, cutting down modestly on the number of its agencies as it consolidated them in rural areas. The national emphasis programs consolidated, and the decision was made that, contrary to the previous expectations of some persons in CAP, they would not be absorbed back into the "local initiative" pot of money whose distribution was determined locally but rather were to remain national programs. A major operating question was the role of CAP with respect to the Model Cities program, which was beginning to be established. Each had some authority to coordinate the other, and who was to do what to whom was unclear. Negotiations over these matters took a good deal of time and effort by the CAP staff. So did the setting up of the CAP Management Information System, which by the end of 1968 had produced many many numbers, signifying what nobody was quite clear.

Indeed, Harding began asking what Community Action was for anyhow. If it was for delivering new and innovative services to the poor in new and innovative ways, then fine, and perhaps even more stress should be put on the national emphasis programs. If not, what was the purpose?

Was it, after all, still to organize and stir up the poor? The problem was brought home sharply by the difficulties of the CAP-funded Blackstone gang before Senator John McClellan's investigating committee and the ultimate demise of that program as well as a few others. Harding received few answers but a good deal of philosophizing on the part of CAP theorists who were far less sure of themselves than the theorists of 1965 had been.

In fact, CAP did begin some innovations; the major new effort was in antihunger programs, as OEO made the most of a small fund for emergency food programs that had been created when the 1967 Congress had found out to its shock that some Americans were starving to death because they did not make enough money to put up the minimum cash required by Department of Agriculture regulations to obtain food stamps. In addition, CAP used part of the allocation to the new Kennedy-Javits urban impact/community economic development funds to initiate a development program in the Hough area of Cleveland that looked good enough to be a prototype for larger efforts in the field. The remainder of the Kennedy-Javits money was distributed among the Labor Department, the Economic Development Administration, and the Agriculture Department for a series of pilots, none of which looked as promising as the CAP program in Hough.

The general uneasiness concerning the role of CAP, however, enveloped not only Harding but also President Johnson, who, as quoted later, reacted to the Blackstone Rangers hearings by accusing OEO of "being run by kooks and sociologists." The role of CAP was being questioned, and it was questioning its own role, but even so, the fact that there seemed to be a necessary role for CAP was generally agreed on. As earlier CAP had dropped the dream of managing massive local antipoverty programs, by 1967 it had ceased to think of itself as the major coordinator of multiagency programs going to the various localities. Having tried, CAP was quite ready to concede that role to Model Cities. But CAP as an advocate of the interests of the poor and an organizer of the poor, in a much lower key than envisaged by the 1965 theorists — organization for cooperation with the establishment instead of overthrow of the establishment — was well settled in. Nobody, not even as it turned out in 1969, Richard Nixon or Daniel P. Moynihan, who had been so critical of the early role of CAP, was quite ready to do away with the program.

Job Corps began and ended the year in somewhat more trouble. Buoyed up by the December 1967 triumph on the Hill, Job Corps morale was punctured in January 1968, when President Johnson and the Budget Bureau cut the Corps back in order to obtain money for other antipoverty programs. After this setback, the Corps seemed unable to get beyond the straightening out and selling job of 1967. It seemed beyond them to solve or even consider many of the problems involved in a program where too many kids dropped out too early to get much in the way of benefits, where 16- to 17-year-old youth were being trained and turned out into a job market they were simply still too young for, and where others were asking serious questions about the utility of "urban" training programs not located in the central city areas where many of the youths would ultimately settle down. Instead of attacking and perhaps experimenting with answers to some of these questions, Job Corps spent its energies refighting the glorious battles of 1967.

Thus, within the OEO direct operating programs themselves, there was little new excitement. The real advance came using OEO funds and OEO ideas but operating outside of OEO. This was the JOBS (Job Opportunities in the Business Sector) program, in which business co-operation was solicited to run an on-the-job training program with on-the-job training slots subsidized as necessary by the federal government. The concept, although not a new one, had been developed largely in the OEO planning staff in 1966 and 1967, and the planning staff and OEO had tried to sell it to the Labor Department and the Budget Bureau. In 1968, it was an idea whose time had come politically, and a pot of money was put together out of the Job Corps reductions, out of the OEO programs delegated to the Labor Department, which had not been spending at the expected rate, and out of Labor Department funds under the Manpower Development and Training Act.

The operations, however, were turned over to a new quasi-public business organization known as the National Alliance of Businessmen, headed by Henry Ford II with one of Ford's Vice Presidents, Leo Beebe, as Executive Vice President. The government end of the program — handling of the subsidies and much of the recruiting of poor people into the program — was operated by the Labor Department. Unlike the Concentrated Employment Program (CEP), where the OEO role had been established by the delegation agreement, OEO's role in JOBS was only peripheral. Representatives of OEO managed to elbow their way by arguing that, "after all, it's our money." But except very indirectly through CEP, the program was not tied in any way to local Community Action agencies, largely because the businessmen were still a little scared of CAP and because the Administration, afraid of kooks and sociologists, was unwilling to push CAP. The lack of participation by the poor seemed to have little effect on the program, whose problems lay more with the businessmen than with the poor. (See next chapter.)

What OEO influence there was on the JOBS program was expressed through the planning staff. The five-year plan stressed the importance of the JOBS program and, having come the full circle, suggested the necessity of a complementary public employment program. A couple of years of full employment together with the prospective outreach of even a successful JOBS program suggested strongly that there were areas in the United States where the only jobs possible had to be created publicly, and there were still far too many Americans even in prosperous communities whose capabilities were simply not up to the training available through the JOBS program. For these people, public employment seemed a necessity.

The focus on income maintenance shifted in 1968 to the New Jersey Graduated Work Incentives Experiment and to the new Heineman Commission, which began to hold hearings and build a record with the aid of OEO and HEW. The Heineman Commission itself may have been an example of the effectiveness of OEO outside its own program. Had not OEO, particularly the planning staff, been pressing hard for income maintenance since the beginning, it seems possible that the issues might never have been brought into sharp enough focus to create the Commission. Certainly without the efforts of OEO the New Jersey experiment would not have taken place.

The other major effort of the planning staff was in the evaluation of OEO programs. For the first time a systematic structure was set up for the rigorous evaluation of the effectiveness of the programs that, at the beginning of 1968, had been running for three years and had produced enough results to make rigorous evaluation a reasonable possibility. Some of the major early evaluations looked at Head Start, the various man-power programs, and the institution-building and institution-changing effects of Community Action. Preliminary results from these evaluations are incorporated in the following chapter.

The year 1968 was characterized primarily by the suspense of wait-ing for the election and after the election by the suspense of waiting to see what President-elect Nixon would do. The early indications seemed to be that things wouldn't be very different after all. (See Chapter 8.) After four years both OEO and the War on Poverty seemed to have become institutionalized. The remaining question was whether innovation itself — the chief function of OEO — could be institutionalized, or whether the two terms are incompatible.

CONCLUSION

Much of what happened in the first four years of the War on Poverty seems in retrospect to have been inevitable. Had things gone differently, many of the trees might have looked different, but the forest would still have been there. However, some of the initial decisions that made what followed inevitable were decisions that could have been made another way: President Johnson's decision to declare War on Poverty was not in itself inevitable; the decision of the President and Shriver to create a separate agency and to go big fast was not inevitable. But given underly-ing forces such as the civil rights movement, some sort of antipoverty program probably was inevitable. And given the theories and theorists that dominated the relevant intellectual landscape in 1964 and 1965, much of the program direction was inevitable. Finally, given this direc-tion together with the escalation of the Vietnam War, much of what happened was likely to have happened under any circumstances.

Particularly likely in any case were the initial effort to organize the poor and the troubles that followed. The militants and theorists were there, and had they not organized within the program, it looked certain that they would have organized against the program, which might have ended up causing more trouble (as in the CDGM case) than finally did occur. Given the initial political troubles and the Vietnam War, the Administration backdown and the limitations of the size of OEO also seem in retrospect to have been inevitable.

It is difficult to see how any initial planning could have avoided the confusion between the antipoverty and equal opportunity objectives, which is one of the themes of this book. These distinctions were simply not known or understood in 1964 or 1965, and they finally were understood only as the *result* of operations. The initial five-year plan was glorious but unreal; and although it became less glorious as the years went by, it became more relevant to what was going on and to what was possible.

The major speculations of hindsight about what might have been center on several questions. What if there had not been a Shriver with all that Shriver's razzle-dazzle style implied, and what if the initial decision had not been to go big? I suspect that a different style would have made a difference, but I also suspect that limiting the War on Poverty to a small experimental program would have become increasingly untenable in the light of increasing pressure from civil rights and other militants.

Another obvious question is: What if Adam Yarmolinsky had stayed or another full-time Deputy who could work with Shriver had been found? It is very tempting to believe that the presence of a full-time politically sensitive Deputy would have muted the wildness of 1965 — not changed it completely by any means but kept it under control — and with that control, the revolt of the mayors would not have taken place and the 1966 legislative year would have been a far more successful one. Perhaps even the 1966 election would have turned out somewhat differently. And so on and so on. Probably the inevitability of history is such that other events now unrecognized because in fact they never occurred would have taken place to keep the direction much as it was.

There is one question that should be asked with the implied answer going in the other direction: What if Shriver had not found Harding? Had Shriver tried another year without a Deputy or had he tried another Boutin, the program that began to consolidate in 1966 and 1967 might have blown apart. The lack of control that would have resulted might have led to bigger, better, and earlier scandals, and Shriver simply would have been unable to devote full time simultaneously to saving the program on the Hill and running it in poverty headquarters. The OEO and

89

the War on Poverty might have gone down in history with the Townsend Plan as something that was really never tried, even though it did have some effect on the future.

In any case, it seems likely that, given the events of November 23, 1963, when Lyndon Johnson committed himself to the antipoverty program that John Kennedy had begun to think of, things would have ended up much as they in fact were. There would be a set of programs randomly distributed over the set of needs, there would be expectations far greater than achievements, and there would be administrative confusion and confusion of program objectives.

There would also have been substantial progress. For in fact the other story of the four years is that in one way or another substantial progress has been made against poverty and toward equality. That is the topic of the next chapter.

5
An Equally Biased Evaluation of the War on Poverty

In the final analysis, the evaluation of the success and effectiveness of the War on Poverty depends on how well it has achieved its objectives, how far it has cut down on low-income poverty in the United States and, if we admit the additional objective, how nearly it has equalized opportunity. But the asking of the "how far on poverty" and "how near on opportunity" questions raises one more question: Near or far compared to what?

At first cut, the "compared to what" question might be answered straightforwardly: compared to zero people in poverty and compared to complete equality of opportunity among groups. In fact, however, because no one expected zero poverty or complete equality at the end of four years, the choice of a reasonable and realistic standard for comparison is important.

On the one hand, science insists that the only meaningful comparison is to what would have happened without the program. It is important to avoid the *post hoc, ergo propter hoc* fallacy; undoubtedly without a War on Poverty there would have been a decrease in the number of poor people and in the degree of inequality from 1964 to 1969. Because of increasing prosperity of the American economy, the poverty population would have decreased. Because of both the social conscience of the American people and the increased strength of the civil rights movement, opportunity would have become more equal. In the first summer of the

91

OEO, data were released by the Census Bureau showing a substantial drop in poverty from 1963 to 1964. Promptly after the release, the Director of OEO received a note from a top White House staffer which said "Nice going, Sarge!" Since both 1963 and 1964 figures were pre-OEO, Shriver's effectiveness in this matter might have been considered open to some question. This sort of assignment of credit for what would have happened anyhow of course is not what we mean by evaluation, but in a more subtle way it is easy to fall into; it is not always possible to separate out accurately those effects that would have taken place even without a program from those directly or indirectly due to the program.

On the other hand, if it is easy to take scientifically unjustified credit for what would have happened anyhow, it is equally easy to receive unjustified political blame for not having realized expectations. The impossible standard of performance can be a heavy political albatross. President Johnson did declare "unconditional War on Poverty" in January 1964; in January 1969, the war was only roughly one-third won in terms of reductions in the numbers of poor people. If the standard were victory in five years — and this certainly was not a standard intended by the President — then obviously the war had failed. In June 1966, Sargent Shriver said that poverty as it was defined (by the Orshansky line) could be abolished in ten years given sufficient funds and proper programs. He was given neither sufficient funds nor proper programs, and poverty has not been abolished in one-quarter of the ten years; he is thus accused of having generated unrealistic expectations and having failed to fulfill them. In fact, the expectations generated by both Johnson and Shriver were unrealistic; they were unrealistic not because of their carefully qualified statements but because hopeful people tend to hear the statements without qualifications. The poor, in desperate hope, heard the declarations but not the statements of difficulties; the rest of America heard what many interpreted somehow to be a promise of the end of all social ills based on income, race, and class.

Indeed, after four years, many politically and economically sophisticated individuals who knew very well at the beginning that poverty could not be overcome in four years or at fund levels like those made available were accusing the War on Poverty of having failed because poverty had not been abolished. And now, because the existing War on Poverty has been "tried" at low fund levels and has "failed," they are ready to begin all over again, forgetting that it is always possible to find the flaws in a program that has been tried, whereas the program to be tried always looks relatively shiny and flawless — until it is tried.

Somewhere between taking credit for the inevitable and taking blame for the impossible lies the truth. This evaluation does not claim to present the truth or even to present an unbiased picture. Four years' experience in trying to present coldly objective evaluations to OEO Directors who needed to know the truth as objectively as it could be presented have been tempered by four years of helping the Directors and others present the program to the public, the press, and the Congress in a reasonably favorable light. The rosy bias as well as strong attempts at objectivity are likely to color what follows, but at least it should be possible to avoid the two extremes: of *post hoc, ergo propter hoc;* and of why didn't you do yesterday what we all know very well can't be done until next week?

Such a statement of personal bias is a necessary warning. But it should be realized that there probably is no such thing as an unbiased evaluation. In March 1969, for example, the General Accounting Office (GAO), the congressional watchdog over federal programs, provided the Congress with an evaluative analysis of the War on Poverty.[1] This report attempted objectivity as I attempt objectivity; given the built-in biases of GAO, it did not succeed any more than I shall. For GAO has throughout its existence been in the business of ferreting out flaws, errors, and peculations; it has not been in the business of analyzing programs for effectiveness. Although the GAO report is objective (and by no means entirely unfavorable to the War on Poverty), the negative biases of the auditor and the investigator do show through. This is not meant as criticism of the GAO report; it is to say that because evaluation is an art and in part like all matters of art is a matter of taste, there is no true objectivity, there are only attempts at objectivity. The GAO has certainly attempted such objectivity. So, I believe, have I.

THE EFFECTIVENESS OF THE WAR ON POVERTY AS A WHOLE

With all the necessary qualifications — about the objectives other than reducing low-income poverty, about not taking credit for what would

1. Comptroller General of the United States, *Review of Economic Opportunity Programs,* March 18, 1969.

Table 5
Number of Poor People and Incidence of Poverty
(Orshansky Line; price-corrected)

	Total		White		Nonwhite	
	Number (millions)	Percent Incidence	Number (millions)	Percent Incidence	Number (millions)	Percent Incidence
1964	34.3	17.9	23.4	14	10.9	49
1965	31.9	16.6	21.4	13	10.5	46
1966	29.7	15.3	20.1	12	9.6	41
1966 (changed series)	28.8	14.8	19.5	12	9.3	40
1967	25.9	13.2	17.6	10	8.3	35

Source: Bureau of the Census

have happened anyhow, and about the arbitrariness of the poverty line cutoff — the changes in the number of people in poverty by the Orshansky measure still provide a reasonable place to start the evaluation. Table 5 shows these changes using as a base year 1964, the year before the explicit antipoverty programs began to operate on more than a very token scale. The table shows very sharp reductions in the numbers of people in poverty, reductions of more than one-fifth in the first three years of the war.[2] It shows, of course, an even sharper reduction in the *incidence* of poverty; among nonwhites in particular, this incidence declined from very nearly one in two being poor to one in three within this same three-year period. Of course, as discussed in Chapter 3, median family income also went up sharply in this period, and a poverty line that moved in relation to median income would have shown smaller drops in the number of poor. Were we trying to measure the change in some absolute concept of "welfare," this would be an important consideration; national welfare would have increased somewhat less than indicated by these figures. For purposes of evaluating the programs of the War on Poverty, however, the possible changes in the poverty standard are not relevant. What is relevant is the comparison to what would have happened to the

2. Note that 34.3 minus 25.9 equals 8.4. Subtracting an additional .9 million for a statistical series change in 1966 leaves 7.5 million, which is more than one-fifth of the 34.3 million base.

numbers of poor people had there been no explicit OEO and related anti-poverty programs.

Such comparison would have shown only a portion, probably substantially less than half, of the overall improvement to be attributable directly to the new programs. There can be no doubt that economic growth unaided is a powerful, probably still the most powerful, generator of additional income for the poor as well as for others. The most important indicator of that aspect of economic growth most relevant to the poor is unemployment. In base year 1964, the national unemployment rate was 5.2 percent, by 1967 it had declined to 3.8 percent. For non-whites, the 9.6 percent unemployment rate of 1964 had declined to 7.4 percent by 1967. These were sharp improvements and to such changes most of the credit for the decrease in poverty numbers must go.

What portion of the credit should go to economic growth, however, and what portion to explicit antipoverty programs is not possible to determine. For one thing, counting the poor is a relatively new activity, and the Census Bureau has had the disconcerting habit of shifting around its estimates of the numbers of the poor years after the event; the numbers in Table 5 may well be obsolete by the time they are printed. These shifts are not likely to be large enough to change the general story of what happened, but they do frustrate any mathematical attempt to factor out specific causes. Indeed, the noise level of standard statistical inaccuracy, compounded by less standard uncertainties due to new concepts and methods, means that the precision of the published numbers is always in substantial doubt. Year-to-year changes in poverty numbers are thus residuals remaining after subtracting one set of conjectural numbers from another, and under these circumstances residuals are notoriously volatile.

For reasons like this, the estimates are not good enough for utilizing the kinds of precise statistical methods that might separate out the various causes for the drop in poverty. Added to such inaccuracies is the fact that among the variables closely related to general economic growth, the one most directly related causally to changes in poverty is unemployment, but unemployment is in itself an "effect" variable that will decrease in part from successes of explicit antipoverty programs. In other words, economic growth affects poverty changes mostly through unemployment, but if we are trying to separate out two streams of causation, growth and explicit antipoverty programs, we must realize that this central explanatory variable on the growth side is directly affected by the explanatory variables like manpower programs on the War on Poverty side. It has thus proved impossible so far to measure directly in any rigorous way that part of the antipoverty improvement of the last few years directly attributable to explicit antipoverty programs.

In another way, some data do suggest, however, that the programs have had a significant effect added to that of economic growth. From 1966 to 1967, for example, the number of poor decreased by almost 3 million, the sharpest drop in the period covered. Yet unemployment rates remained unchanged for these two years, at 3.8 percent. Some of the improvement in the poverty situation may have been due to aspects of growth other than employment (increased wages at the lower end of the scale, for example), but it still seems likely that some of the credit lies outside of growth entirely, that it should go to the antipoverty programs themselves. This is a weak statement, however. The only strong statements that can be made are that poverty has dropped sharply since 1964, that the War on Poverty was associated with this drop, and that the extent of causation cannot at present be known.

If it is tough to estimate precise effects of the programs on low-income poverty, it is even tougher to estimate their effects on equality of opportunity. Table 6 assembles some indicators of relative changes between the white and nonwhite populations. The data are all from the Bureau of Labor Statistics/Bureau of the Census publication of July 1968 entitled *Recent Trends of Social and Economic Conditions of Negroes in the United States*.[3] (In spite of the title, most of the data in the report as well as most of the data used in Table 6 refer to nonwhites, not Negroes.) So far as possible, the base year for these comparisons is 1964, which was also used as a base year for looking at numbers of persons in low-income poverty in Table 5.

The period from 1964 to 1967 (or early 1968) is a very short time for the kinds of fundamental social change implied by increasing equality of opportunity, a much shorter time than it is for the income increase tabulated previously. Nonetheless, there does seem to have been substantial

3. Current Population Report, Series 324–26, Bureau of Labor Statistics Report 347.

Table 6
Indicators of Changes in Equality of Opportunity
(ratios arranged so that higher numbers indicate greater equality)

	1964	1965	1966	1967	1968 (first six months)
A. Improving Series					
1. Nonwhite/White: ratio of Median Family Income	.56	.55	.60	.62	
2. Nonwhite/White: ratio of percent of families with incomes over $8000/year	.41	.40	.46	.51	
3. Nonwhite/White: ratio of percent completing 4 or more years of high school			.68	.78	
4. White/Nonwhite: Unemployment rates of married men	.47	.48	.47	.50	.52
5. White/Nonwhite: Maternal mortality rates	.22	.25	.29		
B. Unchanged Series					
6. White/Nonwhite: Incidence of poverty	.29	.28	.29 / .30 (new series)	.29	
7. White/Nonwhite: Unemployment rates	.48	.51	.45	.46	.47
8. White/Nonwhite: Infant mortality rates under one month	.61	.63	.63		
9. White/Nonwhite: Infant mortality rates, one month to one year	.38	.36	.36		
C. Deteriorating Series					
10. Nonwhite/White: Percent of families with husband and wife			.82	.82	.78 (full year)

Source: Bureau of Labor Statistics/Bureau of the Census

improvement within three or four years in a few basic indices. Because we are talking about equality of *economic* opportunity, the best direct measures are the income measures themselves. Lines 1 and 2 of Table 6 indicate substantial improvements both in the ratio of nonwhite-to-white median family incomes and the ratio of the proportions of nonwhite and white families that are relatively well off, with incomes of $8,000 per year or more. Line 6, however, indicates that the ratio of white-to-nonwhite incidence of poverty has remained almost constant over the measured time period. But this ratio of incidence, which has been in the .29 range since 1964, was substantially higher (relatively more poor whites) in the Census year of 1959 when it was .33, and in fact what apparently has happened is that the War on Poverty, although it has not reduced non-white poverty relative to white, has helped prevent continuation of a dangerous relative nonwhite deterioration that had been going on previously.

Encouraging basic indicators are the relative high school completion rates of nonwhites, which jumped sharply from 1966 to 1967 (the only years with relevant published data), and the continuing catchup of non-whites to whites in the employment of married men. The education and married men's unemployment series indicate underlying factors improving future opportunity. Finally, within the most favorable category, maternal mortality rates, although still shockingly different between the races, are at least becoming more nearly equal.

On the other hand, in addition to the poverty series, two health series on infant mortality showed no substantial improvement through 1966, and one basic economic series, overall unemployment rate, showed no improvement. It is difficult to know how to interpret the unchanging ratio of white to nonwhite unemployment. Since there was an improvement in the ratio of married men's unemployment, there must have been a corresponding deterioration among women and unmarried men. This deterioration is probably dominated by problems among teen-agers, where unemployment rates among nonwhites range around the 25 percent level, and, in turn, teen-age unemployment rates are the most difficult to interpret. What is the relative social importance of a youngster unable to find an after-school job as compared to one who has dropped out and is unemployed, and as compared to an adult who wants and cannot find a job?

Even more important for the purpose of this evaluation, one possible effect of antipoverty programs may have been to increase numbers of teen-agers looking for employment faster than it has increased the number of jobs available to them. Since the unemployed are defined as those actually seeking jobs but not having them, a greater increase in jobseekers than in jobholders would lead to a greater unemployment rate even though there may be more jobs.

All the difficulty of interpretation does not hide the fact that on these series, of which unemployment and incidence of poverty are the most important, there has been no visible improvement in the direction of equal opportunity since the beginning of the War on Poverty. Probably even more disturbing, however, is line 10, which shows deterioration of the relative number of nonwhite husband and wife families. As an indication of underlying conditions leading to inequality of opportunity for the next generation, this could be very bad indeed. It is not likely an effect of the explicit War on Poverty. Almost certainly it has something to do with the welfare regulations that provide an incentive for family breakup, and the situation could therefore be improved by a Negative Income Tax. But at least it can be said that the explicit programs of the War on Poverty have not reversed a deteriorating situation.

Thus, although the progress of equality of opportunity among the races is mixed, the indicators seem at least to show that the situation is improving in the most important areas. In this case, however, comparison to what would have been without the War on Poverty, such as was attempted in the case of the numbers of persons in poverty seems beyond even the kind of inexact and suggestive analysis essayed here.

One more set of indicators should be mentioned. The computations of persons in poverty treat individuals as individuals, and the indications of equality of opportunity treat the experience of racial groups as being measured by the statistical experience of individuals within these groups. The other question for equality of opportunity is: What has been the experience of groups *as* groups? This question is almost as difficult to ask as it is to answer, but what is meant is the ability of the group to help its members and to improve its position relative to other groups. Most of the discussion of program effectiveness in this area will be reserved for the evaluative analysis of CAP later, but it should be mentioned here that the marked change in style of institutional life and socio-political effectiveness in the black ghettos between 1964 and 1969 may in itself be a very important measure of overall program effectiveness. In 1964, the institutional life in urban ghettos was thin. The major institutions of a social or political type were the civil rights movement — but this hardly reached down into the black middle class, never mind those below — and the churches, which seemed to be decreasing in impact.

The nature of institutional life in the urban ghettos is examined in detail by Nathan Glazer and Daniel P. Moynihan in their striking 1963 study of the minority groups in New York City, *Beyond the Melting Pot*.[4] Unlike other New York ethnic groups that have passed through poverty, Negroes did not have the self-created and self-help institutions necessary for the exit from poverty. Now they do. The number and variety of social and political groups in most American ghettos is striking, from an administrative point of view perhaps disquieting and perhaps from some points of view frightening. But the kind of institutions whose existence may be a necessary condition for equality of opportunity and the end of poverty are being created.

There should be added to this set of evaluative statements on the overall impact of the War on Poverty two factors on which Sargent Shriver put great weight, and which may indeed be as important as the rest but are less measurable. The first is that the United States and Americans now recognize poverty as a problem that must be solved; before 1964 they didn't. There can be no doubt that OEO deserves much of the credit for that. The problem cannot be solved unless it is recognized. It is now recognized.

Shriver also argued that the vast outpouring of volunteers to help with antipoverty programs was a major contribution. I frankly have somewhat more doubt about the importance of this increase in numbers of volunteers. There has always been a substantial volunteer spirit in this country, much of which has been devoted to "those less fortunate than ourselves." It is certainly the case that OEO and the War on Poverty channeled these volunteers more effectively than they had been before; it is likely that their numbers were increased somewhat. But then the

4. Nathan Glazer and Daniel Patrick Moynihan, *Beyond the Melting Pot* (Cambridge: M.I.T. Press, 1963).

improvement creditable to the War on Poverty is the improved channeling and the effectiveness, but not the volunteers themselves, most of whom were always there. Perhaps the greatest contribution of this volunteer effort, however, lies in sensitizing the educated upper-middle classes to poverty problems to an unprecedented degree. This sensitization undoubtedly contributed to the OEO legislative victory of 1967, but its greatest payoff may be long-run, as the college youth of today refuse to let similar problems be swept under the rug tomorrow. In any case, it should be said for Shriver that at the very least he discovered and made use of the American volunteer spirit in antipoverty programs some years before George Romney and the Nixon Administration.

To conclude this discussion of the overall impact of the War on Poverty, it seems reasonable (tentative though most of the arguments have been) to state that in fact the efforts of the last four years have had significant favorable effects in reducing low-income poverty in the United States and (slightly more tentatively) in increasing the equality of opportunity. Many of the political troubles of the War on Poverty have been due to the fact that these favorable effects have not been up to expectations. Some of these expectations were unreasonably high; some, however, may have been reasonable expectations not reached. In any case, the effectiveness of the programs of the War on Poverty is best examined through the detailed analysis of the next section.

THE PROGRAMS OF THE WAR ON POVERTY

The overall effectiveness of the individual programs of the War on Poverty can be measured only by what happens to poverty, plus what happens to opportunity if that is considered an objective. In principle, it should be possible to evaluate these by the same measures used for evaluating the total impact of the overall War on Poverty. In practice, however, the *ultimate* effects on poverty and opportunity of these programs are impossible to estimate, and therefore we measure the *proximate* effects. The proximate effects are defined as the effects of a program on its immediate objectives (such as the effects of an antipoverty health program on the health of the poor) as compared with its ultimate effects on poverty itself. Having examined the proximate effects, one may be able to make a connection to ultimate antipoverty effectiveness through a theory. This connection is tenuous, but it is the best that can be done so far except for a few programs, primarily in the manpower area, where the proximate effects on earnings are also direct antipoverty effects.

Evaluation of a government program for its effects — proximate or ultimate — is, however, a relatively new idea. Typically, program evaluation, when carried out at all in government agencies, has been evaluation of operations. That is, programs have been looked at to see whether rules have been followed, administration was working smoothly, unnecessary duplication was eliminated, people were feeding into and out of the programs at a reasonable rate, and so on. Little was done to investigate the effects of a program, that is, whether its impact as measured against its objectives was high, low, or nonexistent. Operational and effectiveness evaluation have been compared by Walter Williams:

> In the past, social action agencies have measured operating "performance" in terms of honesty (no embezzlement), prudence (no profligacy), cost control (not using too many paper clips), and occasionally relatively crude output standards (the number of job placements in a training program). However, under cost-benefit standards, for example, the program manager or operator can be honest, prudent, and thrifty (all no doubt great virtues) and still look like a clod with a shockingly low benefit-cost ratio. Beyond embarrassment, evaluation data have potential for either restricting program funds or forcing major changes in program direction. One can hardly assume passive acceptance of such an outcome by program managers and operators.[5]

In part, then, because it is new, in part because its impact is highly political, evaluation of social programs is not yet "scientific," and perhaps never will be. The claim occasionally heard that evaluation problems can be solved simply by application of "benefit-cost" or "cost-effectiveness" analysis is specious. The ordinary formulation of a benefit-cost ratio means two things. First, a ratio of benefits to costs which is greater than unity (that is, greater than 1:1) means that the dollar benefits exceed the

5. Walter Williams, "Developing an Agency Evaluation Strategy for Social Action Programs," Office of Economic Opportunity, December 16, 1968.

dollar costs; conversely a ratio of less than one means the dollar costs are greater. Second, as such ratios are computed for antipoverty programs, a ratio greater than one means that a greater long-run antipoverty effectiveness per dollar can be obtained from the program being measured than from the alternative of a simple stream of federal income transfer payments paid to the poor recipient; and conversely, if the ratio is less than one, the transfer payments are more effective.

Several points should be made quite clear about benefit-cost ratios as they are used for antipoverty program evaluation:

1. A computed ratio of less than one does not mean that a program is unsuccessful. There are usually many intangibles that cannot be computed into benefits; costs are all too tangible. Further, even though a ratio of less than one might indicate that income transfer payments are cheaper, a program that leads to increased earnings is ordinarily considered socially preferable to one of transfer payments and allowance must be made for this difference.

2. The state of the art and the state of the data for benefit-cost comparisons are both primitive enough that it is almost always unwise to compare even similar programs on the basis of computed ratios, unless the ratios were specifically computed in a single study for purposes of such a comparison.

3. A program is not counted as preferable simply because a benefit-cost ratio (or other quantitative evaluation) is computable, whereas it is not for another program. For most antipoverty programs quantitative analysis is not yet possible; for some it never will be, and these include some of the most important programs. Effectiveness and quantifiability should never be confused. It is an error to substitute the concrete for the important. Benefit-cost analysis, where possible, plays a role in the evaluation of programs, but it is only a part of evaluation.

Thus the program evaluations that follow lay no claim to being scientific. Rather, the evaluations use bits of scientific data, like benefit-cost analysis, embedded in somewhat less rigorous studies of operating structures, and surrounded finally by personal judgments. They draw on science, but they depend on the art of fitting together the scientific pieces. This is so for many reasons, not least of which is that it is necessary. Scientific evaluation is perhaps a myth, perhaps a grail to be sought. It certainly does not exist now, nor has it ever.

The following program evaluations are divided into sections corresponding to the four major program-budgeting categories of the OEO five-year planning effort:

A. Manpower programs. Those programs under the Economic Opportunity Act or elsewhere designed to attack poverty by improving the ability of the poor to enter the labor market and work in decent jobs. These programs include both job training projects and job creation efforts such as Public Employment.

B. Individual Improvement programs. Those programs other than directly job-oriented programs in the first category, whose primary impact is on *individuals* in poverty. Most such programs are educational in nature. In more recent years, health programs have also been put into this category.

C. Community Betterment programs. Those programs designed to change the physical and social environments which cause and perpetuate poverty. They include federal antipoverty housing programs such as public housing and rent supplements, as well as the locally planned and operated OEO Community Action programs.

D. Income Maintenance programs. The poor now receive on the order of $14 billion of federal payments under income maintenance programs, primarily that portion of Social Security going to the poor but also Public Assistance. These Income Maintenance programs together with suggested new ones such as the Negative Income Tax form a fourth category of antipoverty programs.

Table 7 shows the relative size of the four categories and the major programs in each for fiscal 1969. In addition, evaluative discussion within each category begins with a fiscal 1969 budget breakdown for the category to provide the general order of magnitude of the programs discussed. Not all programs listed in the budget breakdowns are discussed in detail, only those for which there seems to be something useful to say.

Table 7
Fiscal 1969 Federal Antipoverty Effort
(millions of dollars)

Manpower		2,114
Individual Improvement		10,005
Education	2,301	
Health	7,002	
Nutrition	702	
Community Betterment		1,503
Housing	405	
Economic Development	293	
"Catalytic" Programs	805	
Income Maintenance		12,190
Social Insurance	8,631	
Public Assistance	3,459	
	Total	25,812
	OEO Programs	1,960
	Other	23,853

Source: Office of Economic Opportunity

MANPOWER PROGRAMS

The antipoverty objective of the manpower programs laid out in Table 8 is to increase the earnings of poor people by getting them more and better jobs. It is hoped that these jobs will be good enough so that these people will then no longer be poor. This formulation, however, suggests one immediate problem with manpower evaluation. The person who gets the job may no longer be poor, but if the job happened to have been someone else's before, then the displaced worker may become poor. Most manpower program evaluations have not been able to handle this problem of displacement. They measure the effectiveness of the program by measuring the employment and earnings gains of the people who have been through the program and make little or no attempt to subtract the losses of those people who may have been displaced by the new employees.

This procedure may not be analytically unjustified. For one thing, in a very hot economy with much inflationary pressure it is likely that any new job is a net new job and the problem does not arise. Indeed, the new employee may reduce the inflationary pressure and thus provide an additional social benefit. In a generally prosperous economy with less steam, it

Table 8
Federal Antipoverty Budget, Fiscal 1969: Manpower

Program	Fund Source	Management	Funds (millions of dollars)
JOBS (Job Opportunities in the Business Sector)	OEO and Labor Department	Labor Department and National Alliance of Businessmen	200
Concentrated Employment Program	OEO and Labor Department	Labor Department and Local Community Action Authorities	115
Manpower Development and Training Act	Labor Department and Office of Education	Labor Department and Office of Education	226
Work Experience	OEO	HEW and Labor Department }	128
Work Incentive	HEW	HEW and Labor Department }	
Job Corps	OEO	OEO (through 7/1/69)	280
Out-of-School Neighborhood Youth Corps	OEO	Labor Department	129
Miscellaneous	–	–	996
Total Manpower			2,114

Source: Office of Economic Opportunity

is likely that some displacement does take place but that some of the effect of the new employment is increased quality or quantity of production rather than displacement. That is, most businesses can get along with a few employees less; people work harder, more mistakes are made, but the thing still works. It works better with more employees, and the businesses are happy to hire more employees; these employees are net additions.

Another effect of new placements of poor people in such a moderately hot economy is likely to be a more spread out kind of unemployment. That is, whereas the previously poor employee gets a job he would not have had at all before — a go–no go matter — the displacement may be spread out because some people who would be employed most of the time anyhow would have slightly longer periods of unemployment or would be employed in slightly less attractive jobs or at slightly lower wages or with less overtime, and so on. This brings us face to face again with the equal opportunity objective. Insofar as the motivations behind the antipoverty program are the opportunity-equalizing objectives of reducing the high incidence of poverty in certain high-risk groups, then even man-for-man displacement of the harshest form may have a favorable effect. That is, if members of a group with 10 percent unemployment displace members of a group with 2 percent unemployment, the net social effect may be beneficial. Were this individual displacement obvious (black for white, for example) it would not work; the displaced members of the 2 percent group would not be likely to take it lying down and the results could be social dynamite. But because displacement is seldom 100 percent man-for-man — some of the new employees increasing production rather than displacing old employees — and because even the true displacement in a prosperous economy is likely to be diffused through longer between-job lags, reduced overtime, and so on, displacement will not ordinarily be obvious. It will not be a matter of a black man walking in and a white being thrown out. Thus it does not seem unreasonable in the first analysis to evaluate manpower programs by their gross effects in getting jobs for their clients and not worry too much about displacement. This conclusion is fortunate because we would not really know how to handle displacement analytically if we had to.

If the gross effectiveness of the total antipoverty manpower effort is examined, then the evaluation must be that the programs are working pretty well overall and particularly well within certain crucial groups and fields but that for others much improvement is needed.

On the whole, the job position of the poor is far better than it was in 1964. From 1964 to 1966, the poor in families headed by able-bodied nonaged males who were less than fully employed went down by one-fourth, so did the poor in families headed by fully employed able-bodied males. (See Table 3 in Chapter 2.) As has been suggested in a number of places, the employable poor have been those most amenable to treatment. Whether this successful treatment has been due more to a prosperous economy or to explicit antipoverty programs remains a question that must be answered as was a similar question about the overall War on Poverty impact: "To each, in part — but we don't know what part?"

More specifically, at overall unemployment rates like 3.5 percent, the manpower effort is beginning to work well in urban areas. It is beginning to work well among adult males; families headed by adult males, regardless of race, are very unlikely to be poor. It is working, although not perfectly, in opening up non-dead-end entry level jobs at least for those who appear relatively "employable," although not among the "hard-core" multidisability (for example, bad health, illiteracy, police record, alcohol problem) unemployed. All of these successes are made possible by the overall prosperity of the economy, which also minimizes the displacement problem. Whatever the cause, however, complaints about no jobs for men are seldom heard in cities anymore.

This is not true, however, for rural areas. It is not true for teen-agers; the unemployment rate for black teen-agers is 25 percent. It is not completely true for women. It is not true for "hard-core" unemployed men. These are problem areas. So is one other, the problem of promotion from entry level jobs into the semiskilled and skilled categories and training for such promotions. Antipoverty manpower programs have not failed here; mostly they have not tried, confining themselves rather to those who are below the poverty level because they cannot even get into entry level jobs. The evaluative result that little has been accomplished above the entry level is thus not evidence of failure of programs but a consequence of utilizing different objectives. More stress on the equal opportunity objective would dictate that far more attention should be paid to upgrading those already above the poverty line. At any rate, the job situation of the poor has been improving greatly and by doing so has had a direct effect in decreasing poverty. To what extent this has been an effect of the major manpower programs discussed in this chapter — JOBS, CEP, Work Experience and Work Incentives, Job Corps, and NYC Out-of-School — is conjectural. The program that works best, JOBS, is the newest and therefore the least likely to have had major impact. Perhaps the greatest effect so far has stemmed simply from the number and variety of efforts that have been tried, each with some success.

Job Opportunities in the Business Sector (JOBS). Job Opportunities in the Business Sector (JOBS) is a program for on-the-job training of the poor in entry level jobs in private business. This training is subsidized in part by the federal government.[6] JOBS is a program of major significance for at least two reasons. It is the first comprehensive large-scale adult training and employment program in the War on Poverty; previous large-scale attempts under the Manpower Development and Training Act have put only a small portion of their efforts into training the unskilled and the poor. And it is the first major effort to subsidize business cooperation in the War on Poverty. The program operates on a "hire first" philosophy under which poor jobless adults over the age of 18 are hired by participating firms and then, depending upon their needs, are given prevocational or vocational training by these firms. Because of "hire first," even the prevocational training can be considered on-the-job training, which is important because actually having a job with a specific firm is important in upholding the motivation of a poor person to come in and stay in. Too often poor people have been taken into institutional training programs where, having been previously failed by the educational system, they are put into a school atmosphere, and, having finished the course, they are turned out onto the streets without a job. For reasons like this, on-the-job training has seemed to be the best technique for entry training for the

6. In the first summer of the JOBS Program, 1968, the attempt was made to hire youth into summer jobs at the same time as adults and older youth were being hired into permanent jobs. The summer job program failed miserably, and that failure in itself may be evidence of the seriousness with which the permanent job program was taken. Participating businesses seriously expected to hire hard-core poor persons into the permanent working force. Given these long-run efforts, they tended to look at the summer program as a somewhat frivolous addition.

poor, and JOBS is the first large-scale federal on-the-job training program for the poor.

The JOBS program is run primarily by the National Alliance of Businessmen (NAB), a quasi-public nonprofit organization, set up initially in 50 cities in January 1968. The National Alliance of Businessmen obtains pledges of job slots from businesses and attempts to make sure that these pledges are filled. At this level, JOBS is one program, but in fact once the pledges have been made, it is a dual program. A business may sign contracts with the Labor Department for "reimbursement of training costs" (the federal subsidy aspect of the program) for the hard-core poor hired into the program, or the firm may redeem its pledges at no cost to the government. In fact, only from one-fourth to one-third of the jobs pledged thus far are in the federally funded portion of the program. And outside of the funded portion, neither the government nor the National Alliance of Businessmen has much control over what is done. As a result, although the funded slots are to be filled by individuals certified by the Employment Service to be hard-core poor according to certain criteria including the Orshansky line, it is less likely that the unsubsidized "free" slots will be filled by hard-core poor.

Again we come up against the question of objectives. If the only objective of the antipoverty program is to decrease low-income poverty, then the free slots contribute little because most of the people filling the slots are likely to be above the poverty line. (Of course the slots cost the government little too, and it is not clear what the benefit-cost ratio of zero to zero is.) If, on the other hand, equalization of opportunity all along the income scale is a major objective and if, as seems to be the case, the free slots are filled by members of minority groups and other disadvantaged individuals, then the free slots may make a vital contribution. They may be training many of the dead-end jobholders of minority groups for open-ended entry jobs with a chance of upward mobility, and by doing so at virtually no cost to the government, they may be allowing federal funds to be concentrated where equity (as compared to effectiveness) would concentrate them, on the poorest. The data are not yet available that demonstrate that the preceding description is accurate, but it does seem to describe accurately many early unsystematic observations.

If one looks at gross statistics for both parts of the program, funded and free, JOBS would seem to be enjoying success as a large-scale man-power program for adults, the success being reflected by the scale of achievement as much as by anything else. In January 1968, President Johnson set a goal for the NAB to place 100,000 hard-core poor in jobs by July 1969. In fact, some imperfect but probably not too inaccurate fig-ures indicate that more than that number had already been placed by December 1968, with another 50,000 or so by mid-1969. The program was thus far ahead of schedule on a scale that seems to make a meaningful dent in job needs. (The job needs of the poor are sometimes quoted at levels like 3 to 5 million. Figures like this are highly inflated with respect to the employable poor, and since the JOBS program through March of 1969 existed only in 50 large cities, 100,000 jobs seems to be a reasonable dent in needs within these 50 cities, which probably total less than 1 million jobs for adults. In March 1969, the program was extended to 125 cities, but still no rural areas, where many of the unemployed or under-employed poor live.) Some of the 150,000 would have gotten similar jobs anyhow in a hot economy — and a fairly warm economy is necessary for JOBS to work at all — but 150,000 is still a large number.

The federally funded contract portion of the JOBS program was moving much more slowly, however. At the end of January 1969, the Labor Department had contracted for 43,000 slots, but only 21,000 of these had been filled, only about one-sixth of the total placements of the overall JOBS program. If the contract portion is taken to consist only of hard-core poor and the free portion only of those above the poverty level, then this small proportion under contract would indicate a failure to penetrate the hard-core. In fact, however, some of the free jobs also went to hard-core poor; *if* from 20 to 50 thousand total hard-core poor had been placed by the overall JOBS program, then this would be rather im-pressive, but we don't know.

A manpower program, of course, cannot be measured by placements alone. It should be measured by subsequent job and earnings history of the group in the program as compared with a control group over a rela-tively long period of time. Now OEO is beginning such an evaluation, but the data will not be available for a while. Even data on immediate job retention experience under a program such as JOBS are not completely meaningful. The NAB reported that, of its 118,000 placements through

December 1968, more than 80,000 were still on the job, that is, a two-thirds retention rate. In the contract portion, 14,000 of the 21,000 placements were still on the job, the same rate as for the overall program. But by mid-1969, the retention rate looked more like 50 percent. Stabilization at this level would still look good, compared with other programs reaching the poor (like Job Corps, Work Experience), but dropping much further would be a strong danger signal.

In addition to placements and retentions, it should also be reported that most of the jobs seem to be at relatively high entry rates of pay. A July 1968 survey showed that two-thirds of the total paid over $1.75 an hour and one-third over $2.00. A later survey over a smaller number of contract jobs indicated a slightly higher wage structure for these. On the other hand, particularly in Northern cities there seems to be difficulty in filling jobs at less than $2.00 an hour or filling the more manual sorts of service jobs at any price. This perhaps is as it should be and indicates that the poor clientele as well as the businessman is taking the program quite seriously as a means of entry into the mainstream of industry.

This somewhat impressionistic analysis of the numbers seems to indicate a program that is working reasonably well. Evaluation, however, also highlights some operational issues:

1. The key operational and theoretical issue is employer readiness to set up programs that will work with the poor as they really are. In the early days of the JOBS program, a high operating official on loan from business told his business boss that what he should expect was what he called "basket cases" — unreliability, drunkenness, unwillingness to come down to the job after the first couple of days. Understanding this, the company was able to overcome some of the disabilities and run a successful program, but many of the participating firms do not understand what they should expect, even though it is made clear in program literature. They are looking for the good, clean, reliable poor person who, having been pushed down time and time again by discrimination and poverty, is willing to rise once more, smile, and go to work for a 40-hour week plus overtime. Mostly he does not exist. Whether people are poor because they have personal problems or whether they have personal problems because they are

poor, most of the hard-core unemployed coming to the JOBS program have personal problems, and until businesses are willing to cope with these realistically, the programs are going to work less well than they should.

This is the major reason for the slower development of the contract portion, particularly the lag in filling slots contracted for. Unlike the unfunded slots, the contracts constrain the employer to look for the true hard-core unemployed, and, having found and seen them, the employer is not anxious to hire them at any federal subsidy. At this point in time, JOBS cannot be demonstrated to have cut deeply into the "hard core." Most of the "unemployable" are still unemployable.

2. Added to this difficulty is the likelihood that the contract portion of the program is probably "creaming" to some extent. That is, it is cutting somewhat above the hardest of the hard-core poor. This is undoubtedly much truer of the free portion. Whether this *should* be the case depends a great deal on the relative balance of the antipoverty and equal opportunity objectives. It does seem quite reasonable for the free portion to select from the top if it still reaches people in need of opportunity-equalizing assistance. Perhaps it is also the case that even the contract portion, although confined to poor people by the Orshansky definition, should work mainly on those within this group for whom on-the-job training is most likely to be successful. The importance of the disengagement of equity from effectiveness by means of an income maintenance scheme that will take better care of the poorest of the poor again becomes obvious here. Both the free and contract portions of the program ought to work with those for whom they can best work if those who need help most but can profit less from JOBS can be taken care of in more appropriate ways.

3. Although most of the entry wage rates seem reasonable and most of the jobs appear to be true entry rather than dead-end jobs, there are certainly some low-wage dead-end jobs included in the program, particularly in the South. There seems little excuse for these, even under the free portion of the program. The poor and members of minority groups have always been able to get jobs as janitors, and it seems dishonest for this program to take credit for such placements. Again, however, it is a mark of the success of the program that most

of the participating businessmen understand and conform to the definition of training and entry jobs.

4. A much ignored issue concerning the JOBS program is that it has been run completely from the top down. Both the NAB and the Johnson Administration feared any aspect of "participation of the poor" in running this program, and the Department of Labor has never been much interested in such participation. The top staff of the National Alliance of Businessmen did meet at least once with some major civil rights leaders; that was the afternoon before the evening on which Martin Luther King was assassinated, and the contacts were never pursued. Frankly, it is not clear that participation should be part of this program. It may be that such a specific and technically oriented program can best be run from the top down; not every institution in the United States can or should be democratic. Business is used to top-down programs and maybe top-down is the only way to encourage business participation. On the other hand, there is little doubt that more participation by the poor could assist the program in recruiting, and difficulty in recruiting may be an additional reason for the slow development, particularly of the contract portion. Furthermore, the knowledge of the poor could be of help to business in understanding how to overcome obstacles to employment. On balance, it would seem a good idea to encourage much more community participation if it can be done carefully and in a less than frightening way, but participation as a shibboleth that must be imposed willy-nilly could run the risk of destroying a very useful program.

5. On the other hand, if JOBS has not become a program of and by the poor because of the desire to keep it a program of and by business, business is distinctly less enthusiastic than it was at the beginning. In part this was inevitable; enthusiasm can never be maintained at peak levels, and, as suggested, the first meetings of businessmen with the poor have scared a lot of businessmen. In part, the cooling was due to the departure after the 1968 election of the charismatic first executive director of NAB, Leo Beebe of Ford Motors.

6. The relationship of the JOBS program to other programs is not clear and could use some improvement. In particular, its relationship to the recruiting and prevocational training mechanism of the Concen-

trated Employment Program (CEP) needs smoothing out. These may be problems of CEP rather than JOBS and will be discussed further in the next section on CEP. But NAB is having trouble in many cities utilizing the recruiting mechanism of CEP and for that matter of the State Employment Services, and is frequently anxious to do its own recruiting. Furthermore, CEP is supposed to provide prevocational training that will turn over to the employer relatively cleaned-up versions of the hard-core poor, thus ameliorating some of the traumas stemming from the businessman's first look at a true member of the hard-core poor. In many places, CEP has not been doing this very well, and again NAB has argued for control over its own prevocational training. The "hire first" principle is important enough that business proposals to hire as a pool to do prevocational training leave something to be desired; if the poor individual goes into the JOBS program, he should go into the employ of a *specific* company, not a pool. But if business could take over some of the already existing prevocational operations of CEP, there might be some improvement.

Nonetheless, given all of these operational problems and given some doubt as to the reliability and meaning of the placement and retention figures, the JOBS program seems to be working somewhere between reasonably well and very well indeed. This is the first *large* program attacking the training needs of the poverty and unequal opportunity groups where they must be attacked, in the private sector, and in the way they must be attacked, by a government-business combination. It has always been possible for the best experts in training to set up small-scale high-quality training programs that provide excellent placement and retention records although some of the best reputed of these turn out upon later examination not to have deserved their reputations. But it has not been possible to mount even a reasonably good program on a large scale, and in this sense the utilization of the government-business combination of the JOBS program may have provided a breakthrough in program size as well as type.

The JOBS program has worked reasonably well even among the hard-core poor. Twenty thousand is not a small number. But it certainly has not broken through here. If anything, the lagging contract program experience may indicate that some of the hardest hard-core unemployed may simply not find it possible to get into private industry. This is not a criticism of the JOBS program. It is a suggestion that even though JOBS might exceed the wildest expectations of its admirers, it is not a substitute for all other programs, past, present, and future. It is certainly not a substitute for economic prosperity, which is an absolutely necessary support for all these training programs.

Some new techniques should be tried within JOBS, a few of which will be suggested in the next chapter. But business and the multiproblem hard-core "unemployable" may be incompatible, and solutions outside the private sector need looking at too. In particular, the next chapter will discuss the need for a residual public employment program in addition to JOBS.

Concentrated Employment Program (CEP). The Concentrated Employment Program (CEP) is not really a program. It has suffered from a dual or perhaps even triple confusion of identity since its inception. Begun in January 1967, it was (1) an attempt to tie together the various manpower provisions of the 1966 Congressional Amendments of the Economic Opportunity Act into the coherent pattern of a comprehensive manpower program; (2) an attempt to concentrate manpower resources on small sections of poverty communities, sections small enough to be only portions of CAP target communities of poverty; and (3) a program patterned after a pilot Chicago effort called Jobs Now, to provide prevocational (literacy, disciplinary, cleanliness, etc.) training to poor people who were then fed into on-the-job training programs in business.

In addition, CEP was the fruit of a delegation agreement that gave the Department of Labor the authority to run the program nationally with OEO/Labor Department funds but built in the strong presumption that locally the "prime sponsor" of a CEP would be the Community Action Agency. Although the Community Action tie focused CEP sharply on the poor and this tie was considered necessary for CEP to work at all in many target areas, it did cause administrative problems.

The subarea concentration of CEP has pretty much gone by the board, but the problems consequent upon a confusion between the other objectives remain in part. As a comprehensive manpower program, CEP has never taken hold, or at least it has not taken hold as *the* comprehensive manpower program for an area. In relation to the JOBS program, for example, CEPs have performed poorly enough as prime or sole recruiters of poor people for JOBS slots that the National Alliance of Businessmen has ceased to depend upon them in many places. This has not necessarily been the fault of the CEPs; the businessmen of the Alliance have sometimes feared that CEPs would send them the truly hard-core poor and have instead gone directly to the State Employment Service, which is typically more employer-oriented. Nonetheless, this has made the comprehensive functioning of these CEPs impossible.

In any case, what has apparently happened with regard to the comprehensive function of CEP is in microcosm what has happened to OEO at the national level. Given the task of running some programs and coordinating others, the CEP administrators have run programs and failed to coordinate, the result being just another set of programs. The reasons are multifold, but the main ones are that existing programs have been too strong to succumb easily to being coordinated and that suspicion of the operator of one program trying to coordinate (or give orders to) another has made the coordination even more difficult. The latter has been compounded by the fact that CEP marks a shotgun marriage between local Community Action Authorities and local Employment Service offices, which typically have been hostile parties. Although the marriage has lasted because the shotgun has remained loaded, the two parties have failed to bring much community property into it. They prefer to keep their other programs outside of the CEP complex and thus away from the conjugal enemy.

As a prevocational training program, CEP has also been less than perfectly successful although no absolute standard should be applied here more than anywhere else; no prevocational program has been highly successful. In the first instance CEP suffered from lack of flexibility on the part of the Labor Department. The Chicago Jobs Now Program, run by the YMCA, appeared to be working well by providing intensive training to hard-core poor in improving literacy, reliability, discipline, and so on, preparatory to turning them over by prearrangement to private businesses for entry level training jobs. Even after they entered their on-the-job training the enrollees in Jobs Now were helped by "coaches" from the program who helped counsel and get them through their first days in a new company. This seemed to be working in Chicago, although data coming in after the model was introduced into CEP indicated a less spectacular success than had been believed: retention rates in particular remained low. In any case the working of Jobs Now depended upon a complex relationship among the YMCA, Chicago businesses, and other powers in the city. The Department of Labor tried to impose this very specific model on 75 other communities without being able to reproduce the political pattern that made the model workable. It didn't work very well elsewhere. Indeed, although the CAP relationship caused administrative confusion and program jealousy, it may be all that prevented the combination of the centralized rigidity of the Labor Department trying to impose a single pattern plus the unsympathetic orientation of many independent State Employment Services from making the program completely unworkable. A possibly workable system might have been the reverse: standards set nationally for who should be helped and what the objective of the assistance was, models adapted to local conditions designed locally. But as it did work out, local CAP participation helped concentrate many programs on the target populations without typically being able to force them to operate flexibly.

Perhaps the most important flaw in CEP as an operating program, however, was that outside of Chicago it was a prevocational training program without sufficient connection to on-the-job training and placement; business was insufficiently committed to the program, and business alone could provide on-the-job training and jobs. Report after report on local CEPs showed that the programs brought enrollees through completion of prevocational training and perhaps some institutional vocational training (in classroom settings) but then simply couldn't find entry slots in industry for them. The trainees either dropped back into the casual labor force or joblessness of the ghetto, thus losing the benefits of the program, or they recycled again through classroom training, a frustrating experience indeed. These experiences negated the benefits the program had in remotivating those who had previously had every reason for low motivation. It built up their hopes even higher than before and then dashed them.

The failure of the business community to come around and the lack of a national program with available federal subsidies led the next year to such a federal program, JOBS. In part JOBS was a response to just this problem in CEP. And completing the process by feeding CEP prevocational graduates into JOBS vocational training makes possible substantial improvement of the workings of CEP. Whether CEP is good enough to facilitate JOBS, however, remains a question.

Because of the confusion of objectives and identity in CEP and because of the lack of reliable data, it is impossible to evaluate quantitatively. What can be said is that where it exists, it is reasonable to hope for its working fairly well as a prevocational program coupled with JOBS and as an outreach mechanism, finding the people in need of training programs.

But CEP has not proved to be so successful a mechanism for doing what it does do that it should be replicated much more widely throughout the country. A prevocational mechanism connected to programs like JOBS is needed, but it would seem useful to experiment with other alternatives, including alternatives managed directly by the National Alliance of Businessmen.

Work Experience and Work Incentives Programs. The third antipoverty manpower program concerned primarily with adults — chronologically the first — is the Work Experience Program under Title V of the Economic Opportunity Act. From the very beginning of the effort, data showing low program retention and placement rates supplemented by operational evaluations filled with horror stories indicated that Work Experience as a whole was not working well although, as usual, there were a few outstanding programs.

The Work Experience Program was supposed to be a work and job-training program for people on relief and those in categories eligible for relief. By the latter is meant unemployed fathers who, prior to the Public Assistance amendments of 1962, were ineligible for the Aid to Dependent Children Program in most states. At that time ADC had been confined to female heads of households without a man in the house. The incentive for family breakup caused by this restriction led to the 1962 amendments changing the law so that states were able to provide ADC to male-headed families also. Work Experience then was to be not only for female relief recipients but also for males in states which the Department of Health, Education and Welfare hoped to coax into the unemployed fathers section of the ADC program. Work Experience was supposed to demonstrate to these states that a work program coupled with Public Assistance could be a way to get both men and women out of the dependence category.

Work Experience suffered from the beginning because of the duality of the objectives implied by its use for training poor people on the one hand and its use as a demonstration program to the states on the other. In particular, the demonstration objective led to a geographical spotting around the country by the Welfare Administration of HEW that related not to community needs or abilities to utilize the program but rather to HEW's felt need to demonstrate the program in various states.

Added to this difficulty was, first, the fact that welfare authorities may not be the best vocational trainers in the world. Local welfare authorities proved in most cases to have neither the experience to carry on vocational training nor the ethos. They were more experienced and concerned with providing social services to the trainees than they were in providing them with skills.

And, second, those people on Public Assistance or eligible for Public Assistance comprise a group categorized by a characteristic other than their relative trainability. Relief recipients (and eligibles) form an odd category for purposes of training. Perhaps, as some defenders of Work Experience claim, the low retention and placement statistics (50 percent and 20 percent) were understandable, given the population being treated with. But the question is: Why make this population the object of a single separate job-training program? Some recipients of relief may be highly skilled but on welfare because, for example, they simply have too many children to take care of to work; others may be illiterate and close to untrainable. This indicates a wide spread of training needs. And, added to this, the fact that Work Experience reimbursed its recipients through relief payments and supplements to relief payments rather than through wages made the connection of the whole program to the world of work very tenuous.

The program obviously did not work well, and in 1966 Congress amended the legislation to turn the training over to the Labor Department while keeping recruiting and social services in the Welfare Administration. By this time, however, it was decided to phase out Work Experience and substitute for it a new program known as Work Incentives, outside of the Economic Opportunity Act, to be run primarily by the Department of Labor for the same groups of people. It is too early to say how well the program is operating. On the one hand, it does substitute trainers for social workers in the training business, and it does make payments in the form of wages rather than relief. On the other hand, it seems to be blended into other training programs for the poor less than might be hoped, thus again categorizing recipients according to their need for welfare rather than their trainability.

In addition, the Work Incentives Program seems to be getting off the ground slowly, but this might not be a bad idea. The original intention of the program was to make possible the enforcement of the punitive go-to-work-or-get-off-the-welfare-rolls provision of the 1967 Welfare amendments by making sure that work programs were available. Given this intention, it is probably a good thing that Work Incentives Programs are building up slowly rather than being jerry-built to force welfare recipients into jobs for which they may be very ill-suited. For it remains the case that recipients of relief simply do not seem to be a prime category for manpower programs. If one-half the poor are in families with "non-labor force heads," the proportion for the poor who are on relief must be nearer 75 to 90 percent. It seems a bad place to start a major manpower program.

Job Corps. If vague concept and objectives make it difficult to carry out quantitative evaluations of some adult manpower programs, Job Corps, for 16- to 21-year-old youth, is relatively clear-cut and should be easy to evaluate quantitatively. This is so obvious that OEO and others started early to do benefit-cost evaluations of Job Corps. The difficulties of these evaluations and their failure to show consistent results perhaps tell more about the primitive state of benefit-cost analysis than they do about Job Corps itself.

Job Corps is one of the initial major Economic Opportunity programs. It came into being on the basis of a strongly felt need for vocational training for hard-core poor young men who had dropped out of high school without completing it or who had completed high school

121

without having learned very much and were on the streets. Many legislators had fine memories of the Civilian Conservation Corps of the 1930s and wanted to apply the concept to a new antipoverty program. In fact the needs of the 1960s for vocational training did not relate too well to CCC types of programs because conservation work provides little such vocational training. The lack of training fit the 1930s, when many boys needed training less than they simply needed jobs from an economy that didn't provide them. In the sixties, the problem was different.

In any case, Job Corps was divided into two portions: a conservation program, intended to fill the educational needs of functional illiterates while providing them with useful work experience and providing the public with recreational and other facilities, and so-called urban centers, rural in location but designed to train the somewhat more literate in urban vocational skills. In addition, Congresswoman Green added a provision for women's centers as well as the men's. These centers were actually located in cities, unlike any of the others.

Given this three-way division and confusion of concept together with the difficulties discussed in the previous chapter of meeting initial enrollment goals, Job Corps was in trouble from the beginning. It filled up fast and was not prepared to treat the educational or vocational needs of its enrollees. This led both to jerry-built curricula at the beginning and to a failure to channel youngsters to those camps that might best meet their needs. Indeed, it was never possible to distinguish the typical characteristics of Job Corps youngsters from those of youngsters being channeled into the lower-cost less-intensive Neighborhood Youth Corps, a fact that plagued OEO's efforts to justify Job Corps. Perhaps some of the NYC kids were more difficult to deal with since the really hard cases were likely to cause disciplinary problems in the Job Corps's residential settings.

The early difficulties of the Job Corps, including the 1966 difficulties before the Powell committee discussed in the previous chapter, did lead the Corps to try very hard to obtain data to justify itself. On its public face, Job Corps appeared to be a set of troubles with few benefits; and starting with 1967, when William Kelly took over the program, data to reverse this impression were gathered in greater abundance than in any other OEO program. These data, including detailed data on enrollee characteristics and follow-up data on post-Corps experience (as of August

1966), enabled OEO to make its first attempts at benefit-cost analysis. In 1967, Glen Cain of OEO's Office of Research, Plans, Programs and Evaluation did a study based on educational gains in Job Corps and on initial placement experience after Job Corps that indicated a benefit-cost ratio conservatively estimated at 1.2:1.[7] Cain used as a control group "no-shows," those who had signed up for Job Corps but never showed up to be enrolled. Sample data on these as well as those who had got through Job Corps had been gathered systematically and periodically by the Louis Harris polling organization.

The difficulty was that the educational data were not very good, and the Harris placement data both for Job Corpsmen and no-shows were biased by the impossibility of including the large portion of both groups that could not be located by the surveying organization. It was difficult to figure out how to allow for this bias. The Cain study was acclaimed within the small world of benefit-cost analysis as a methodological breakthrough but was thrown into doubt as a definitive study of Job Corps because of the data problems. Subsequently, another OEO analysis indicated that different treatment of control groups might lead to a range of benefit-cost ratios anywhere between 1:1 and 32:1. Then the Resource Management Corporation (RMC), under contract to the General Accounting Office, did one more study, using essentially the same data, that argued that still another treatment of the control group would show practically no earnings gain stemming from Job Corps, with a consequent benefit-cost ratio of .3:1. For the *aficionado* of benefit-cost analysis these and other benefit-cost studies of Job Corps are tabulated in Table 9.[8]

A further study not included in the table was done on the basis of a new sample gathered by the General Accounting Office (GAO) itself for its own study. This sample also used no-shows for a control group, and it indicated the difficulties of benefit-cost analysis even when data are available. It showed those who had been through Job Corps to have virtually the same wage and employment rates as the control groups, and GAO thus concluded that Job Corps had had very little beneficial effect.

7. Glen G. Cain, "Benefit Cost Estimates for Job Corps" (University of Wisconsin Institute for Research on Poverty Discussion Paper, September 1967).
8. This table and the analysis on which it is based were prepared by Lillian Regelson of the Office of Economic Opportunity.

Table 9
Benefit-Cost Ratios for Job Corps

Source	Basis for Benefits	Trainee Sample	Control Group Sample	Cost (dollars)	Average Hourly Wage Gain	Working Lifetime, Years	Employment Rate Job Corps	Employment Rate Control Group	Net Annual Adjust.[1]	Pre-Job Corps Average Hourly Wage	Discounted Benefits (dollars)	Benefit-Cost Ratio
Cain Benefit Cost Estimates for Job Corps Done for OEO/ RPP&E 9/67	Educational Gains	2000 corps members Jan. '67	2000 corps members Oct. '66	3580[6]	—	—	—	—	3%	—	3583-5949[2]	1.02-1.70[2]
									5%	—	2203-3994[2]	.60-1.14[2]
	Wage Gains	Harris Sample of Aug. '66 terminees[3]	Late — no shows from Harris Sample[4]	3508[6]	.12	48	81.25%	81.25%	3%	—	5124	1.45
									5%		3666	1.04
Wagner, Wheeler Done for OEO Job Corps 9/68	Wage Gains	Harris Sample of Aug. '66 terminees[6]	New enrollees with same age, race, time in job market	3613[6]	.44	47	88% men 50% women	88% men 50% women	3%	—	18075	5.0
				3991[7]	.44	47	88% men 50% women	88% men 50% women	3%	—	18075	4.5
RMC Report UR-054, Done for GAO 12/13/68	Wage Gains	Harris Sample of Aug. '66 terminees, male	0-3 month terminees, Harris Sample Aug. '66 terminees,[5] male	3840[7]	.07	46 diminished by death rates	68%	68%	5%	—	1596	.4
									7.5%		1175	.3
									10%	—	917	.2

Study	Comparison group	Sample	Cost	Hourly / income gain	Working lifetime	%	%	%	Net rate		Present value	Benefit-cost ratio
Regelson,[8] Evaluation of the Job Corps, Done for OEO/ RPP&E 1/69 — **Wage Gains**	Same, Female	0-3 month terminees, Harris sample, Aug. '66, females	3840[7]	.14	46 diminished by death rates	50%	50%	50%	5% 7.5% 10%	— — —	2301 1697 1303	.6 .4 .3
Income Gains — 8a	Harris Survey of Aug. 1966 terminees[5] Men's Urban Centers only	New enrollees with same age, race, time in job market	4100[8a]	.44	47	88%	88%	88%	3%	—	—	4.9
8b			5125[8b]	.44	47	88%	88%	88%	3%	—	—	3.9
8c			4100	.44	47	67%[8c]	67%[8c]	88%	3%	.50	—	3.7
8d			4100	.44	47	88%	67%[8d]	88%	3%	.50	—	8.9
8e			4100	0[8e]	47	88%	67%[8e]	88%	3%	—	—	4.0
8f			4100	.44	42[8f]	88%	88%	88%	3%	—	—	4.7
8g			4100	.44	47	88%	88%	88%	5%[8g]	—	—	3.5
8h			4100	.34[8h]	47	88%	88%	88%	3%	—	—	3.8
8i			4100	.54[8i]	47	88%	88%	88%	3%	—	—	6.0
8j			4100	.22[8j]	47	88%	88%	88%	3%	—	—	2.5
8k			4100	30¢ 1st hr. increasing evenly for 10 yr. then constant[8k]	47	88%	88%	88%	3%	—	—	28.0
8l			5125[8l]	.22[8l]	42[8l]	67%[8l]	67%[8l]	88%	5%[8l]	—	—	1.1
8m			4100	30¢ 1st[8m] hr. increasing evenly for 10 yr. then constant	47	88%	67%[8m]	88%	3%	1.50	—	32.0

1. Discount rate minus growth in earnings.
2. Assuming even gain, 5-month stay, and various assumptions concerning comparable education groups.
3. Measured in February 1967.
4. Harris no-shows.
5. Harris 18-month follow-up, February 1968.
6. Computed by economic method, which eliminates transfer payment of food, clothing, pay and allowances, adds foregone earnings, and deducts appraised worth value of conservation centers.
7. Computed as total cost to Job Corps of maintaining center operation.
8. This paper examined the effect of variations in assumptions related to costs and benefits. The base case uses the assumption used by Wagner and Wheeler. Variations are:

8a: Base Case.
8b: Cost increased by 25%.
8c: Employment rate decreased to 67%.
8d: Employment rate decreased to 67% for control group only.
8e: Employment rate decreased to 67% for control group only. Average hourly wage gain reduced to 0.
8f: Working lifetime reduced to 42 years.
8g: Net discount rate increased to 5%.
8h: Control group earnings increased 10¢ an hour.
8i: Control group earnings decreased 10¢ an hour.
8j: Average hourly wage gain cut in half.
8k: Average wage gain made linear for 10 years.
8l: Combined assumptions reducing benefit-cost ratio.
8m: Combined optimistic assumptions.

However, the study also showed that the control group had started out in the pre-Job Corps period at much higher wage rates than the Corpsmen. Thus the wage *gains* of Job Corpsmen were higher since the Corpsmen had achieved the same post-Corps wages starting from a much lower level. But the GAO did not choose to interpret this as a gain attributable to Job Corps. The point is not that the GAO is necessarily wrong but rather that benefit-cost analysis even carefully done is seldom definitive; the results depend on how one chooses to interpret what figures. The summary statement on the quantitative evaluation of Job Corps is that equally objective studies of the Corps indicate that the ratio of benefit to cost lies somewhere between .3:1 and 32:1, so that it follows that these studies either justify Job Corps or do not. My own belief is that the bulk of the statistical evidence reasonably interpreted at least leads to benefit-cost ratios greater than 1 and perhaps even substantially greater than 1. Even with all its drawbacks, the Corps can be justified by this analysis. But because RMC and GAO have produced studies throwing this result into question, I certainly cannot prove that my bias is justified.

The studies do agree on one numerical result, however, that those who stay in Job Corps the longest — at least up to six months — do much better than shorter termers who drop out without completing a course. Benefits increase more rapidly over time than do costs. Were the averages not dragged down by the very large number who stay in shorter times, the Corps would be unambiguously successful. This is the first of a set of operational facts that, if they could be corrected, would greatly improve the experience of Job Corps and its enrollees:

1. If some device could be found to keep Corpsmen in for long enough to receive maximum benefits, then the Corps would be much more successful. Under Kelly's leadership, each new enrollee was asked to sign a statement promising he would stay in for six months. It didn't work; they all signed, but too many of them still didn't stay. Job Corps has thought of various systems of incentives to get enrollees to stay, but these are limited by law in their applicability.

2. Job Corps is a high-cost program, and even if benefit-cost analysis could indicate unambiguously that benefits are greater than costs, the Corps would have to undergo a second test comparing it with

other possibly lower-cost means of achieving the same results. Difficult as the data problems of Job Corps are, the problems of comparing Job Corps to another program (to the out-of-school Neighborhood Youth Corps in particular) without specially gathered common data are such that a comparison of this sort has seldom been tried. Resource Management Corporation did try it and came up with the ironic conclusion that since neither Job Corps nor NYC provided much in the way of substantial demonstrable and measurable benefits, NYC was better because it was at least cheaper. Aside from what this conclusion says about benefit-cost analysis given the current state of data, it also brings out an important substantive point. Job Corps has tried to justify itself by comparing its benefits to those of alternative programs for the same populations; as noted earlier, however, statistically the populations are difficult to distinguish, and operationally little effort has been made by recruiters to distinguish what kid should go into which program. One way for Job Corps to improve its performance and evaluation record would be to try to find out once and for all what has been promised since the beginning of the program, that is, for which distinguishable kind of youth is Job Corps the best program? If Job Corps gained this knowledge and concentrated on these youngsters, then justification for the program, as best not for poor kids in general but for specified subportions of the population, might be much easier to achieve.

3. Similar to the last point is the fact that Job Corps makes little effort any more to distinguish what sort of youth might be benefited by the education/work experience programs of the conservation centers as compared with the vocational training programs of the urban centers.

4. Job Corps is now open to 16- and 17-year-olds, but even if they go all the way through the training program (and few do) they are too young to get jobs. This fact drags down the overall measurable effectiveness of the program. It may be that the 16- to 17-year-old kids receive long-run benefits that will be manifested in their later job experience, but this has not yet been demonstrated.

5. One of the reasons for the high cost of Job Corps has been the fact that it has been almost exclusively a residential program, thus carrying the cost of housing and feeding as well as training enrollees. Job

Corps has been reluctant to experiment with lower-cost variants that would preserve the essential training features of the program but move the Corps into cities, where Corpsmen would live at home. In the last year or so such experimentation has been forced upon the Corps by Congress, the Budget Bureau, and OEO, but it has been small in scale and no evaluative results are yet available. Perhaps the new city "mini-centers" announced by Secretary of Labor George Shultz will provide some data.

The fact that Job Corps has been reluctant to face up to problems of the sort just listed is a more damning point of evaluation than the variable benefit-cost ratios. In fact, the most accurate summary statement about Job Corps seems to be that it has helped many kids and that at least some studies indicate that this help justifies even the high cost but that the management of Job Corps has failed to engage in the introspection and experimentation that could lead to a far better program with no ambiguity about its success. All of this criticism does not imply that Job Corps has been a failure and should be abolished. It does indicate, however, that substantive changes beyond the recent shift to the Department of Labor are needed.

Neighborhood Youth Corps (NYC) — Out-of-School. The Neighborhood Youth Corps Program (NYC) for 16- to 21-year-old youths has been divided among three parts: a program for part-time jobs during the school day for 16- to 21-year-olds still in school; a summer program of jobs to take kids off the streets, in part as a continuation of the in-school program; and an out-of-school program for youths in the same age group who have dropped out of high school or completed it.

The first two of these are intended to enable and encourage kids to continue their education and are thus considered under the educational portion of the Individual Improvement category below. Out-of-School NYC, however, is as much a manpower program as it is anything.

Few data are available to evaluate quantitatively the effectiveness of out-of-school NYC in increasing the earnings of its enrollees. What little quantitative information is available — primarily from surveys by Dunlop Associates and by the Resource Management Corporation for the GAO —

shows little effect from the NYC Out-of-School program with the possible exception that it may increase the return to school of younger dropouts. The problem of getting a valid control group for NYC, however, is even more difficult to overcome than for Job Corps; it is so easy for a youth to drift into and out of an NYC program in his own neighborhood that the question of why a "control" didn't drift in is particularly crucial. In any case, with or without the control group NYC seems to have little effect on increasing the earnings of those who do not return to school.

Thus NYC seems to make little permanent change in the lives of its enrollees. If the program is examined institutionally rather than quantitatively, this is what one would expect. Although NYC does very little training, counseling, or teaching, these services were intended, and OEO frequently requested Budget Bureau permission to increase the cost per enrollee so as to add more "enrichment" of this type. The Labor Department was not interested, however, the Budget Bureau never agreed, and after a while OEO stopped trying. So what the NYC has been all along is not a training program but rather a work experience program for the most part in quite low-level public employment jobs. A few of the job slots such as nurses' aides and clerical jobs for young women have had some training potential, but most of the boys' jobs have been of the maintenance type. Because of the lack of enrichment in the NYC, unlike the Job Corps, most of the cost has gone to payments to the enrollees rather than for training and education.

Because of the ineffectual attempts at training, it is hardly surprising that the training and upgrading effects of NYC have been small. Rather it has been a program that has performed a service keeping kids off the streets and giving them a little work experience at an age when jobs for dropouts are tough to come by and their potential for getting into trouble is very high indeed. It has undoubtedly performed a service, but it is not a readily quantifiable service.

With regard to the cost structure of NYC, it might be considered almost a transfer payment program; technically a transfer payment is a payment for no work, and the NYC kids are paid for work, but the objective is more to get the money into their pockets than it is to get the work done. This brings up another quirk in benefit-cost analysis that can further confuse the quantitative evaluation of NYC. A benefit-cost analysis of manpower programs ordinarily subtracts payments to enrollees from both the cost and benefit sides of the ratio in order to get a better measure of the cost and effectiveness of the training components of the program.[9] When payments to enrollees in NYC, which form the bulk of the costs, are subtracted from the cost and benefit sides, not much is left in either place. As stated before, the measured benefits in terms of earnings are small if they exist at all. The measurable costs after deducting payments to trainees are also small. So the benefit-cost ratio is the quotient of two inexact small numbers and can be very volatile indeed and not very meaningful.

In sum, Out-of-School NYC can be considered an ineffective training program that also costs very little plus a device to give poor kids some money and keep them off the streets. Viewed this way, it may or may not be justifiable.

Further analysis, however, also suggests that the NYC technique of treating kids in their home communities may be profitably combined with the Job Corps technique of intensive educational and vocational training. In addition, for youths 18 or above it might be best to train them not separately but with adults, with other adults who are over 18 and out of school. This bringing 18-year-olds and older youths into mainstream training programs has been happening in the JOBS program in particular. What is left, then, is a need for new programs for kids 16 or 17 who may be a bit too young for the programs of JOBS, Job Corps, or NYC Out-of-School. If NYC Out-of-School has been effective in getting these kids back into school then it may be doing as well as we can do.

New Careers. Although not specifically carried in the budget list because it is quite small and funded as a subcategory under the Concentrated Employment Program, New Careers for the Poor is different enough from the others that it needs special mention. This program was begun under

9. Some recent benefit-cost studies, in recognition of the kinds of problems mentioned here, have supplemented the analysis of benefits and costs to society, in which transfer payments are taken out of both the benefit and cost sides because they do not change the total resources available to society, with analyses of benefits and costs to the individual, in which benefits of transfers count, and to the government, in which transfers are added in on both the benefit and cost sides. See Ralph E. Smith, "A Cost-Benefit Analysis of a Program to Train Licensed Practical Nurses," an unpublished paper (Washington, D.C.: Georgetown University, May 1968).

the Scheuer amendment of 1966 to train poor people as subprofessional aides to professionals in such fields as education, health, and welfare. Its objective was not only to obtain jobs for the trainees but also to open up professional structures in these fields by breaking down professional jobs so that some of the parts could be done by nonprofessionals. Thus it was hoped that a new stratum of highly respectable jobs would be found for the poor and at the same time the outreach of professionals in short supply would be multiplied.

It hasn't happened that way. Useful jobs of this type have been found for many poor people, but for the most part the structure has not changed in any fundamental way but merely opened up to accept a few more people. In other words, it has been demonstrated that federal funds can provide jobs for the poor in public or private nonprofit organizations, that these jobs are useful and help the people in them, and that perhaps they are somewhat new in style. But it also seems likely that the structures are stronger than the innovations and little longer-run structural change has been achieved.

What this means, then, is that the public and quasi-public sectors of the economy can accept the kinds of relatively capable people who can be taught subprofessional jobs, just as the private sector can. In deciding whether to fund training and job slots for these "capable poor" in private or in public pursuits, the basis of the private-versus-public decision must be the estimated *needs* of the private and public sector; for the individual, either is about as good a job as the other. This conclusion also implies that New Careers is no more a breakthrough in increasing the total number of jobs for the poor than would be a full federal subsidy to private employment. With some assistance the "capable poor" can be put in jobs in the public or private sector; the less capable poor are no more capable of taking New Career jobs than they are of taking private or public training.

As a public employment program for the "capable," New Careers may be considered the prototype of a new program with the unfortunate acronym of JOPS, Job Opportunities in the Public Sector, a public employment analogue of JOBS. Because JOPS is just beginning, it has provided no experience to discuss in this evaluative chapter. It is taken up in more detail in the next chapter on recommended programs.

131

INDIVIDUAL IMPROVEMENT

A summary of the federal antipoverty budget for programs for individual improvement, fiscal 1969, is presented in Table 10.

Education.[10] There has been remarkably little systematic comparative evaluation of different educational techniques for reaching the underprivileged. The Office of Education, which disposes of a billion dollars or more a year for the education of the poor under Title I of the Elementary and Secondary Education Act of 1965, is beginning a comprehensive evaluation program. It will not be simple to carry out this program because the Office of Education statutorily provides monies without being able to control them, and local school authorities don't like to be evaluated. Up until this effort, virtually no evaluation had been attempted on a systematic basis.

Table 11 brings together an inventory of federal programs that are intended to contribute to the compensatory education effort or can be used to contribute to the compensatory education effort. In addition to identifying federal programs and administering agencies, Table 11 contains estimates of the number of beneficiaries and the amount of funding through fiscal 1967.

The two right-hand columns briefly summarize the kind of evaluation information available about each program. It is important to note that while there are several inventories of federal educational programs for the poor, this table represents the first attempt to summarize what is known about the impact of such programs on the amount or rate of learning whether this be measured in cognitive, behavioral, or attitudinal terms.

What Table 11 clearly brings out is that we know virtually nothing about what techniques of education, compensatory or otherwise, work to improve the education of the poor. Our ignorance has been summarized by Mary Robinson of OEO as follows. We do *not* know:

1. The most advantageous age or school level for compensatory intervention — infancy, preschool, early elementary, secondary, postsecondary and higher education.

10. Much of this section on educational evaluation, including both the table of evaluative results (Table 11) and the summary statement about what we do not know, should be credited to Mary Robinson of the Office of Research, Plans, Programs and Evaluation, Office of Economic Opportunity.

Table 10
Federal Antipoverty Budget, Fiscal 1969: Individual Improvement

Program	Fund Source	Management	Funds (millions of dollars)
Education			
Head Start	OEO	OEO (through 7/1/69)	2,301
Follow Through	OEO	Office of Education	318
Upward Bound	OEO	OEO (through 7/1/69)	30
In-School Neighborhood Youth Corps	OEO	Department of Labor	30
Summer Neighborhood Youth Corps	OEO	Department of Labor	51
Elementary and Secondary Education Act (Title I)	Office of Education	Office of Education	122
Miscellaneous Education	—	—	1,123
Health			623
Neighborhood Health Centers	OEO	OEO (CAP) (through 7/1/69)	7,002
Medicare	Social Security Admin.	Social Security Administration	60
Medicaid	Social and Rehabilitation Services Administration	Social and Rehabilitation Services Administration	2,553
Miscellaneous Health	—	—	2,400
Nutrition			1,989
Food Stamps and Commodity Distribution	Department of Agriculture	Department of Agriculture	702
School Lunch Program	Department of Agriculture	Department of Agriculture	273
Emergency Food and Medical Program	OEO	OEO	59
Miscellaneous Nutrition	—	—	17
			353
Total Individual Improvement			10,005

Source: Office of Economic Opportunity

Table 11

Summary of Federally Funded Compensatory Educational Services and Financial Assistance

Name of Program	Federal Agency and Authority	Beneficiaries (thousands)			Funding (millions)			Impact on Learning of Disadvantaged	
		1968	1969	1970	1968	1969	1970	Experimental (controls)	Operational (norms or judgments)
PCC	OEO – CAP	3.6	3.6 . . . families . . .	3.6	5.7	5.0	5.6	NA – Program in first year of development	Baseline data on parents and children are being gathered; information and first evaluations of programs will not be available until end of first developmental year.
Head Start (exclusive of PCC)	EOA (64); II OEO	695[a]	664[a]	664[a]	310.5[a]	(322.6)[a]	(322.4)[a]	Experimental studies indicate modest immediate gains. Long range surveys indicate that students not exposed to HS by and large catch up to HS students by first 3 years of schooling.	
Follow Through	EOA (64) (amended PL 90–222) OE	18	33	60	14.6	30.0	60.0	Limited evidence shows little if any gains made by FT students; unmatched control groups show consistent, slightly (not significantly) better test scores.	
In-School Children (5–15) Poor	ESEA; I, II OE	9000.0	9000.0	9000.0	[1187.0]	[1123.0]	[1226.0]	Title I Statistical Report and National Survey of Compensatory Education, school year 1968–9 being written.	cf.: Title I, Year I Title II, Year I Profiles in Quality Education

Source: prepared by Research, Plans, Programs and Evaluation, Office of Economic Opportunity

Program	Authorization									
Dropout Prevention	ESEA (65, 67) VIII OE	—	244	270	—	[5]	[24]	NA	NA	NA
In-School Children (5–15) Indian Children	25 USC	51.6 4.2[b]	(53.6) 4.5[b]	(54.4) 4.1[b]	78.5 9.1[c]	(81.9) 9.9[c]	(89.5) —	NA	NA	NA
		these are both regular and compensatory program figures . . .								
Upward Bound	42USC 2781 OEO	26	(26)	(26)	31.1	(29.8)	(30.0)	Grade point average shows downward drift (despite UB) for UB and nonUB groups (Syracuse study, 1967). UB enrollees drop out significantly less than control or older siblings (Segal, OEO). College enrollment improves significantly (Educational Association, Inc., 1967). School retention rate is significantly better (EAI, 1967)	NA	Attitudes toward school and college improve (Syracuse, 1967)
In-School Youth (16–21) Counseling and Guidance	NDEA (58); V-A OE	4000	4000	—	[24.5]	[17.0]	—	N/A	N/A	NA
Vocational Education	Voc. Ed. Act (63); A, B, D (grants to states)	87.5	105.0	255.8	[4.5]	[5.8]	[29.6]			
	Voc. Ed. Act (63); F, G (consumer, home-making, coop.)	465.0	465.0	504.0	[2.6]	[2.6]	[7.8]			

Table 11 (Continued)

Name of Program	Federal Agency and Authority	Beneficiaries (thousands)			Funding (millions)			Impact on Learning of Disadvantaged	
		1968	1969	1970	1968	1969	1970	Experimental (controls)	Operational (norms or judgments)
	Voc. Ed. Act (63) work study	50.0			[50.0]				
In-School Youth (16–21) NYC	EOA (64); IB Labor	109	(98)	(120)	58.9	(50.9)	(62.5)		GAO report claims program fails to keep students in school; in each of four locations dropout rate increased. Also fails to reach those most likely to drop out. Work experience may not have good scholastic effect but may have good social, disciplinary effect.
Educational Opportunity Grants	HEA (65); IV-A OE	293	259	309	131	134	176	N/A	
Higher Education Loans	NDEA; II OE	223	230	219	93	99	85	N/A	
Guaranteed Student Loans	HEA (65); IV-B OE	139[d]	203[d]	249[d]	9[e]	18[e]	28[e]	N/A	
Higher Education Work-Study	HEA (63); IV-C OE	229	233	231	82	91	97	OE questionnaire to all recipients 3 years ago. Data available July '69.	
Educational Talent Search	HEA (65); IV-A OE	115	115	140	4	4	5	N/A	

Program	Legislation/Agency	—	[139]	[150]	—	[7.5]	[10.0]		
Bilingual Education	ESEA; VII OE	—	—	—	—	—	—	First year of operation; all projects are innovative	None yet
Out-of-School Youth (16–21) Job Corps	EOA (64); I OE	73.5	65.0	(42.0)	282.3	(280.0)	(180.0)		Pre and post testing of Corpsmen indicates reading and math gains are made during stay in JC centers no follow-up testing of retention of gains has been done
NYC Out-of-School	EOA (64); IB as amended OEO	161.6	(120)	(120)	93.6	129.9	(134.0)	Slightly more NYC students than control students resume school after brief stay in NYC	No indications either of educational gains or of any but very slight employment gains
MDTA Institutional	MDTA (62); II-B OE and Labor	50.5	56.1	58.1	[40.0]	[43.6]	[44.4]	N/A	N/A
OJT-Coupled		4.1	1.9	1.9	[6.8]	[7.0]	[7.3]	N/A	N/A
Adult Education Adult Basic Education	Adult Ed. Act (66); III elementary and second. amendments OE							Such information as is available is to be found in the "Adult Education Information and Reporting System"	
Grants to States		408	480	533	[30.6]	[36.0]	[40.0]	Xerox report, funded by OEO after transfer to OE, could not collect attainment data from states involved in the sample survey	
Special Programs		39	42	48	[6.6]	[7.0]	[8.0]		
Teaching Training		2	3	3	[1.5]	[2.0]	[2.0]	N/A	N/A
Adult Education	EOA (64); II OEO-CAP	44	(45)	(96)	5.9	(6.1)	(13.0)	N/A	N/A
MDTA Institutional	MDTA (62) OE and Labor	81.3	85.0	88.0	[65.7]	[72.8]	[74.3]	N/A	N/A
Adult Education OJT-Coupled	MDTA Labor	4.1	2.0	2.0	[7.6]	[3.2]	[3.2]	N/A	N/A

Table 11 (Continued)

Name of Program	Federal Agency and Authority	Beneficiaries (thousands)			Funding (millions)			Impact on Learning of Disadvantaged	
		1968	1969	1970	1968	1969	1970	Experimental (controls)	Operational (norms or judgments)
Vocational Education	Voc. Ed. Act (63); A OE								
Basic Grants to States	Part B	37.5	35.0	105.0	[1.9]	[2.5]	[9.9]	N/A	N/A
Consumer and Homemaking		202.0	202.0	202.0	[1.1]	[1.1]	[1.2]	N/A	N/A
Work Incentive Program (WIN) formerly Work Experience and Training	PL 90-248 Labor	18	(102)	(300)	—	117.5ᶠ	—	No analysis of educational components available	
G.I. Bill	38 USC 1651 VA	687ᵍ	890ᵍ	927ᵍ	429	(620)	(669)	Recipients of G.I. Bill funds enroll in standard universities	
PACE formerly New Careers	42 USC 2740 Labor	4.8	5.1	14.3	12.3	18.6	(50)	As of late 1968, the first year of operation, there was little quantitative or qualitative effect measured (AVCO Economic Systems Corp, 1968). Academic components are weak or nonexistent; same is true of OJT program	
Mainstream	EOA (64); I Labor	14.6	14.7	(10.7)	32.3	(50)	(41)	There are two parts of the program: job creation for rural communities of people who could not otherwise get jobs (Mainstream A); intensive training (ABE, OJT) for urban jobs for which the participants would not otherwise qualify. Very limited evaluation of either (US Research and Development Corp.)	

Program							
Adult Education							
Concentrated Employment Program	EOA (64)	65[h]	105[h]	(170)[h]	73.0[i]	83.0[i]	(133.0)[i]	As yet no information on specific educational programs (content, method effectiveness)
	MDTA				22.1[i]	31.8[i]	(105.0)[i]	As yet no information on specific educational programs (content, method effectiveness)
JOBS	EOA (64)	39.0[h]	66.7[h]	(140.0)[h]	60.1[i]	152.0[i]	(180.0)[i]	As yet no information on specific educational programs (content, method effectiveness)
	MDTA				44.6[i]	48.0[i]	(240.0)[i]	As yet no information on specific educational programs (content, method effectiveness)

a: Includes summer and full year
(): Estimated
[]: Estimated obligations – OE figures
b: Students in dormitories financed by Bureau of Indian Affairs who attend local off-reservation public schools
c: Supplemental funds
d: Number of loans approved
e: Total amount lent: FY 68, 118; FY 69, 173; FY 70. (214)
f: Educational component not broken out; figure represents total financing
g: G.I. Bill recipients are not subject to means test, so there is no way to estimate number of disadvantaged who benefit
h: EOA and MDTA figures combined
i: Total financing; educational component not distinguished

Table 11 (Continued)

APPENDIX A

Adult Basic Education

Adult Education Act of 1966

Systematic Evaluations

1. *Title:* Adult Education Information and Reporting System

This study consists of four phases, two of which have been completed. Phase I involved the development of a conceptual model of an Adult Basic Education Evaluation System. Phase two was a full-scale system development plan for the design and development of an operational unity for the continued evaluation and feedback on Adult Basic Education programs.

When completed, this system will be designed so as to be capable of answering the necessary questions required for immediate, short-range decision making; establishing the parameters for a full and final Central Office Information and Reporting System; and afford the ability to design, test, and implement an Adult Education Information and Reporting System which will provide a uniform means at Federal, State, and local levels of measuring the quality and quantity of output, efficiency of operation, achievement of objectives, and a basis for day-to-day and long-range decisions.

2. *Title:* Evaluation of Teacher Training Institutes

The primary purpose of the study is to determine the effectiveness of past efforts and to establish viable goals and directions for future training programs. The objectives are: to provide the Office of Education with data to assist in the further planning, control and evaluation necessary for effective, efficient and economical operation of the over-all program; to provide the office of Education with guidelines for teacher-training institutes; to provide an information and feedback system designed to answer the need for immediate evaluation and short-range decision making; to provide a basis for an information retrieval system which will aid in competent program review and decision making at all levels; to develop a standard program reporting procedure according to accepted OE definitions and interpretations of teacher-training activities.

2. The kinds and levels of educational attainment required for social and economic effectiveness, on which assumptions and hypotheses about program goals, objectives, and content of compensatory educational undertakings rest.

3. The interactions between affective and cognitive aspects of learning, and how programs of general education, functional skill training, and motivational factors interact.

4. The kinds and intensities of educational inputs (qualities and quantities of curricula, methods, materials, teachers, etc.) that are required to increase cognitive and/or affective learning, what inputs are more important or what input mixes are necessary to achieve a learning threshold.

5. [How educational] skills and abilities are related to the exit from

poverty or the adoption of nonpoverty styles of living and behavior.

6. The length of time a compensatory treatment must be sustained if retention and expansion of educational gains is to be assured.

7. The importance and the ways of using other institutions, including the home, as alternatives or supplements to the school, in providing and/or reinforcing compensatory programs.

8. The methods of turning new educational approaches and techniques developed in demonstration units into accepted practices by schools and other performers.

9. The importance of the skills, attitudes and styles of teachers in relating to poor learners, and in relation to the manipulation of the multiple compensatory inputs to the teaching-learning situation. Thus, the unknowns are many and the knowns are few; while we have posited much we have really tested little. As a result, in almost no case can compensatory education programs be formulated and undertaken by schools or other performers with any assurance that stipulated kinds, qualities, and quantities of educational services will produce predictable kinds and degrees of attainment with given kinds of disadvantaged learners. Tried and true compensatory models do not yet exist.

Indeed, we may be more specific than Miss Robinson. We also know virtually nothing about whether the following more or less highly touted programs work:

1. New York's More Effective Schools program. Evaluation of MES has caused much controversy among such interested parties as the United Federation of Teachers (which sponsored More Effective Schools) and the New York City Board of Education (which generally objects to real innovation). A summary of this controversy appears in *The Urban Review*.[11] What it seems to come down to is that MES is hopeful but has shown little hard evidence of across-the-board success. Some gains may be measurable among those students who stay put in one school for a few years, but in the ghetto this is a very special sample. MES might be considered successful if some

11. "The Controversy Over the More Effective Schools: A Special Supplement," *The Urban Review*, May 1968.

of the better techniques could be replicated on a broad scale, but broad-scale replication of detailed techniques is a hard thing to come by. In any case, we don't really know which of the techniques work.

2. Decentralization and community control. There is no evidence that community control of schools either works or does not work toward better education. The analogy with rich suburban schools sometimes drawn by advocates of community control is a faulty one. Rich suburban school systems provide good education because the kids are well off and easy to educate, two factors not typically applicable to most city school districts that might be put under community control. Certainly, community control in some New York City school districts has engendered, in addition to violent controversy, a vigorous and progressive spirit within the schools. It feels good, but that doesn't mean it works, and there is no evidence that it does (or doesn't).

3. Desegregation. The Coleman Report does present evidence — weak evidence, but evidence — that children of low "socioeconomic status" going to school with kids of high "socioeconomic status" seem to benefit from that fact, whereas the better-off kids do not suffer.[12] This would seem to indicate that desegregation would be an effective technique to raise the achievement levels of now-segregated children. Desegregation on the scale required, however, seems so far down the pike and its indicated effects, though not insignificant, are so far from overwhelming that this seems as little like a large-scale solution as anything else.

Add to all this the fact that available studies, particularly the Coleman Report, indicate that a child's home life and general environment are far more important in determining his educational achievement than is his experience in school. A poor child receiving a good educational experience at an early age has many chances to dissipate the value of the experience before he reaches an age when it can directly benefit his earnings; that is the nature of the poverty environment, and it does not lead to putting great weight on educational programs.[13]

12. James S. Coleman and others, "Equality of Educational Opportunity," Report submitted to the President in response to Section 402 of the Civil Rights Act of 1964 (Washington: U.S. Department of Health, Education and Welfare, July 1966).

13. This differs from the economist's use of discount rates in cost-benefit analysis, which makes education programs difficult to justify as antipoverty efforts because

In general, then, the evaluation of educational programs shows that very little is known about what works and even throws doubt on the importance of anything that might work. These flaws are brought out in the discussion of the very popular Head Start program, which, as the major OEO effort in education, has been the one that has been more evaluated than any other.

Head Start. The Head Start Program of educational and other treatment for preschool poor children was based in large part upon the theories of child psychologists, who pointed out that poor children enter school at a distinct disadvantage because in their preschool years their total environment is a home life inferior in educational and other stimulation to that of the middle class. Basing their suggestions on a few experimental programs antedating OEO, psychologists pushed hard to establish programs to right the balance for preschool children. As discussed in the previous chapter, Shriver, who was worried about getting all his money spent in the first year of OEO, accepted these suggestions eagerly.

The Head Start program got under way very rapidly, and in the first summer it brought in more than a half-million children. This was an administrative triumph that, despite expectations, did not seem to harm the quality of the program severely. Some initial advocates criticized Head Start for not following the models. Perhaps they were right, but no large-scale program ever follows the model, and Head Start seems to have come pretty close. Certainly as compared with Job Corps, which suffered and ultimately came close to dying of the first pains of expansion, Head Start did very well.

It was an extremely popular program, partly because 4- and 5-year-old kids are appealing and because the program mobilized a generous outpouring of American volunteer spirit but partly also because it really seemed to be helping these kids. They seemed happier. At the end of the

---

earnings are distant in the future and heavily discounted as compared to current costs. See, for example, Thomas Ribich, *Education and Poverty* (Washington, D.C.: The Brookings Institution, 1968). It might be argued that an implicit social choice of long-run once-for-all solutions implies a zero discount rate so that the future when earnings are gained is weighted equal to the present when costs are incurred, or even a negative rate, so that future earnings are overweighted. But the risk of a poverty environment overcoming the favorable effects of a good education program is a matter of the real world, not an artifact of economics.

first summer, President Johnson proclaimed Head Start to be "battle-tested — and . . . proved worthy."[14]

Unfortunately, later evaluations threw some doubt on this statement. In evaluating Head Start, it is necessary to distinguish between two objectives: the improvement of the educational and other capabilities of the children in the program and the improvement of the communities in which these children live. The latter effect may be very important. Head Start is a Community Action program and as such has a community-changing role that it has performed well. The school boards of the United States have been changed irreversibly for the better because they have been challenged by Head Start programs oriented toward innovation, parent participation, and poor kids, none of which many school boards had been particularly interested in before. This community effect alone may partly "justify" Head Start, but in the final analysis, Head Start is a program for children and must be evaluated primarily on its effectiveness in helping these children. Furthermore, although the auxiliary assistance, such as medical examinations for Head Start children, has been important, the test of the program must be on its ability to improve children's educational capabilities.

By educational capabilities, we mean those things classed by child psychologists as "cognitive" and "affective" abilities, each of which is related to the child's ability to absorb learning. (Roughly, the word "cognitive" relates to what might be termed "ability" to learn, the word "affective" to "willingness" to learn.) These educational capabilities may be affected by the direct "instruction" (if this term applies to preschool children) taking place in the Head Start classrooms, through the atmosphere of the classrooms, through the parents of the children, or through the community. But evaluatively, whatever the sources of improvements, the measures must be tests of cognitive and affective capabilities of the children involved. Head Start may be a fine Community Action program, and the indications are that it is. It may improve the health of its kids. But it is *primarily* a program to improve children's learning abilities, and on this criterion it must finally stand or fall. If the program does not bring about educational improvement, then the other favorable effects may be brought in much more cheaply.

The evaluations completed thus far on Head Start all seem to indi-

14. *The New York Times,* Sept. 1, 1965, p. 1.

cate that it fails the educational test. There is little evidence that the program does significantly improve the learning capabilities of the children in it. Head Start began in the summer of 1965, but for various reasons having to do in part with the unwillingness of program managers to risk comprehensive evaluations that might shake the program's high popularity, evaluations until 1968 were partial and particularly deficient in the establishment of control groups. There were evaluations of techniques and of individual programs, but no evaluation seemed to represent the whole. Even so, they did begin to show a pattern: Gains were made by enrollees during a summer in Head Start, but the gains were wiped out as children who had not been in the program caught up with the Head Start children during the first year or so of regular school.

In fact, this was not unexpected. It was generally conceded that the summer was too short a time to bring about lasting results, and Head Start and OEO pushed for a full-year Head Start program, which it was hoped would be substantially more successful in achieving lasting educational gains. But the first comprehensive evaluation of Head Start, carried out in 1968–69 by the Westinghouse Learning Corporation for OEO, threw doubt even upon the utility of the full-year program. The study confirmed the earlier findings that summer programs had no lasting effects; in fact, the rigorous use of control groups brought into doubt even initial gains. The evaluation showed a very slightly greater effect for the full-year program, but even this was doubtful. The Westinghouse summary stated that "Full-year programs appear to be ineffective in regard to the measures of affective development ["willingness"] used in the study, but appear to be somewhat effective in producing gains in cognitive development ["ability"] that could be detected in grades one, two, and three,"[15] but even in the cognitive area, the report shows that of the three types of test used, only one, applicable only to first graders, showed statistically significant effects. Of the other two, one, for all grades, did not confirm the successful test; the other, for grades after the first, seemed to indicate that any gains at the beginning of first grade were soon matched by the children in the control group.[16]

A few subordinate results indicated areas for further probing: be-

15. Westinghouse Learning Corporation/Ohio University, *The Impact of Head Start*, Preliminary Draft, April 1969, pp. 0–4.
16. Ibid., pp. IV-22 through IV-32.

tween some experimental and control groups of black children, Southern children, and core-city children the differences associated with the full-year program were significant though partial. In general, however, the Westinghouse study not only confirmed but reinforced the earlier findings that Head Start, even in its most intensive and longest form, was bringing about no lasting educational improvements and perhaps no improvements at all. These findings, plus the fact that any preschool program is going to be hurt evaluatively because direct antipoverty benefits, earnings, are fifteen uncertain years in the future, throws into strong doubt the effectiveness of Head Start as an antipoverty educational program.

At this point, it is necessary to ask "What did we expect anyhow?" Head Start, even full-year Head Start, takes kids after four years of home life, treats them to perhaps as much as six hours a day of programs out of their waking fourteen hours, and after a year turns them over to slum schools. There is no reason to believe that this system would have any lasting effect. Head Start thus shares the difficulty not yet overcome by any educational program, that even a high-quality program for poor kids is likely to be embedded in a countervailing environment that is so powerful that the evil is very likely to outweigh the good. And for Head Start, the time gap between program and ultimate effects is greater than for any other educational program, thus increasing the uncertainty.

It may be that the ultimate solution in education will come from a Head Start program starting even earlier and being followed up intensively through the grades of primary and perhaps even secondary schools. We do not have the knowledge now to say that this would work better than anything else, but particularly on the post-Head Start end, a good deal of experimentation is going on. The Follow Through program, to stay with children after they move from Head Start to school, which is delegated by OEO to the Office of Education, is being held at the experimental level of $30 million (experimental as compared to the more than $300 million going to Head Start), and it is in fact being handled as an attempt at a set of controlled experiments, so that we may find out whether Head Start gains can be revived and retained. The Parent-Child Center program for children even younger than those in Head Start is also being carried out on a pilot basis, but the quality of experimentation is such that little information is likely to be provided.

On the basis of the information summarized here, I would not recommend doing away with Head Start, which is fortunate. Because of its political popularity the program is likely to survive a good deal of negative evaluation. The Community Action effects and health effects of Head Start do provide a partial justification although if these were expected to be the only effects, then the summer program, which can reach about four times as many kids for the same money, would seem to be more cost-effective than the full-year. In fact, the full-year program is likely to survive. If far better experimentation and evaluation can be done with different teaching techniques, if more emphasis and more rigorous evaluation is applied to the Parent-Child Center program for pre-Head Start children and the Follow Through program, then perhaps Head Start deserves to continue.

Neighborhood Youth Corps (NYC), In-School and Summer. The In-School Neighborhood Youth Corps provides part-time jobs to 16- to 21-year-old students in order to enable and induce them to remain in school and continue their educations. It has been a mixed success in achieving this objective. As with Out-of-School NYC, data are insufficient for any comprehensive national evaluation, but some local studies of a high quality have been done. On the one hand, they show that a few programs are, in fact, achieving their purpose. In Washington, D.C., for example, a rigorous study showed that the dropout rate within a group of high school youth who were demonstrated to be prone to drop out was significantly decreased by NYC. (The study also showed some slight lowering of school grades for the NYC enrollees; this may or may not be significant.)

On the other hand, it is generally the case throughout the country that most NYC programs are not used primarily for dropout-prone students; the programs can thus have little effect on decreasing dropouts. Rather the after-school jobs of NYC are typically used as rewards for the better students who are likely to remain in school in any case. To the extent that this remains true in the future — and it would seem very difficult and perhaps not even desirable to force school teachers and administrators to favor their less successful low-income students over their better ones — the NYC In-School program is not going to achieve its anti-dropout objective.

Of course, like Out-of-School Neighborhood Youth Corps, In-School NYC provides quasi-transfer payments to youths in need of the money — they *are* poor — and (perversely in terms of the objective of reaching those prone to drop out) to those who "deserve" the money and jobs because they are doing well in school. As such, it may be a very useful program.

The same may be said of summer NYC. This was originally conceived as a follow-on to the In-School program, continuing the in-school jobs on a more nearly full-time basis during summer vacation. In fact, it quickly became a much larger program with an only partially euphemized antiriot goal. The objective was to keep kids off the streets during the day as much as possible and give them spending money they could use at night so at least they wouldn't be looking for low-cost trouble. It is difficult to evaluate the antiriot effectiveness of the program. The profile of the *average* urban rioter is that of an adult male, not a teen-ager, and somebody with a steady job at that; on the other hand many rioters have been younger, and it is difficult to believe that having fewer and more content teen-agers on the streets during a long hot summer is less desirable than having more discontented ones. The decrease in civil disturbance between the summer of 1967 and that of 1968 is undoubtedly attributable to a lot of other things. In some places (e.g., Buffalo, Minneapolis), however, making jobs available to poor youths certainly seems to have been a coolant. Again, at worst, summer NYC provides payments to those who need money, and this in itself should go a long way to justify the program.

Upward Bound. The objective of the Upward Bound program, begun in 1965 as an innovative program of CAP and transferred by law to the Office of Education on July 1, 1969, is not well understood. Indeed, the misunderstanding is one reason for the transfer although that may have been justified in any case.

Upward Bound is not a scholarship or financial aid program for poor youth who can make it into college intellectually but simply lack the funds. The Talent Search Program of the Office of Education with which Upward Bound is being combined is such a financial aid program, but Upward Bound is different. It is specifically a program for kids who lack *both* financial resources and good grades, but in whom teachers see a spark that can be fanned into an intellectual fire. This is done by a couple of summers of intensive classroom work and counseling for high school students on college campuses, together with school year follow-throughs.

The program seems to be working well. An early benefit-cost analysis done by OEO using lifetime income differentials among high school dropouts, high school graduates, college entrants, and college graduates, together with early estimates of the effects of Upward Bound in moving students from one of these categories to another, indicated that even modest program success would lead to favorable benefit-cost ratios. Just as Head Start suffers in benefit-cost analysis from the uncertainties incurred in the long time period between program and maturity, Upward Bound gains because the enrollees enter the adult world relatively soon after they have incurred program costs. Among the benefit-cost ratios computed for this OEO study, the highest was attained simply by keeping kids in high school through graduation; college entry was less important, but college retention and finally graduation built the ratio up again.

The OEO study was done on the basis of data available in the spring of 1967. In March 1969, the General Accounting Office reported that Upward Bound students:

—have substantially lower high school dropout rates than is considered normal for the low-income population,

—have considerably higher college admission rates in comparison with the admission rates of both their older siblings and the national average of all high school graduates, and

—have college retention rates above the national average of all college students in spite of lower than national average scores on a standard test which measures college potential.[17]

In addition, Upward Bound has been very important in the current movement to open colleges to low-achieving poor youth who would not have been admitted in the past.

One important contradictory point of evaluation should be men-

17. Comptroller General of the United States, *Review of Economic Opportunity Programs*, p. 118.

tioned, however. In various attitudinal, motivational, and achievement tests given Upward Bound enrollees after the program but before college entrance, only the measures of motivation to continue school show significant gains.[18] Thus for those Upward Bound students who do not enter college, only the symbolism of a high school diploma rather than a dropout really helps them in future life. For those who do go on to college, both the real achievement in college and the symbolism should count.

On balance, the program looks quite successful. It is to be hoped that the combination of Upward Bound with Talent Search will not lead to a softening of focus and a lessening of success.

Health Programs. Aside from income maintenance, health is the largest category of program expenditure within the War on Poverty. Seven billion dollars of the total $25.8 billion goes to health. Of the $7 billion, $2.5 billion each go to Medicare for the aged (that portion of Medicare going to the poor) and Medicaid for the "medically indigent," as defined by the states, which administer the Medicaid Program. The major OEO health program, Neighborhood Health Centers, costs $60 million, slightly less than one percent of total antipoverty health expenditures.

The first question to be asked is: Why do health programs loom so large in the War on Poverty? The answer has very little to do with program planning or evaluation, much more to do with the way things happen in the real political world. From a planning/evaluation viewpoint, health should not be of such high priority. It cannot be doubted that bad health can cause poverty, but how large a proportion of poverty is caused by bad health is conjectural. Although the figure is somewhat suspect, Table 3 in Chapter 2 showed that fewer than 5 percent of the poor are in families headed by a disabled nonaged male. If antipoverty health programs were concentrated on wage earners whose physical abilities made the difference in their abilities to attain nonpoverty jobs, then the connection between better health care for these people and decreasing poverty would be easier to establish. In fact, very little of the $7 billion is spent that way. The Medicare program goes almost entirely to retirees.

18. David E. Hunt, and Robert H. Hart, *Characterization of Upward Bound, Academic Year 1966–67* (Syracuse University Youth Development Center, July 1967), and David E. Hunt, Robert H. Hart, and James B. Victor, *Characterization of Upward Bound, 1967–68* (Syracuse University Youth Development Center, August 1968).

The Medicaid program goes mostly, though not entirely, to welfare recipients, the large majority of whom are incapable of working. If we start from these observations, it is difficult to see why so much antipoverty money goes to health care programs that are likely to have only limited antipoverty effectiveness.

In fact, the justification for Medicare lies not in any antipoverty effectiveness but in achieving two other very valuable social objectives: the direct objective of better medical care for the aged and the relief of many middle-class earners who support aged relatives. Not every federal social program must be an antipoverty program, and even though a substantial chunk of Medicare does go to the poor, this is part of an overall program with a different objective. Medicaid is another matter; it just seemed to have come along with Medicare. It is a program primarily for the poor, and it is by no means clear that it is the best expenditure of that money for the poor, particularly in light of the fact that too much of the money seems to go into increasing demand for medical services without increasing the supply, thus bidding up the price. But just as the popularity of children made Head Start popular, the universal fear of ill health makes health care programs relatively popular. In addition, one suspects the existence of liberal doctors who are just as effective medical lobbyists as the anti-public-health-care doctors of the American Medical Association. In any case, Medicaid as well as Medicare exists and is likely to remain.

Neighborhood Health Centers. It is in the context of these massive expenditures that evaluation of the much smaller OEO Neighborhood Health Center program becomes important. At its $60 million or any level approachable from $60 million, the Neighborhood Health Center program is not likely to have a significant impact on the total health of the poor, even if it works very well. But the health center program is more a new way of *organizing* existing expenditures on health than it is a new way of spending health money. The Neighborhood Health Center program is an effort to deliver high-quality medicine at a reasonable price through a system of organization that combines the old-time style of comprehensive family health care with the availability of specialists, and supplements both of them by the use of paramedical aides. If it works, it may be a device to improve the effectiveness of the other $6.942 billion spent on the health of the poor and indeed the effectiveness of non-hospital medical care at all income levels.

Evaluative data are not yet available to say how well it does work. The test of the Neighborhood Health Center program is whether it does, in fact, improve the health of its target population, and baseline medical data are so difficult to come by that no comparisons have yet been made to any such baselines. Some straw-in-the-wind indicators are available: In Columbia Point, an isolated community in the city of Boston where one of the first centers was set up, hospital admissions have dropped, perhaps indicating the success of preventive medicine in the center. But this result is merely indicative, and it may be a while before real evaluation is available. Like Head Start, the Neighborhood Health Center program is popular and is not anxious to have its boat rocked. At any rate, it does seem to be the case that the health center program brings in its medical care at a price lower than a similar high level of care if provided by the private market. This is something of an indicator of the organizational effectiveness of the program, which in turn has favorable implications for the desirability of replicating the organizational structure throughout health programs. But none of this is very firm, and the best that can be said definitely at this time — on a basis far different from benefit-cost — is that the program is a popular one both among its recipients and in Congress and that it does benefit in a major way the clientele who come in. This statement is different from saying that it has a major impact on the target population at which it is aimed. The last could be an important evaluative statement, but we simply do not know.

Family Planning. The poor live in larger families than the nonpoor, but the poor want families of the same size as the nonpoor. These two facts make a family planning/birth control program potentially very important to the War on Poverty. For if the families of the poor are larger than they want, they are also a major reason for their poverty; preventing unwanted future births can prevent a good deal of poverty. In one way this has to do with the definition of poverty. The poverty line is a function of family size, but the earnings that support the families are not. Beyond this simple numerical relationship, however, the fact of a too large family, leading from economic stringency to insufficient attention paid to all the children and so forth seems to be an important factor in perpetuating poverty.

Because of the importance of family size in both defining and causing poverty, many benefit-cost studies have been done of family-planning programs. For example, OEO did one using as a measure of the benefits the $500-per-person increases in the poverty line for families of larger sizes; one undesired child fewer would bring the family's ability to get out of poverty $500 closer. Other studies have been done using different kinds of benefit estimates. All of these show a fantastically high benefit-cost ratio for a successful family-planning program. If it is possible to reduce the number of children born among the poor at any kind of reasonable cost, it is worthwhile by this calculation.

The trouble is that nobody has data measuring the effectiveness and workability of family-planning programs as they actually exist. The computed benefit-cost ratios are all based on "if it works" reasoning. It probably does work, but nobody is sure, and nobody knows how well. Measurement of how well is what evaluation is all about, and until such measurements are made of undesired children actually prevented by specific family-planning programs, the best that can be done is to fall back on the statement that family planning is very important indeed to the War on Poverty if it works, and we think it works, but we aren't sure.

Nutrition. The nutrition programs of the federal government are in a state of flux. Hunger and starvation, which are discussed in Michael Harrington's *The Other America* (1962), a book that contributed to the War on Poverty, were rediscovered by the Senate Labor and Public Welfare committee in 1967 and re-rediscovered in 1969. This last discovery bids to stick, and the future nutrition programs of the federal government are likely to be vastly different from the ones discussed here. The Nixon Administration's proposals not only would increase federal nutrition programs greatly but would rationalize them and aid in getting them to the poorest and most in need.

Nutrition is undeniably important. Medical evidence is increasingly demonstrating that malnutrition of pregnant mothers and of children can lead to irreversible brain damage, and this aside from being tragic in it-

153

self most certainly leads to poverty. The quantitative potential for poverty prevention through nutrition programs is not known, among other reasons because the number of badly malnourished people in the United States is not known. Horseback estimates have been made that there are from 9 to 15 million hungry poor Americans, but these figures seem too large to describe the population liable to damaging malnutrition, and it is difficult to say what they do describe. Much more certain, however, is that there is some significant amount of such damaging malnutrition, that *any* is intolerable, and that even less damaging hunger is bad enough so that getting rid of it seems a high objective of national policy. Postponed for the next chapter is a discussion of whether the best antihunger policy is direct feeding or income maintenance or a combination.

Although OEO has carried out no specific evaluation of nutrition programs, all of which thus far have been run by the Department of Agriculture, it is clear that the feeding programs of the federal government are in sad shape. Commodity Distribution is one such program based initially on the desire to get rid of surpluses rather than the desire to eliminate anyone's hunger. Of late the commodities distributed have been a bit more varied and nutritionally complete than the earlier ones, yet a commodity diet is unbalanced, inevitably dull, and useful mainly for preventing literal starvation. Early in President Kennedy's Administration, Congress passed his proposal to supplement the Commodity Program with a Food Stamp Program, under which poor people could purchase stamps that would greatly increase the reach of their food dollars and that could be used almost as flexibly as money, thus giving recipients as varied a diet as they desired. The food stamps have the advantage over commodities of variety, but until recently they have had the disadvantage of requiring some money for purchase.

These two programs have been alternatives, with the choice made by the administering counties. The counties could choose either one or could choose none, which indicates a major flaw. The programs are federally funded, but they have not been federally administered. Not only has the choice of which program to accept or whether to accept a program been left up to a county, but recipient eligibility is largely locally determined, and so is the extent of any effort to reach people ignorant of the program. Publicity early in 1969 has indicated that at least some county officials are remarkably insensitive and even brutal, and it seems unlikely that any nutrition program left to their mercy will succeed in the places it is most needed.

In 1967, Congress mandated OEO to carry out a small "Emergency Food and Medical" program. This has been used mainly to provide the money with which people with no money at all could buy food stamps (in those areas where food stamps are available). Rural Community Action Programs have also performed some of the outreach necessary just to find starving people in backwoods areas and tell them what is available.

Not only are the Commodity and Food Stamp programs carried out at the discretion of local authorities, so is the school lunch program, which provides federal subsidies for lunches for poor children to make sure that they will get at least one nourishing hot meal a day. The lunch program has been spotty, not only because of local school board discretion but also because many schools don't have the kitchens necessary to prepare the food. Again this is mostly the case in areas of greatest need and, indeed, the school lunch program has some tendency to go more to kids above the poverty line and less in need than those below the poverty line. Middle-class schools are more likely to have facilities.

Nonetheless, at least for those poor children it reaches (children of school age only, of course) the program is a valuable one. In general, like the other programs affecting nutrition, drastic reorganization seems needed. At a minimum, feeding programs should be taken away from the Department of Agriculture with its prime interest in commercial farming and turned over to the Department of Health, Education and Welfare. But when one thinks of the tender mercies of some welfare workers, particularly welfare workers in poor rural areas, one wishes that the program could be temporarily administered by OEO. For OEO, whatever its disadvantages, has the virtue of having maintained the antipoverty focus of the programs it has innovated and managed and even the programs it delegated. Perhaps it could preserve the antipoverty focus of federal nutrition programs, and this more than anything may be what they need.

COMMUNITY BETTERMENT

The programs classified under Community Betterment, as shown in Table 12, are those whose main objective is to change the environments in which the poor live and which help perpetuate poverty, not merely, and

Table 12
Federal Antipoverty Budget, Fiscal 1969: Community Betterment

Program	Fund Source	Management	Funds (millions of dollars)
"Catalytic" Programs	—	—	517
CAP	OEO	OEO	443
Legal Services	OEO	OEO-CAP	42
VISTA	OEO	OEO	32
Housing	Mainly Department of Housing and Urban Development	Mainly Department of Housing and Urban Development	405
Economic Development	Many Agencies	Many Agencies	293
Miscellaneous	—	—	288
Total Community Betterment			1,503

Source: Office of Economic Opportunity

perhaps not even mainly, the physical environment but also the social environment of injustice, inequality, and despair in which the poor exist. Housing programs and a few others like rat control and garbage pickup do attempt to change the physical environment, but the awful impact of environment on poverty can be understood only by looking at the total environment in all of its aspects.

Programs for environmental change do not put the same emphasis on all the poor. They are target-area programs aimed at the poor who live among the poor and near-poor and whose physical and social environment is thus that of poverty. As shown by Table 2 in Chapter 2, only one-seventh of the poor live in the slum areas of central cities, with the number in similar suburban slums bringing the proportion up to one-fifth. Adding in roughly one-half of those poor who live outside of Standard Metropolitan Statistical Areas, primarily those who live in the poorest rural counties, which are equally environments of poverty, brings the total of target-area "concentrated" poor up toward, though probably not as high as, one-half of the poor of the United States. These are the poor in the environment of poverty; both because their total environment is the worst and because programs for Community Betterment cannot operate effectively outside of these communities of poverty, they are the poor for whom Community Betterment programs are primarily designed.

Community Betterment programs, in addition to being a necessary part of any solution to low-income poverty in target areas of concentrated poverty, are essential to the achievement of the opportunity-equalizing objectives of the War on Poverty. Not only do most poor nonwhites live in poverty target areas, whether urban or rural, but so do most nonwhites above the Orshansky poverty line. This is true of Negroes both in urban slums and in the poor counties of the rural South, and it is particularly true of reservation Indians. In addition to those classified by the Census as nonwhite, it is true of urban and rural Mexican Americans and of Appalachian and other rural Southern whites. These are the unequal opportunity groups, and much of the reason for their unequal opportunity stems from the physical and social environments in which they live. These are the environments of dilapidation, crowding, garbage, and rats; they are the environments of hopelessness and despair. They are also the environments of injustice, brutality, and powerlessness, and these aspects of environment as much as the others must be changed by Community Betterment programs if the effort to achieve equality of opportunity as well as an end to low-income poverty can be successful. Although poverty is by definition a family and individual matter (low income for the family, low earnings for the individual) and so is unequal opportunity — opportunity to get ahead is essentially opportunity for an individual to rise — the causes and cures of these individual phenomena lie in substantial measure in the ethnic and other groups that the individual and family belong to. Both poverty and opportunity for the individual are severely constrained by the powerlessness and inability to help on the part of the group. The group can help the individual pull himself up and can help support him economically and psychologically if he falls back, if the group is strong enough. But when the group is powerless and looked down upon, it drags the individual down with it. Racial discrimination is the major cause of unequal opportunity, and racial discrimination is in its very definition the treating of an individual not as an individual but as a member of a group deemed "inferior."

Powerlessness and hopelessness thus lead to the failure of the War on Poverty programs designed to help individuals. Powerlessness leads to the failure to apply programs like manpower and education to the right populations in the right ways, and hopelessness leads to the failure of the programs to take hold of the individuals. That is why the largest subcategory of Community Betterment programs is catalytic. These programs are designed to change the institutional environment of hopelessness and powerlessness and thus catalyze the building of new institutions and changing of old institutions so that they will work more effectively against poverty and inequality. In this they have been quite successful.

Catalytic Programs
Community Action Program. The $443 million of programs covered in the Community Action Program segment of the Community Betterment category are less than one-half of the total Community Action programs funded under Title II of the Economic Opportunity Act. The method of classification here puts Community Action programs like Head Start and Health under the heading of Individual Improvement because improvement of the individuals receiving their services is their primary function. In addition the Community Action Legal Services program is different enough to require separate treatment later in this chapter. What is left in the $443 million, then, in addition to certain central administrative costs of the overall Community Action Program, is the set of programs planned and operated locally by more than 1,000 Community Action agencies throughout the country plus about $30 million of mostly similar programs run from Washington under the heading of Research and Demonstration. These locally planned and operated programs plus Research and Demonstration thus form less than one-half of the CAP budget, less than one-fourth of the OEO budget, and less than 2 percent of the total War on Poverty. But they provide well in excess of 50 percent of the controversy surrounding the War on Poverty, and indeed the Research and Demonstration programs, which are less than 10 percent of the CAP total, themselves provide the bulk of the controversy. Why?

The short answer to the question is that these programs have been relatively successful in achieving a particular type of antipoverty objective that is relatively unpopular. This is the objective of changing the way things are done, and there are many, many people in the United

States who either have a stake in the way things are done or at least are comfortable with the way things are done. What I am suggesting is that although Community Action at the local level is not highly efficient in reaching its objectives, if it were *more* effective in achieving these objectives, it would be even *less* popular than it is.

To understand Community Action, it is necessary to realize that it has three distinct objectives: *delivery* of new services to the poor or delivery of old services in new ways; *coordination* of the services reaching the poor in target areas; and *changing* the institutions which surround and perpetuate poverty. These are not either-or objectives, nor are they separate objectives of separate components of a CAP program. Each of these is an objective of every CAP program and every portion of a CAP program, a fact that some members of the 1966 Congress failed to understand fully when they tried to cut down on the agitational institution-changing effects of Community Action programs by earmarking most of the money for specific service delivery. These services too were changing institutions.

The effectiveness of CAP can be evaluated separately for each of its three objectives. The mark on service delivery is high. Most of the major specific services such as Head Start and Health Centers have been discussed already; Legal Services will be discussed later. Although, as has been suggested, not all of these new services have been equally effective against poverty, CAP has been effective in utilizing them as pilots for entire new modes of service delivery to the poor. The other major category of services delivered by CAP locally is contained in the Neighborhood Service Center program. This is the attempt to pull together the wide variety of services delivered to poor people in poor neighborhoods so that they will fit a pattern comprehensible to poor people (or to anybody else for that matter). Putting the Employment Service counselor cheek by jowl with the welfare advisor and perhaps representatives of Head Start and other programs and mixing all of these with "outreach" workers recruited from among the poor themselves to find and help their fellows has worked well. It has given the poor access to knowledge they did not have before, and to those working with the poor it has given an invaluable immersion in and sensitivity to the problems and feelings of the poor. These results have been attained in most of the urban target areas of poverty by the Neighborhood Service Centers of the Community Action Program, and, like other aspects of service delivery, the Centers have been relatively successful.

The second objective of Community Action, coordination of all services coming into the target areas, has been far less successful. The Neighborhood Centers have done some, but even bringing certain services together has not eliminated the duplication, overlapping, hostility, and failure to mesh programs that coordination is supposed to overcome. Throughout the entire set of activities in CAP target areas, little coordination is visible; because services and activities are much larger and more varied than before CAP, the lack of coordination is if anything worse than before. Programs under different auspices still compete with one another; program operators may or may not talk to one another, but if they do, it does not typically result in a smooth overall system in which areas are assigned, people fed in and directed to those services they most need, and programs meshed so that the educational program feeds the prevocational program, which feeds the vocational program, and so forth. One reason for this failure is that just as the federal government has had its competing agencies and bureaucracies, so has every local community: the school authorities, the welfare people, the manpower trainers, and many more. Each of these has some power, and none wants to give up any power to the others although most would be willing to coordinate the others. The federal government has made the situation worse by piling in new operations, each with some authority to coordinate the others. It did not take long before CAP's operating authority was partially superseded (but only partially) by Model Cities and by CEP. In some communities, Kennedy-Javits Special Impact programs became additional rivals for attention and operational control. Nor is any of these organizations necessarily unitary in itself. Not only has CAP spawned neighborhood organizations overlapping in geographical and functional authority, but each of these, like each of the others, set up a vested interest that does not like to be coordinated.

The major reason for the lack of coordination in target areas is not bureaucratic, however; it is the real division of the world among competing interests. Many interests are present in and around poverty areas, and they all want representation; at this stage they prefer and need autonomy more than they need coordination and smooth program operation. Community Action has failed to coordinate because coordination of many interests, within and without the ghetto, has not been compatible with CAP's other function of advocating one of these interests, that of the poor in the target areas.

Advocacy of the interests of the poor and of those without opportunity is the activity that goes with the third objective of Community Action, institutional change. This objective is the new and unique one. Services have been delivered to target areas for a long time, coordination has been attempted (almost always unsuccessfully) for a long time, but institution changing is new. Its two aspects are the building of self-help institutions in ghettos and other target areas, and the changing of the institutions of the larger communities in which the target areas are embedded in order to make them more willing and effective in helping end poverty.

The evaluative evidence on institution building must be anecdotal and impressionistic, but it does imply a marked degree of success. As noted earlier, in 1963, when Glazer and Moynihan published *Beyond the Melting Pot,* the institutional life in New York's black urban ghettos was thin, and it was probably richer in Harlem than elsewhere, at that. The lack of institutions carried with it real psychological and economic disabilities for individuals needing the support of group institutions. Psychologically, surroundings of failure, feelings of belonging to a failure-doomed group are not conducive to personal success.

But the conditions for failure were not only psychological, they were concrete and economic too. Things have probably reached the point in the United States where the really capable members of any race have a good chance of succeeding, maybe even an equal chance. But no race is composed mainly of capable people. Who is to help the second-raters? Where in the black community are the Workmen's Circles of the Jewish ghetto or the businesses that would provide a job because "After all, he's Max's second cousin's nephew"? Where are the saloon-based political organizations of the New York Irish? Where are the street societies of the Italians? For reasons having to do with discrimination, slavery, and all the rest, these did not exist in the black community in New York or the other urban black communities of the United States.

What institutions did exist were largely either too middle-class to meet the needs of the vast majority of the black ghetto dwellers or becoming obsolete. The civil rights movement, for example, achieved much in removing social and political disabilities from those who had the economic ability to take advantage of these gains, but even the Urban League had not broken through on large-scale programs to raise economic capabilities; other institutions, like the store-front churches, were obsolete and fading. New institutions like the Muslims were beginning but were infinitesimal and so far distant from people's ordinary beliefs that their prospects for growth looked small.

All this was true in New York as described by Glazer and Moynihan and much much more so everywhere but New York. It is not true in the major cities of the United States today, and this is to a substantial extent a triumph of Community Action. Social, economic, and political institutions proliferate and flower in a tangled undergrowth so thick it is impossible to find a way through without a seasoned guide. Many cities have "Black United Fronts" partially united and partially in rivalry with other organizations. Cities have organizations for different purposes in different neighborhoods, organizations for people in different age groups, organizations with different political outlooks. Washington, D.C., in addition to the more or less old-line NAACP, Urban League, SCLC, and SNCC, and to the local version of the Black Panthers, has MICCO, FAIRMICCO, Rebels With a Cause, Pride, Inc., and the Black United Front among others. Los Angeles has the same variety of organizations with additional Angeleno quirks such as shaved heads and the threat and potential of paramilitary violence. And between the coasts the variety is almost as rich. It is a Hobbesian political situation, a state of nature, with the unpleasant aspects as well as the pleasant aspects associated with unconstrained freedom. There is a lack of control verging on chaos, and there is occasionally the threat or even carrying out of violence, not excluding murder.

Nonetheless, it is necessary to pass through the Hobbesian state of natural freedom in order to reach a state of controlled freedom, and both are preferable to no life at all. Before 1964, there was little institutional life and without the institutional life no real hope for group support for the efforts of the individual to rise from poverty, and now there is. It's that simple.

In the real world, single effects seldom stem from single causes. Much of the change has been due to the evolution of the civil rights movement and to the summer riots of 1965 through 1967. But CAP demonstrably has also had very much to do with the beginnings of this life in each community, although the life is certainly now out of CAP's control, as it should be. Except for one or two early demonstration programs started during CAP's radical period and except for one or two later aberrations, CAP organizations have had little to do with the more extreme manifestations of this life, whether violent or not. It would be specious to deny that people associated with CAP have been associated with some of the more far-out aspects, but for the most part they have had the political intelligence to separate such activities from their Community Action connections. The extremes have been deplorable as extremes always are, but there can be no doubt that if ending poverty and equalizing opportunity are the objectives, the overall activity of institution building has been vital.

The other aspect of the institutional change function of Community Action is changing the institutions of the overall community within which the target-area poverty community exists. Again, these changes are necessary for ending poverty and equalizing opportunity. It is not only in the old Confederacy that school boards have deliberately segregated and downgraded slum schools, Employment Services have discriminated, welfare authorities have degraded the poor, courts have provided unequal justice. This has happened in every state and probably every community. Changing it is necessary to ending poverty, but change is inevitably unpopular both with the bureaucracies that man these institutions and with the constituencies that have benefited from them.

Because of the combined necessity and inherent unpopularity of such changes of institutions, carrying the changes through is a difficult process, and doing it right, with minimum friction, is a markedly subtle process. By no means has it always been done right, and the occasions on which it has not been done right have been publicized well enough to characterize much of the War on Poverty in the public mind. "Done right" does not mean done with no conflict; it does mean managing the conflict well. No conflict at all means no progress. Strong institutions seldom simply get religion and change their ways; they must be pushed a little.

But the poor and the blacks are minorities on the order of 10 to 20 percent, and too much conflict inevitably means uniting majorities of 80 to 90 percent against these minorities with inevitable results. The middle way is the political way, the policies of coalition as compared with the more violent methods of confrontation.

Sundquist and Davis describe three types of Community Action agencies:

1. The innocuous ones, found mainly in smaller communities. They were the ones of whom it was said, "Oh, they're all right; they're not doing much." That type of CAA [Community Action Agency] had found its place in the cluster of social agencies in its community, as another specialized organization quietly administering a few programs designed in Washington. Sponsored initially by the power structure, it had not challenged the institutions and leadership of that structure.

2. The respected ones — those that were aggressive, even militant, but with a quality of leadership and administrative competence to match. The respect was accorded not willingly but grudgingly — usually not because of their achievements but because of their political strength, which rested upon the mobilization of the poor. And they stood apart from, and in a position of confrontation with, the established institutions of their communities.

3. The outcasts — those that had not been able to match their militancy with a leadership and competence that compelled respect. They were effectively contained, left to administer the programs financed from Washington but otherwise ignored or even shunned.[19]

Of these it seems to be the middle way that works. As put by one OEO evaluation summary,

In the short run, the optimum course for Community Action Agencies is clear: a limited form of pressure and antagonism is preferable

19. James L. Sundquist with the collaboration of David W. Davis, *Making Federalism Work* (Washington, D.C.: The Brookings Institution, 1969), pp. 46–47.

to the extremes of vehement antagonism or docility. Vehement antagonism, although it may be brought about by the recalcitrance of the public agency, is likely to result in a communication breakdown. Docile CAAs, on the other hand, are unlikely to bring about any improved focusing of existing services for the poor.[20]

These are the ideal types, and on the basis of logic the middle way, "a limited form of pressure and antagonism," is the most likely to work. In fact, evaluative data are beginning to show that it does work. Institutional change is not inherently quantifiable, but anything that exists in definable units can be counted, and OEO, utilizing a fairly powerful evaluation technique, has begun to count institutional changes. The technique is one in which relatively unbiased local observers with no stake in program success answer a carefully structured set of questions about changes in local institutions and about the contribution of Community Action to bringing about these changes. The carefully worded questions specify four institutions: a major private welfare agency, the public welfare program, the Employment Service, and the school system. They ask for information on very specific kinds of changes. In regard to the Employment Service, for example, they ask about

> Change in decentralization, outreach. (For example change in geographic location of existing and new services, use of neighborhood workers, transfer of function to suboffices, degree of autonomy of outstationed personnel; money spent for building material at central office relative to outstations.)

In regard to the school system:

> Change in training regarding programs for the poor. (For example change in orientation programs for staff, starting new training programs, participating in such CAP programs, change in content or method of existing training programs.)

The answers are not merely yes or no. They are graded on a five-point scale according to degree of significance of the change and on a seven-point scale according to degree of CAP participation.[21]

20. Unpublished OEO memorandum.
21. The contractor responsible for analysis of the data has been Barss, Reitzel, and Company, of Cambridge.

The results can be tabulated in various ways, and, as more data on this pilot study and follow-up studies come in, more sophisticated compilations will be available. But the very significant tabulation already available shows that approximately two-thirds of the sample city Community Action agencies "played a vital part in significant changes . . . that is . . . those changes which the observer thought significant and not likely to be reversed" in at least one of the four institutions.[22] In more than a third of the sample the significant changes had been effected in two or more of the institutions, in about one-sixth in three or more, and in 2 percent in all four institutions.

Of the four institutions, changes were spread fairly evenly over the schools, the public employment services, and the public welfare system, with slightly less frequent changes in the private welfare agency. The most frequent type of change was increased demand for services by the target community. The pattern was even enough, however, that no single institution or type of change dominated the sample. In other words, Community Action authorities in different communities varied their targets as opportunities presented themselves, but in two-thirds of the communities the Community Action agencies had found at least one target where real improvement was possible. The kinds of changes are exemplified by the following:

> The Community Action Agency in Portsmouth, Ohio, got the public schools to launch job-oriented adult education courses in CAP neighborhood centers, and to commence school bus service for poverty areas. In Fremont, California the Community Action Agency prodded the school board into requesting and obtaining a Labor Department grant for a child care center, stressing the use of nonprofessional aides from poverty groups. In Leominister, Massachusetts, CAP was responsible for changing a school board requirement that teachers' aides be college graduates, making possible the hiring of the poor.
>
> In Lowell, Massachusetts, the Community Action Agency induced the Welfare Department to participate in a surplus food program that had been available within the state for fifteen years; the CAA runs the program out of its neighborhood centers. The CAA in Mil-

22. Memorandum from Jonathan Lane to Robert Levine dated January 9, 1969, which includes quotations from the questionnaires used.

waukee has obtained the decentralization of Welfare services to CAP neighborhood centers; and has forced the Welfare Department to accelerate the processing of special-needs payments.

In virtually every major city in the United States, local offices of the State Employment Service, which had been in downtown office buildings with typically difficult access from poverty areas, have moved into the poverty areas, mostly into the CAP neighborhood centers. In Atlanta, not only the Employment Service but the Welfare Department and City Hall itself have set up local offices in the centers.

These are clear instances of institutional change stemming directly and demonstrably from local Community Action. In addition, one significant evaluative finding shades toward the radical from Sundquist and Davis's and OEO's finding that CAP moderation is most successful:

> We found that a type [of CAP] thus identified — one on the whole innovative, somewhat oriented toward institutional change, independent of local government, and involving the poor significantly — had a great deal of impact. Another group — which placed no emphasis on institutional change, was totally noninnovative, under firm government control, and allowed the poor no authority or influence — showed extremely limited impact. Two other clusters — with mixed characteristics — had moderate impact on institutions in their communities.[23]

In other words, perhaps a moderate type of confrontation does pay off.

To sum up my discussion of Community Action, the most controversial program in the War on Poverty has been one of the most vital because delivery of services alone is never likely to end poverty and equalize opportunity. It is also the most novel part introduced thus far although a Negative Income Tax would rival it on this score. And, finally, although Community Action fails miserably on any evaluation of its results on coordination, it succeeds well on new services and delivery of services, and when evaluated for its institution building and changing effects, it may be the most successful of antipoverty programs.

23. Barss, Reitzel and Associates, *Final Report on Phase I Data Analysis* (in fulfillment of OEO contract B99-4730).

Legal Services. The Legal Services Program of OEO shares at least two objectives with the overall Community Action Program, of which it is part. Legal services delivered to the poor are services by and large not available before. For the most part the Legal Services Program provides help in civil law cases, and such help has frequently been out of reach for the poor. It has been remarked that at the beginning of many Legal Services programs, the bulk of the cases were in domestic relations, mostly divorce. This is sometimes considered shocking, but it is less shocking than the thought that up until then poor people were forced either to remain in miserable marriages or to live in extralegal arrangements simply because of lack of money. In many other cases — landlord/tenant, welfare, and the ordinary run of automobile cases, for example — Legal Services has made something available that was seldom available before to the poor.

The other objective of the Legal Services Program has been institutional change, change in the legal systems delivering unequal justice to the poor. The change thus begun and brought about by the Legal Services Program has not been political change, not changing the laws, which would be an illegitimate use of federal money. Rather it has been the legitimate function of changing legal practices so that they fit the written laws, including the Constitution of the United States. In the field of welfare law in particular, suits brought by OEO Legal Services projects have had major effect. They have been responsible for abolishing the length-of-residence requirements under the Constitutional clause requiring each of the states to give equal rights to residents of the others. Legal Services programs have weakened or abolished man-in-house rules, and in local cases, they have forced the welfare authorities to conform with state law (for example, in Contra Costa County, California). They have achieved similar successes in landlord/tenant litigation and in other fields.

The Legal Services Program is difficult to evaluate quantitatively; not all the cases taken up are taken to court; not all the judgments are in money. It has been estimated that outlawing the residence rule alone was likely to bring to the poor enough money to be able to pay the annual cost of the entire Legal Services Program, but this kind of calculation is always a bit dubious. It does seem certain, however, that both on its own terms of making available to the poor good law and good lawyers and on the broader terms of breaking the institutional barriers to people getting out of poverty, the program should be marked a success.

Volunteers in Service to America (VISTA). The so-called "domestic peace corps" is the most difficult of all programs to evaluate for effectiveness. It shares with CAP a coupling of the goals of delivering services to the poor and changing the institutions of poverty. On service delivery, marks for effectiveness have generally been good; total annual costs averaged over the number of volunteers come to between $7,500 and $10,000 per man-year, which is low compared with the full average man-year cost of a social worker in most parts of the country. In addition, since many of the volunteers have been assigned to duties in places where skilled and sym-pathetic social workers are in short supply — in 1968 a third were rural, mostly in very poor rural areas, an additional 5 percent each went into Indian and migrant programs — the cost-effectiveness score is likely to be high compared with alternatives, including no outside assistance for many areas and groups.

The other major VISTA function is to help the poor change institu-tions much in the manner of CAP. Whereas beginnings could be made on measuring the extent of this change for CAP, it is unlikely ever to be measurable in any general sense for VISTA. Community Action is a large enough portion of the entire set of activities in a community that its effects may be singled out as they were by the observers whose views were tallied in the CAP evaluation discussed previously. Almost always VISTA is too small for such separation of effects. What can be said is that over the four years of its existence, VISTA itself has changed in a direc-tion necessary for building any kind of institution-changing ability. In the beginning, VISTA carried many hallmarks of a "lady bountiful" type of outfit — bringing bread, goods, workers, and the Word to the poor. In addition, many of the volunteers came in for inner- rather than outer-directed motives. Dissatisfied with college, they dropped out to discover themselves rather than being motivated primarily by a desire to help others. Much of this has changed as volunteers have worked more with the poor and as VISTA has discovered through its own evaluations what kind of volunteers can be most effective and stressed recruitment of these.

Much more stress has gone into recruiting "indigenous" volunteers, not necessarily poor but at least members of minority groups. At the end of 1968, more than one-fifth of the volunteers were nonwhite, and one-sixth of total volunteers had a high school education or less.

Lacking good evaluation of the effectiveness of VISTA, however, little can be said about its importance compared with other antipoverty programs. What can be said is that such evaluations are also lacking on the effectiveness of American youth in the Peace Corps, in the Teacher Corps, and in military service.[24] Under these circumstances, it seems reasonable to state that so long as youth and others are called upon for a year or more of public service, VISTA is a reasonable option that should be continued. The $30-million VISTA budget is small compared with overall antipoverty budgets or with the total spent on youth services. This evaluation provides no basis for decision at the margin as to whether to increase VISTA 10 percent, decrease it by a like amount, or cut it in half, but decisions like this are likely to be political decisions in any case.

HOUSING

The OEO has only a very small portion of the total federal antipoverty housing budget — some $14 million out of a total of $405 million — and most of that is catalytic, used for organizing groups to take advantage of the financial provisions of various federal housing laws. For this reason, OEO has done little evaluation of federal housing programs. Nor for that matter has the Department of Housing and Urban Development, which manages most of them.

What can be said about housing, then, is that it is difficult to establish a causal connection running from bad housing to poverty, except as the bad housing is a part of the overall stifling environment of poverty. By and large, it seems likely that if people can get out of poverty, they can get decent housing (although it may take an income higher than the Orshansky line) and that bad housing will not keep them in poverty if they could make it otherwise. Bad housing may be a spectacular symptom of poverty about which we want to do something simply in the inter-

24. Actually, more than a third of VISTA volunteers are over 25 and one-eighth over 35, but the image and center of gravity of VISTA is still as a program that mainly utilizes youth.

est of ameliorating the worst effects of the disease; largely for this reason, it is a frequently expressed concern of the poor. But because of the doubt about causation and particularly the apparent difficulty in doing much about housing on a national basis, no matter what our intentions may be, antipoverty housing programs have never had high priority in any comprehensive plan.

One aspect of housing that does seem more directly connected to causing poverty, however, is segregation. Leaving aside here any arguments over whether desegregation is a proper public goal as compared to internal development and improvement of ghetto life, it is quite clear that any evaluation of the effectiveness of antihousing-segregation programs would indicate so little immediate prospect for large-scale success of desegregation among the poor and near-poor that such housing desegregation cannot now be a major part of an antipoverty program.

The other aspect of evaluating housing programs for the poor is their immediate effect on improving housing. Here conventional wisdom has it that public housing has become slum renewal, building bigger and higher tenements that initially at least may provide better physical facilities than the old ones but balance out this improvement with regimentation, arbitrary regulations, coldness, and extreme social disorganization. Urban renewal as it has been run has become Negro removal, replacing homes, albeit mostly deteriorating ones, with much nicer luxury apartment houses and offices and ensuring either the growth of new slums or the compounded overcrowding of old ones. I see no reason to challenge these judgments.

So far as the future is concerned, newer programs and modes of operation like rent supplements (which is a new housing construction program, not a program for dispersing poor people in existing housing), turnkey operations by which a private builder builds housing under flexible rules and turns it over to a Public Housing Authority, and highly automated rehabilitation operations may each or together make it possible to increase the supply of housing faster or at lower cost than was previously possible. But none of them seems to show much promise of breaking through on the social and institutional conditions that have led housing programs for the poor to be impotent at best and perverse at worst.

ECONOMIC DEVELOPMENT

Economic Development of one sort or another is thought by some to be the new antipoverty panacea. In fact, however, economic development so far has done very little for the poor, and there is no reason to believe the prospects to be changing. Economic Development programs can be grouped into three categories:

1. Economic Development of rural areas or small towns and cities. As discussed in Chapter 3, such development may be a legitimate public objective either for itself or for its effects on retaining middle-class social stability in declining areas, but poor areas are not to be confused with poor people, and it is the effectiveness of such rural economic development on the poverty of people with which this section is concerned. Rural economic development is supposed to work as an antipoverty program by reversing the rural-to-urban migration stream or at least by stopping it. It is believed that this will keep people in areas where they are likely to be better off.

2. External Economic Development in urban target areas. By external is meant attracting of plants and facilities of existing outside firms with the primary objective of providing jobs in the target area. It should be noted that successful programs of this kind are likely to counterbalance any successful effects of the rural development programs in staunching or reversing migration flows.

3. "Black Capitalism" programs. These are programs for new business development in ghettos, owned or controlled by the residents of the ghetto on an individual ownership or cooperative pattern. Although "job creation" is an objective of this variety of economic development program, it is less important than ownership and control as a building block for social and political power. Because of the importance of the latter sort of objective, aid from outside business may be solicited but only on the clear understanding that control will remain with or be turned over to local people and groups.

All three of these types of programs are more often than not misunderstood by their advocates as being true "job creation" devices. They are not. Jobs in our economy are "created" by the demand for the goods and services produced by these jobs. General national economic growth produces jobs; economic development, insofar as it has effects separate from general growth, merely redistributes the jobs. Were the American economy static, not growing at all, a job "created" in a specific area by economic development would necessarily be a job destroyed in another area. Since the economy is dynamic and growing, however, the effects of economic development are less obvious; development moves new jobs that *would have been* in one area into another area with no necessary net loss to the nondevelopment area. Nonetheless it remains the case that public expenditures on economic development do not create new jobs that would not have existed otherwise except by accelerating economic growth a bit as would any government expenditure of the same size. The specific effect of successful public promotion of economic development is to move jobs around.

This does not mean that it is necessarily undesirable to promote a geographical distribution of jobs different from what it would have been in the absence of development programs. Rather it means that development must be evaluated according to whether the new job location is more desirable than the old, and expenditures of public monies for development must be measured by the relative value of job moving as against other objectives.

It has been suggested that rural development programs may have legitimate objectives other than fighting poverty. If so, that is the basis on which they should be evaluated, for there is little evidence that most past rural economic development programs have had particularly favorable effects against poverty as an individual and family phenomenon. For example, local agricultural station evaluations of Mississippi Delta economic development projects point out quite casually that the new employees are all white — this is an area in which poverty, although generally endemic, is very heavily black.[25] This case is not typical. The racial extremity of the outcome may be peculiar to Mississippi, as is much racial extremity, but the general failure to help most of the poor goes beyond the bounds of the Confederacy. This failure insofar as the poor are concerned is indicated by the fact that the local Economic Development

25. Sheridan T. Maitland and George L. Wilber, "Industrialization in Chickasaw County, Mississippi A Study of Plant Workers," *Mississippi State University Agricultural Experiment Station Bulletin*, No. 566, September 1958.

District planner under the programs of the Economic Development Administration is a local official or local businessman interested in bringing the plant in, and then interested in operating in the most efficient way with good sound labor needing a minimum of new education, training, and so on. As a result, the typical rural economic development program has been more likely to bring already trained middle-class people into an area than to help the poor who started out there. This may be good for the area and its business and governmental infrastructure, but it provides trickle-down help to the poor, at best.

There are honorable exceptions to this general rule. In some communities, particularly in programs utilizing OEO monies, local businessmen have made substantial and successful efforts to train the people most in need. This has been the case in North Carolina in a program under the Kennedy-Javits Title I-D of the Economic Opportunity Act, funded by OEO and administered by the Department of Agriculture (but to achieve program effectiveness, a new local organization had to be set up in order to get around the existing local Economic Development District); it has been the case in Congaree, South Carolina, where a steel firm has been succeeding with a large-scale development with great emphasis on training the local black poor. These are exceptions, however, and an attempt to replicate them on a large scale would not only be extremely difficult because of local indifference or hostility in most of the areas most in need, but it would fail because the total economic demand for the products of viable rural manufacturing operations utilizing the poor is small enough that building the supply of such goods above the current pilot levels would sop up the demand.

The same is true of another type of rural economic development, agricultural development as typified by the Southwest Alabama Farmers Cooperative Association (SWAFCA). This vegetable-growing and marketing cooperative must be marked a success in spite of the fact it has run into accounting, management, and sales difficulties; it is a success because it continues to exist at all in the face of boycotts and harassments by local white officials, canning plants and so forth. Even counting SWAFCA as a success, it is a success on a limited scale only. Its maximum potential is to help only a small portion of the poor in the target areas and the better-off poor at that, since the major beneficiaries are landowners. An analyst for a pro-agricultural co-op organization offers the following conclusion: "The co-op built about crop diversification and group marketing has been the most successful of all recent efforts. It has, however, with few exceptions, included only men who own their own land. The base upon which farm co-ops must build is small and getting smaller . . . 44,000 owners and renters [with net annual incomes over $2,500] represent only 17 percent of the Negro farm operators in the United States."[26] In addition, as in the case of nonagricultural development, too many vegetable-growing cooperatives in the South could very quickly glut the market for such vegetables. In the ensuing national competition it would not be Del Monte that would lose out.

The importance of stemming or reversing the rural-to-urban migration stream is open to question in any case, but to sum up the evaluation here, feasible rural economic development is not going to do it anyhow.

Parallel statements can be made about the second type of economic development, bringing jobs into the ghetto by bringing in plants of existing businesses. Looking at recent experience leaves little room for optimism. It is always possible to point to some programs that have worked. The Bedford-Stuyvesant area of Brooklyn provides a good example of success, success based on pressure from both New York Senators and participation by such giants of the business community as Thomas Watson of IBM, both of which would be difficult to replicate generally. Sar Levitan describes the Bedford-Stuyvesant program as follows.

> Possibly best known are the economic efforts of the Bedford-Stuyvesant development corporations in Brooklyn, N.Y., involving two organizations working closely together. The Restoration Corporation is controlled by local residents and the Development and Services Corporation represents the white establishment and includes on its board national business and civic leaders. In operation since June 1967, the corporations claimed the development of 27 businesses by the end of 1968 with an employment potential of 1268. This success must be tempered by the fact that five firms which will create potentially three of every four jobs received no funds or other tangible as-

26. Al Ulmer, *Cooperatives and Poor People in the South* (Atlanta: Southern Regional Council, March 1969).

sistance from the development corporations and their location in the area was presumably not a product of any efforts made by the corporations. The other 22 firms, potentially employing 357, were given federally subsidized grants and technical assistance for development and operation. The average direct funding per firm amounted to $35,000, while the total management assistance costs are averaging around $7,000 per business. In other words, it cost close to one million dollars to develop 22 firms which will potentially average 16 employees. Additional subsidies may be necessary when the 22 companies open for business. Obviously, this type of local business development is not cheap.[27]

And this is one of the best programs. In Los Angeles the Department of Labor, using OEO funds intended for economic development under the Kennedy-Javits Special Impact amendment (Title I-D), managed to attract a new bottling plant to the City of Industry. The City of Industry is a tax haven in the midst of Los Angeles county with a population of only several hundred people, which already had many large plants and which is a substantial distance from either the South (black) or East (Mexican-American) Los Angeles poverty areas; it is difficult to see how this might help the target-area poor. It should also be noted that in the late summer of 1967 the Johnson Administration began with much fanfare Project TEST, designed to utilize the not inconsiderable sum of $40 million to attract businesses to ghetto areas on a pilot and experimental basis. The result of the experimentation was so negative that in 1968 the JOBS Program, which institutionally and politically stemmed directly from Project TEST, stayed completely away from economic development and stuck to developing jobs in existing plants. Project TEST had tested very badly.

What it comes down to is the fact that industry plant location is determined by powerful economic factors, that among these factors, the congestion and cost of inner-city development play a strong negative role, and that it seems unlikely that any federal program is going to overcome this in any major way except at fantastic cost. For reasons of public spirit,

27. Sar A. Levitan, "Are We Planning Ersatz Manpower Programs for the 1970s?" (Mimeographed paper, dated March 21, 1969), pp. 13–14.

some companies are willing to do some things, but for large-scale operations, costs outweigh civic duty (and in our economy, they should).

The third type of economic development, Black Capitalism, is somewhat different. Although, like the effort to bring plants of large firms into the ghetto, Black Capitalism also has a job-developing objective, its major objective is institution building, much like Community Action. This makes for two important differences in evaluation, as compared with rural and existing-business ghetto development. First, as has been noted, institutional objectives are difficult to measure, and evaluation of Black Capitalism thus must be more indefinite than for other economic development programs. Second, if rural economic development and major ghetto plant development must be marked failures primarily because of their impossibility on any large scale, perhaps the scale of expenditures needed for successful institution building by Black Capitalism is much smaller than that necessary for meaningful job creation. The institution-building scale might be calibrated by comparison with Community Action, which spends $400 million a year on institution-building programs. Although the analogy is not a precise one, the wage bill, say for a million decent jobs for poor people — not an unreasonable estimate — would be $5 billion a year, which is quite a differently calibrated scale. The point is that if "Black Capitalism" can fund say $50 million of successful programs a year, this might mean a significant 10 percent or greater increase in institution building, but $50 million is only one percent or less of job development needs.

What I am suggesting, then, is that if Black Capitalism programs are successful institution builders, they may be significant and useful parts of the War on Poverty. The same argument that produces this conclusion, however, demonstrates equally that the institution-building aspect of Black Capitalism may be meaningful only *because* of the small scale needed.

The attempts by some blacks and whites to treat Black Capitalism as the new panacea are demonstrably weak. They depend on easily dispelled mythic analogies, like that of a ghetto to an underdeveloped country (unlike an underdeveloped country, people can move from the ghetto to jobs in the developed economy). They vastly overestimate the potential of the black ghetto for adding to its own income stream (the outflow of funds to white ownership is not large compared to the flow to black labor working for the white owners). They put onto shaky new businesses the extra burden of helping support community activities and then expect them to compete with firms that reinvest profits. But most of all, they fail to look at the questions of scale. Institution-building success depends on smallness.

How well have Black Capitalism programs worked? Some of them apparently are quite successful. In the Hough area of Cleveland, for example, CAP, also using part of the Kennedy-Javits money under the Economic Opportunity Act, has begun a program that is working smoothly and seems likely both to continue in operation and to expand. And if institution building is the criterion, continuation and expansion of business operations as a core for such institution building is the crucial factor. In Philadelphia, the Opportunities Industrialization Center under the highly dynamic Reverend Leon Sullivan has opened a substantial shopping center that is too new to be evaluated but at least looks very promising. In Washington, D.C., on a smaller scale, Pride Inc., has begun a number of small businesses, notably in landscaping and retailing of gasoline.

There are also many examples of failures. It should be remembered by those advocates of Black Capitalism who understand that the chief objective is building institutions rather than providing jobs, that successful institution building depends on program success, and program success in a business operation is largely an economic question. One cannot get away from considerations of economic feasibility by arguing that the objectives are not economic. Small business is and will remain a very risky operation. Carefully planned "large-scale" businesses of the shopping center type with enough outside financial backing may have enough prospect for success to be willing to take a chance.

Institution building is in its essence an activity that depends on variety; any effort to impose a single pattern is almost certain to fail and cause the institutions to fail. For this reason, careful Black Capitalism, well thought through economically and on a scale that shows some promise for success economically, seems a useful part of the pattern. Black Capitalism as *the* solution for the ghetto — the economic solution, the social solution, or the political solution — comes close to nonsense.

Table 13
Federal Antipoverty Budget, Fiscal 1969: Income Maintenance

Program	Fund Source	Management	Funds (millions of dollars)
Old Age, Survivors, and Disability Insurance (Social Security)	Social Security Fund	Social Security Administration (HEW)	5,782
Public Assistance (Federal contribution)	Social and Rehabilitation Services Administration (HEW)	Social and Rehabilitation Services Administration (HEW)	3,459
Unemployment Insurance	Employment Insurance Fund	Department of Labor	422
Miscellaneous (primarily other pension systems)	—	—	2,507
Total Income Maintenance			12,190

Source: Office of Economic Opportunity

INCOME MAINTENANCE

The Income Maintenance system of the United States as it affects the poor can be divided roughly into four parts (see Table 13):

1. Old Age, Survivors, and Disability Insurance (Social Security), which is intended to be a system of pensions for the aged and certain others by "right" of being earned. As will be discussed later, the earnings basis is tenuous, but the myth persists and is probably useful.
2. Public Assistance, which by contrast is not considered income by right but rather income by gift of the people of the United States to those who without the gift would starve or otherwise suffer (and mostly do anyhow).
3. Unemployment Insurance, which the title describes adequately.
4. Various other large and small assistance programs, primarily pension systems such as Veterans, Civil Service, and Railroad, which, like So-

cial Security, may be considered income by "right" although the legal basis differs.

The two basic components Old Age, Survivors, and Disability Insurance (Social Security), and Public Assistance are the only ones discussed specifically in the following two sections. One evaluative statement should be made initially, however, concerning the entire income maintenance system of the United States: In coverage and adequacy it is insufficient. More than half the poor are not covered by any federally assisted forms of income maintenance. Income maintenance systems are categorical, and the categories are delineated partly according to need but also according to some moral standard of who is "deserving." Need does enter. No American is allowed to starve except in certain counties. Most children can obtain support, although if their father is present in the house, the fact that he is undeserving because he should be out working rather than receiving income maintenance has a substantial effect on the payments to the children. Although most states now have put into their Public Assistance laws the federally sponsored provision for assistance to unemployed fathers, the fact that only some 50,000 wholly unemployed fathers out of a national total on the order of 10 to 20 times that implies that anyone trying to take advantage of the provision has a good deal of difficulty.

The aged generally have a relatively easy time in receiving income maintenance even if their pension rights under Social Security are low because the aged are generally clean, white, and deserving, and they tend to vote. On the other hand, nonaged adults without children are generally undeserving and have a hard time. The major difficulty in applying the classification of deservingness is that it is difficult to withhold money from the mothers of illegitimate children without starving these children even though some states might like to try. In any case, whatever the reasons, coverage of current American income maintenance programs is spotty and irregular.

Furthermore, in many places income maintenance is absolutely inadequate. Minimum welfare payments of $8 a month — $96 a year — in Mississippi are too tragic to be laughable, but they form the bottom end of a continuum on which only a very few of the wealthiest and most liberal states approach adequacy.

Any evaluation suggests that on both criteria, coverage and levels, income maintenance taken as a whole fails badly. Of the two major components, Social Security works far better than Public Assistance, but as discussed next, Social Security does not work best as an antipoverty weapon.

Old Age, Survivors, and Disability Insurance (Social Security). Rights to pensions under the Social Security System are "earned" by the aged, the disabled, and the widows and orphans of the deceased because these rights are dependent upon the payment into the Social Security fund of taxes by both employee and employer. In fact, as is frequently pointed out, in reality the pensions are not fully earned. Payments to most individuals are higher than actuarial benefits that would be based on the contributions of the pension receiver and his employers, retained in the Social Security Fund at compound interest, and paid out at a rate based on average life expectancies.

The system can keep on paying out benefits higher than actuarial ones without going bankrupt because of the continued growth of the total taxable wages upon which employee and employer contributions are based. If the system were truly sound actuarily, this year's pension payments *out of the fund* would be based on wage taxes *previously* paid by fewer contributors with lower wages, and this year's tax payments *into the fund* would be based on this year's greater total taxable wage bill. Since this year's tax input would thus be greater than this year's pension output (substantially greater), the fund would grow rapidly. In fact, pension payments have continuously been greater than they would have been if computed on the basis of contributions, compound interest, and life expectancy, so the fund grows less than it would otherwise.

This means that Social Security pensions are not precisely earned since any individual gets more from the fund than his own contributions and those of his employers would warrant by the straight computation. Nonetheless, the earnings relationship is far more than a social myth; payments are based on earnings and are related to earnings even if not precisely earned. Social Security, then, is not intended primarily as an antipoverty device in the sense of maintaining minimum incomes; rather it is intended to guarantee maintenance of incomes at levels related to what they were during the earning years of the individual. The $5.8

billion of Social Security payments listed in Table 13 as part of the anti-poverty budget is little more than one-fifth of the total $26.8 billion of Social Security payments made in the same fiscal year. (The concept used to determine what portion of the Social Security should be part of the antipoverty budget is a slightly odd one. The $5.8 billion are those payments going to people who are still poor *after* they receive Social Security payments. If payments going to people brought above the poverty line *because* they receive Social Security were added in, the total would be substantially more than one-half of the $26.8 billion. Either concept is arbitrary; the one used here seems as acceptable as the other so long as we know what it means.)

Social Security can be evaluated as a highly effective antipoverty weapon because without the system far more than the roughly 30 percent of the aged now in poverty would be poor. But parodoxically, increases in Social Security would be far less effective against poverty. The reason is that the pension system has done most of what it can in raising people above the poverty line; most of those who have pension rights under the system receive payments high enough that, together with other income, they are across the line, and increasing payments would have its greatest effect in raising the incomes of those already above the poverty line. It has been estimated that only 20 percent of any across-the-board increase still goes to the poor. Future Social Security increases will be relatively ineffective against poverty even if they are increases in the minimum payment level (now at $55 a month for a single individual, which is slightly less than half of poverty income) because many of those with minimum Social Security rights also receive additional pension or other income, with the total raising them above the poverty line.

Two devices that might be relatively effective against poverty would be "blanketing in" all those with no rights under this or other federal pension systems (in the past, many wage earners were in industries not covered by Social Security and thus earned no rights and now receive no pensions), and changing the concept of minimum payment so that it would be related to *total* Social Security and other income available to the pension receiver rather than being based only on contributions as now. The latter, relating the minimum Social Security payments to other income, could be quite effective, but it would bend the semimyth of the relationship of pension payments to contributions paid into the fund. Or so it is argued by those who feel that the relative smoothness and popularity of Social Security as compared to other maintenance systems is dependent upon the earnings relationship and who therefore fear the risk of questioning the ethos.

Neither across-the-board increases in Social Security nor increases in minimum payments (unless these are related to total available income) can therefore be evaluated as very effective weapons against the poverty of the aged. This is not a criticism of the system; its primary objective is not antipoverty. But on the other hand, this does imply that any decision between increases in Social Security and other income maintenance devices must be based upon a political choice between antipoverty and other objectives; since Social Security increases are typically sold in the name of the War on Poverty, this distinction is important.

Public Assistance. Public Assistance payments go almost entirely to the poor. When they do not, it is because of minor definitional discrepancies between the Orshansky poverty line and local computations of the needs of welfare recipients. Most states do not pay up to their own estimate of minimum need anyhow, so the questions of payments to those whom Orshansky would count as nonpoor seldom arises.

Of the 3.5-billion-dollar federal contribution to Public Assistance, $1.2 billion goes to Old Age Assistance (OAA) and $1.7 billion to Aid to Families with Dependent Children (AFDC), with the remainder to miscellaneous categories. Old Age Assistance is intended for those without earned pension rights under Social Security, and as a supplement to Social Security for those whose pension rights are not high enough to guarantee them a decent minimum. Although Old Age Assistance shares in a number of the problems of AFDC listed in this section, OAA is relatively smooth compared with the other, mainly because the aged poor are primarily white, they vote a lot, and they have few illegitimate children. They thus make it easy for the vast washed mass of the American people to sympathize.

However, AFDC is different. Families with dependent children need aid either because the male wage earner is no longer in the house and thus the family is incomplete and un-American, and besides some of the dependent children may be illegitimate, which is really un-American; or because in some few cases there is a legitimate father in the house who is not working and therefore can be presumed to be sinful. The AFDC system has the following defects:

1. Payments are far too low. As noted earlier, Mississippi pays a minimum of $8 a month; and most of the states pay less than their own computations of the necessary minimum.
2. The determination of eligibility is frequently capricious. In some jurisdictions anyone can get on welfare quickly by an assertion of need; in others standards are strict and arbitrary depending upon the welfare worker's view of deservingness.
3. The system has a built-in incentive not to work. Although some states are somewhat more flexible, the national system takes away 67 cents of welfare payments for every dollar earned, which provides little incentive to earn that dollar and get off assistance. Even this is a move in the right direction from the recent system of taking away a dollar of payment for a dollar earned, however.
4. The system provides an incentive for family breakup. Even in states with AFDC programs for families with unemployed fathers, it is far easier for a woman head of a household to receive assistance than a man. And an employed man, a member of the "working poor," is not covered at all.
5. Recipients of Public Assistance payments are required to receive the ministrations of a welfare worker whether they want or need them or not.
6. A basic deficiency common to a number of the others is that, although the basic rules of the system are national, the applications are state and local. This as much as anything leads to the arbitrary nature of the application of eligibility requirements, the difficulty of male family heads getting on the rolls, and the unwelcome intrusion of services, not in all states but in many. It is important to point this out because many of the defects such as payment levels and eligibility rules, and even antiwork and anti-family-stability incentives might be corrected in part by the recasting of federal rules. But so long as these federal rules are applied by state and local welfare workers, in

Mississippi as well as in New York, it is basically going to be the same old Public Assistance system. Evidence may be found in the fact that so few male family heads are on the rolls even though almost half the states have adopted the federal Aid to Families with Dependent Children–Unemployed Parents (AFDC-UP) Program, which makes payments to male-headed as well as female-headed families.

Added to all of these defects of the system is the fact that the costs and the numbers of people on the rolls are increasing frighteningly. No definitive statement can be made as to the reason for this rise. To some extent it has to do with liberalizations of the law. It is conceivable also that it results in part from real deterioration of social structure; increasing illegitimacy figures are always alarming, and so is the decline in the proportion of Negro families with both husband and wife, as noted in Table 6.

Nonetheless, it seems likely that the real reason for the increase in rolls and costs is far less any increase in the number of eligible persons than it is an increase of the proportion taking advantage of their eligibility. During his preparation for the various defenses of OEO before Congress, Shriver occasionally appealed somewhat plaintively for someone to provide him with evidence that the War on Poverty was decreasing the number of persons on welfare. He once got some evidence from Pittsburgh when an increase in antipoverty efforts happened to coincide with the revival of the steel industry. But such evidence was difficult to come by because, although it seems likely that the War on Poverty did have a real effect in decreasing poverty, some of its programs played a major role in getting eligible recipients onto the welfare rolls. It seems very probable that after balancing out the decrease in poverty against the increase in applications by those who were eligible, the net result of antipoverty efforts was an increase in the welfare rolls attributable to OEO rather than a decrease. I think that this increase is one of the most positive accomplishments of OEO, but I recognize that mine is not a universally shared viewpoint.

In any case, questions like this should not arise. The current Public Assistance system of the United States, particularly AFDC, deserves to go down in history with the British poor laws of the early Industrial Revolution. The abominations of welfare have frequently been written about — by Edgar May,[28] by Gilbert Steiner,[29] and others — but Public Assistance has yet to find its Dickens. It is clear, however, that some new system is called for.

ADMINISTRATION

In addition to the evaluation of the programs of OEO and the other programs of the War on Poverty, there has been much discussion of the administrative effectiveness of OEO, a subject for detailed, knowledgeable, and effective evaluation. Such evaluation has not yet taken place. The General Accounting Office[30] and Sar Levitan[31] have both evaluated OEO administration relatively objectively, but unfortunately they evaluated its administrative smoothness rather than its relationship to the effectiveness of the programs administered. Different styles of administration are likely to have different impacts on program objectives, and these should be measured.

Nor am I in a position to carry out a disinterested evaluation of administration of OEO. Having been in the business of evaluating War on Poverty programs with at least attempted objectivity for four years, I feel that stating my background and bias so that the reader may allow for them makes it possible for me to discuss these programs sufficiently objectively. But having been part of the OEO administration for four years, that degree of objectivity is simply not available. So let me note for the future evaluator of effectiveness and impact that it seems to me that, whereas OEO administration did indeed range from the confused to the chaotic, careful consideration should be given to the tradeoffs between smooth administration on the one hand and program effectiveness on the other. Observation of other agencies in the poverty business at the same time seems to indicate that those that worked most smoothly ad-

28. Edgar May, *The Wasted Americans: Case of Our Welfare Dilemma* (New York: Harper & Row, 1964).
29. Gilbert Y. Steiner, *Social Insecurity; the Politics of Welfare* (Chicago: Rand McNally, 1966).
30. Comptroller General of the United States, *Review of Economic Opportunity Programs.*
31. Sar Levitan, *The Great Society's Poor Law* (Baltimore: Johns Hopkins, 1969), Chapter 2.

ministratively did so at the cost of engendering a bureaucratic deadliness of a kind that leads to effectiveness only in a bureaucratic world, which the world of poverty, the poor, and the ghetto is not.

It was contended earlier that the local administrative disorder caused by CAP-based institutional growth was very important and favorable in any attempt to end poverty. Similarly it seems to me that the disorder of OEO and the disorder caused within the federal government by OEO were the only possible substitutes for having bureaucrats do the same old things in the same old ways with the same old ineffectiveness against poverty. The history of the writing and operation of the agreement delegating manpower programs to the Labor Department (Chapter 4) provides one example. Had these manpower programs been turned over to the Labor Department directly and without fuss, there is no doubt that they would have operated much more smoothly. They would have been integrated into ongoing manpower systems by State Employment systems operating according to the Washington-provided Jobs Now model. And they would have failed to reach the poor, continued to impose rigidity where flexibility was called for, and ultimately disappeared, at least as antipoverty programs.

Without claiming the objectivity to prove it convincingly or even to make the case, it seems to me that what is still lacking is an evaluation of OEO administration that examines and tests these tradeoffs between smoothness of operations and effectiveness against poverty and for equality of opportunity.

CONCLUSION

To sum up a very long set of numbers, statements, arguments, and wisecracks about evaluation, the War on Poverty for the first four years has been neither a complete success nor an absolute failure. The question of success or failure still must be asked: "Success or failure relative to what?" It seems very likely that the War on Poverty has reduced the number of poor people substantially compared with what this reduction would have been without a War on Poverty. It seems only slightly less likely that opportunity is more nearly equal than it was before the War on Poverty, but no attempt has been made to make a comparison with what would have happened if there had been no War on Poverty.

Among the programs of the War on Poverty, manpower programs seem to have been working well recently compared with pre-War-on-Poverty standards; educational programs seem to have had little effect measured by any standard.

The most controversial set of programs, the CAP programs for community change, have been coterminous with marked favorable institutional change in the poverty communities of America, and substantial evidence indicates that this is more than coincidence, that CAP has been one crucial causative factor in these changes. And finally, any evaluation of the income maintenance systems of this country indicates that they are in poor shape indeed.

My conclusion is that the War on Poverty has been a success compared with what would have been without a War on Poverty. The many many flaws in many many programs indicate that many things could have been done better, and thus the success is less when measured against some standard of what might have been.

But Moynihan's third-person conclusion of the summer of 1968 is at best premature. He reported regretfully that

the painful truth that a great national effort, so bravely begun not four years earlier, was . . . widely deemed to have failed.

This is not to say that the war on poverty actually has failed. Its success or failure is a question for historians, and the final verdict may be very different from the perception of the moment, not only as to what happened, but as to what was relevant. Nevertheless, there is no doubt that for the present moment the confidence of many persons in the nation's ability to master the congeries of social, economic, regional, and racial problems which were subsumed under the heading of poverty in the winter and spring of 1964 has been badly shaken.

The main Agency responsible for conducting the war on poverty is, of course, the Office of Economic Opportunity (OEO), and accordingly much of the blame for the presumed failure of the war has been directed to that particular quarter.[32]

32. Daniel P. Moynihan, "The Professors and the Poor," *Commentary*, August 1968, p. 19.

This was premature in 1968 and it still is. If this "failure" was intended to represent Moynihan's own conclusion, hedged by his use of the third person and by a future opening for changing his mind, then he is right only if the "failure" is measured by some standard he has in mind, but which is not stated. And if the statement is to be taken as a description of general political failing, then the Nixon Administration's attempt to continue virtually all of the programs of the Johnson War on Poverty (including Community Action), with Moynihan in the vanguard for retention, may be an indication that even the consensus on political failure was overdrawn, as it had been in 1966 and 1967.

6
Future
Directions

The programs proposed in this chapter are designed to aid in the solution of two problems and two problems only: low-income poverty and inequality of opportunity. It is my belief that these programs can end low-income poverty at any time at which sufficient funds become available; and they can accelerate rapidly the achievement of the national objective of equalizing opportunity among racial and ethnic groups.

But it should be clear that this particular set of recommendations is not aimed at solving all the problems of the United States, not even all the social problems or all the urban problems. The programs here do not solve such problems as:

Improving the quality of education for all the nation's children
Improving the health of the nation
Enriching the life of the aged
Student revolt
Crime
Civil disorder
Decline of national morals
Urban congestion
Deterioration of the urban tax base
The fiscal crisis of the states
Maintaining the quality of life in rural areas
Housing

Some of the programs here will help with some of the problems. For example, it seems very likely that ending poverty and equalizing opportunity will in fact go a long way toward decreasing crime rates. But without a great deal of analysis establishing the connection between poverty and inequality on the one hand and crime on the other, this is merely an assertion; with such analysis it would be another book. The important point is that although all social problems are related, none can be solved if each waits for a solution upon the other. Ending poverty and equalizing opportunity are very important social objectives in themselves. The fact that they are likely to help gain other social objectives is important, but any feeling that with the solution of these problems the United States will become a social paradise is illusory indeed.

What I do claim for the programs suggested here, then, is that, together with continued prosperous economic growth and low unemployment, they can solve one of these problems, low-income poverty, and go a long way toward solution of the other, unequal opportunity. And they can do so at costs that while not modest by any absolute standard are not high by the standards we live by. A rough estimate, tabulated further on, on page 239, is that the additional cost would be $6 billion above the current $25 billion antipoverty budget in the first year of the recommended programs and perhaps $18 billion a year above the $25 billion when the new programs reach a peak at which further increases are unnecessary and some decline is possible. These are not really large numbers as such things go. Six billion dollars is less than half of the annual increment of federal tax revenues at current rates. And assuming the $18 billion level is reached, say in five years, the same tax rates will have produced an annual revenue increment over current intake of over four times $18 billion.

I am not trying to be disingenuous about the so-called "fiscal dividend." Former Budget Director Charles Schultze's chapter in the Brookings volume *Agenda for the Nation* makes clear that even after Vietnam the demands on the "fiscal dividend" are going to be much higher than the supply of funds from this dividend.[1] Indeed, even within the antipoverty budget, the $6 and $18 billion increments would pay only for the

1. Charles L. Schultze, "Budget Alternatives After Vietnam," Kermit Gordon (ed.), *Agenda for the Nation* (Washington: The Brookings Institution, 1968), pp. 13–48.

specific programs suggested here; realistically other substantial additions are going to be imposed on the antipoverty budget. For example, no major increases in either health or housing programs are recommended here. Yet in the health field, Medicare and Medicaid will continue to increase more or less automatically; built into current housing legislation also are somewhat less automatic increases in federal expenditures. Still less automatically, expenditures in other fields like education will be politically so popular that they will increase whether or not it can be demonstrated that the monies are being spent effectively. So the increments of $6 to $18 billion are only parts of total increments for programs in the same general categories.

Nonetheless, $6 to $18 billion is the bill for the recommendations made here, and the costs of these recommendations must be part of the consideration. Such costs must compete with other demands, but the point to be made is that they are by no means impossible to meet if we want to.

CRITERIA

The programs recommended here are selected primarily on the basis of three criteria:

1. What is needed. Much of the previous discussion has been directed toward the question of what kinds of programs are needed if we are to do the job of ending poverty and of equalizing opportunity. A new Income Maintenance program of the Negative Income Tax type, for example, is the central recommendation here, both because it is needed to reach the half of the poverty population which is not likely to be helped by other programs and because it is needed to satisfy the equity criterion of reaching those in greatest need, thus disengaging other programs from the requirement that they go only to those below the poverty line whether or not the programs are likely to be most effective that way.
2. What has worked. The previous chapter discussed in some detail the workings of specific antipoverty programs. From this analysis it is possible to select both programs that seem to have worked well and approaches that seem to be workable. Perhaps even more important, it is possible to avoid some approaches that once looked promising

but have not yet proved workable. The recommendations here, for example, put little stress on education because we don't know how to make education work for the poor and for the blacks and for other minority groups.

3. What is flexible. Too many earlier programs would have been beautiful indeed if they worked perfectly as planned, but having missed perfection, they turned into disasters. Public Assistance and Urban Renewal provide examples here. The Public Assistance system was designed in exquisite detail to do all sorts of good things: to take care of those who needed care, to encourage productivity on the part of those who could be productive, and so forth. It just didn't work out that way, and in not working out it turned into the counterproductive program described in the previous chapter. Similarly, Urban Renewal was designed in large part to rehouse slum dwellers. It didn't work out that way either, and it too turned perverse, becoming the well-known program of Negro removal.

The problem here is the arrogance of planners.[2] Planners are not nearly good enough to hit precise objectives on the nose, nor for that matter are managers able to manage according to the plans. But few plans are flexible enough to hedge against their own failure or imperfection. What are needed are planning techniques that stress movement in the right direction rather than precise ultimate goals and make iterative changes as the plans are executed. And to execute such flexible directional plans, we need stronger efforts at understanding the incentives that move bureaucrats,[3] heavier dependence upon those forces in society whose incentive structure is already relatively well understood (e.g., business), and utilization of economic and social bargaining, so that groups of people can do for themselves rather than fitting into someone else's master plan. Techniques like these are not going to bring about perfection in either planning or management. They are, however, likely to work fairly well even when they don't work very well and to avoid the kind of disasters associated with Public Assistance and Urban Renewal.[4]

2. As a planner, I suppose I can get away with saying this.
3. And as an ex-bureaucrat, with this, too.
4. For a more explicit discussion of the need for flexibility, see my "Rethinking Our Social Strategies," *The Public Interest,* No. 10, Winter 1968, pp. 86–96.

For this reason preference is given to programs like JOBS, which attempt to manipulate the business profit incentive in a socially desirable direction, and like Community Action, which changes the balance of social bargaining forces in a desired direction. The Negative Income Tax also goes a long way toward satisfying the criterion of flexibility. One of the greatest appeals of the Negative Income Tax as compared with the current Public Assistance system is simplicity. Public Assistance depends upon federal rules implemented by state rules that are in turn implemented by county welfare departments and finally applied by county social workers, and such a rules-within-rules system is least likely to work even moderately well. It must work perfectly or not at all, and it does not work perfectly.

In addition to these three criteria, one constraining factor is considered at a somewhat different level. That is political feasibility. Unlike the first three criteria under which programs can be measured along scales — those more needed, more workable, or more flexible being preferable to those scoring lower on these scales — a politically more palatable program is not necessarily preferred to one less easy to pass. After all, that's what this book is, an input into a political process by which I hope that the arguments I can bring to bear for those programs I favor will in themselves perturb the political calculus to the advantage of those programs. This political calculus is thus more an output than an input of the system.

There are those who argue, for example, that any device like the Negative Income Tax, which provides benefits only to the poor and near-poor, is simply not going to sell politically. They therefore favor some variety of "Children's Allowance" that would go to all families with children regardless of income, and thus, they argue, might be politically very popular. The troubles with this reasoning are two. First the political analysis demonstrating the superior popularity of a Children's Allowance has not been carried out, and the popularity of such an implied redistribution from families with fewer children to families with more may not be straightforward. Political "analysis" of the "we can buy votes in the following way" type sometimes appears to be quite simple-minded, limited to elementary interpretation of public opinion polls. Yet public opinion polls on Negative Income Tax and other income maintenance devices have been extraordinarily badly worded, with the words implying the answers desired by opponents of these devices; other polls with different implicit biases would provide opposite results.

But even if good political analysis showed a Children's Allowance to be politically more feasible than a Negative Income Tax, it would still be necessary to weigh this in the balance against the relative desirability of the two schemes. A Children's Allowance, even with some tax recapture of allowance payments from those toward the upper end of the income distribution, would still give half or more of its payments to those who are neither poor nor near-poor. Compared to a Negative Income Tax, which would go entirely to the lower end of the income distribution (with the balance between the poor and the near-poor depending on the particular scheme), a Children's Allowance just seems so ineffective as either an antipoverty or equal opportunity device that the relative desirability of a Negative Income Tax outweighs any likely margin of political feasibility favoring the Children's Allowance scheme.

Even though political feasibility is not a carefully scaled factor, some thresholds of feasibility must be considered. Some programs are so impracticable that there seems no point in talking about them. Such proposals as Marxian Socialism in the United States; turning the states of Mississippi, Louisiana, and Alabama into a black Republic; or on another level, instituting an Israeli *Kibbutz* system for all black kids in the United States are, aside from any question of desirability, just not within the range of possibilities worth discussing seriously.

PROGRAMS

Three basic sets of programs are proposed: for Income Maintenance, a Negative Income Tax; for Manpower, a continuation and expansion of the JOBS program plus the establishment of a low-skill residual public employment program to employ those who cannot enter the competitive market through JOBS or any other program; and for Community Betterment, a continuation of CAP or something like CAP to act as an independent goad, yardstick, innovator, and institution builder at the local level. Administratively, such a goad, yardstick, and innovator is also needed at the federal level, and continuation of an independent antipoverty operating agency is also important.

Although the basic structure of recommended programs is built on this threefold Negative Income Tax, JOBS–Public Employment, CAP framework, other programs are recommended as support. For Individual Improvement, carefully designed educational research and evaluation is extremely important. Although our current lack of knowledge about what to do in education should limit major program expenditures in this area, we do know that *if* we could improve the education of the poor, we would be able to go a long way in the desired directions. Another important group of programs is concerned with Nutrition. Although Nutrition has been treated as an Individual Improvement program, it might also be considered an alternative form of Income Maintenance, and the question should then be asked: Why provide people with food or food stamps rather than giving them more money and letting them buy their own food? Free consumer choice is a useful principle even for the poor, and should they thus not be given this freedom? The answer to this is that decent nutrition, particularly for children and pregnant mothers, is just too important to ending poverty and creating equality to be left wholly to individual choice at this point in time. The evidence of irreversible brain damage stemming from malnutrition seem in this case to override the desirability of free consumer choice.

The same cannot be said of housing, which might also be considered a substitute form of Income Maintenance. The causal connections between bad housing and poverty and unequal opportunity have not been established, and for this reason, direct support of housing for the poor seems less important than free choice through cash income maintenance. Housing, like health programs and many many supporting programs contained within the War on Poverty, is substantially less important to stress than those just mentioned. In fact, however, activities are going on in this area and will continue to do so; efforts to channel them in the most effective direction must thus continue. Programs to enable the poor and members of minority groups to take advantage of existing federal housing funds are useful and important so long as the funds are there. Similarly, the fact that $7 billion is being spent on antipoverty health programs means that relatively small-scale innovative efforts like the Neighborhood Health Center Program promise a substantial payoff in showing the way for far more effective uses of immense sums of money. Thus I am not contending that all antipoverty activity outside of the central thrust should be discontinued but rather that the important question is one of stress and allocation. The major stress should be put on the threefold Income Maintenance-Manpower-CAP effort. Available monies should be allocated primarily to these (to Income Maintenance and Manpower really; the innovational-institutional effort of CAP may need less new funding).

Before entering a more detailed discussion of individual program recommendations, several connections among the major recommendations need to be established. One question that arises is that of priority. Which comes first among the three categories depends primarily on the pattern in which funds become available. Ideally, Negative Income Tax should come first. As has been argued throughout, this is really the crucial need. It is crucial because of the half of the poverty population that cannot be reached well in any other way. It is crucial because this proportion is increasing. And it is crucial because only by instituting such a program can the equity criterion of reaching those in greatest need be disengaged from the criterion of program effectiveness so that the opportunity-equalizing programs can be aimed and organized most effectively.

But there is no point in starting a Negative Income Tax that is too small. Indeed, there is good reason not to. The way such a program starts will strongly affect its future direction. A Negative Income Tax starting at a level that would fill, say, 10 percent of the income gap for a poor family ($150 a year for a family $1,500 below the poverty line) would remain indefinitely a small supplement to a whole range of Income Maintenance devices. It would thus avoid virtually all the advantages of the Negative Income Tax: simplifying the Income Maintenance system of the United States, getting rid of the arbitrary application of welfare by states and counties, and so on. For this reason, a minimum sum estimated at $2 billion would be necessary to start. For this kind of money, it would be possible to fill 50 percent of the gap for families with children, and although it would be desirable to do more, particularly to extend the scheme to all the poor, such a start would make it easy to broaden later as more funds became available.

If initially available funds were much less than $2 billion, then, emphasis should be put on increased manpower efforts, which can be brought in at lower cost for meaningful levels. As noted earlier, although the third leg of the stool — Community Action — is as important as the others, the incremental funds needed there are smaller as are the funds needed for other important programs like educational research.

Thus Income Maintenance comes first in importance; insofar as chronological implementation is concerned, Income Maintenance or Manpower comes first, depending on fund availability. Another relationship between Income Maintenance and the recommended manpower programs stems from criterion 3 — flexibility. Difficult though it may be for some to accept, we simply do not know how many of the poor are amenable to successful treatment in different sorts of manpower programs, nor if we knew how many, would we know which individuals. For this reason, when the National Manpower Policy Task Force states its position, it is recommending a policy that cannot be implemented.

> We express serious doubts concerning the desirability or political acceptability of any guaranteed income program offered as a substitute for employment or for the provision of services to the needy. We strongly favor national minimum standards of income maintenance at an adequate level for all of those who cannot or should not work.
>
> But we believe it is far better to provide the able-bodied with useful work . . . according to public opinion surveys, in our work-oriented society, overwhelming majorities reject a universal "guaranteed income" program, but equally large majorities support a "guaranteed employment" program. We believe that this preference has a reasonable basis and that national policy should be shaped accordingly.[5]

We *cannot* separate on a priori grounds the "able-bodied" (or more important, the "able-minded") — those who will succeed in one sort of employment program or another — from the probable failures who thus "deserve" income maintenance. Any program that tries to make such a distinction is going to guarantee personal disaster for those who fail in manpower programs even though they looked as though they should be "able-bodied."

The only good test of an individual's ability to succeed in such pro-

5. "The Nation's Manpower Programs" (a position paper by the National Manpower Policy Task Force, January 7, 1969), pp. 14–15.

grams is to put him into a program and let him try to succeed. What is suggested here, then, is that a flexible set of programs would try to develop the best abilities possessed by each person, but if these abilities were just not good enough, a fallback position would be provided. Thus, if JOBS is the highest-quality program in the sense of really integrating the underprivileged into the mainstream of the private American economy, then everyone in need should be encouraged to enter the JOBS program. In fact, however, industry will continue to turn down those whose looks it does not like, and among those who are taken on, many will fail, and *we don't know which ones.* For those people who do fail in JOBS or other training (or who cannot get in for one reason or another), a residual Public Employment program may provide a partially satisfactory substitute. Although not completely integrated into the American life, those with low-skill Public Employment jobs will still be getting the self-respect that is supposed to stem from gainful employment. But not everybody is going to make it in Public Employment either, and the Negative Income Tax thus provides a final fallback for some (and again we don't know in advance who they will be).

The recommended programs are thus connected to one another fiscally, chronologically, and through fallback linkages. But none of these connections, not even the last one, implies that the recommendations will succeed only if implemented in a precisely specified way or order. This is the final flexible aspect of the overall system. The chain of programs is not linked in a way by which the failure of any one, failure to work well or failure to be enacted, implies the failure of all. As stated, Income Maintenance is both primary and central. But a decent Income Maintenance program may be harder to achieve quickly than any of the others. And the others can go ahead without waiting; they can go ahead with less impact than if connected with Income Maintenance but at least with some prospect for partial success.

Income Maintenance: Negative Income Tax. The importance of Income Maintenance has already been argued. It is based on two notions: that about half the poor can be reached only by Income Maintenance programs, so that if we are serious about ending poverty, such programs are a requirement; and that without Income Maintenance to help those in low-income poverty, opportunity programs in fields like manpower and education will continue to focus on those most in financial need rather than those in need of training and learning who can be effectively helped by such programs.

These two core arguments are reinforced by others. Income Maintenance is not merely a program of personal assistance to those in need; it is also a key support to opportunity programs at all levels. A guarantee of some minimum level of income to a family may well help stabilize that family, and the income and stability will in turn contribute to the success of family members in other programs, from Head Start on up. The Coleman Report and much other evidence indicate that educational success is far more dependent upon family background than upon in-school factors, thus an Income Maintenance program, which helps stabilize families and provide them with some security, may turn out to be an important educational program.[6]

But it is not only among young children that Income Maintenance supports other programs. In January 1969, I attended a hearing of the President's Commission on Income Maintenance in Tucson, Arizona. A parade of witnesses, mostly Mexican-Americans in the depths of poverty, all painted a picture in which lack of income itself led to failure of all sorts, from school dropouts to ill health. One woman, however, stood out as an exception. Although poor by the Orshansky definition, she and her family had a small guaranteed income because of their "good fortune" in being the survivors of a dead husband and father with Social Security rights. They lived austerely, but unlike the other witnesses this degree of security put them on an upward path. One daughter was going to a community college, and the whole family seemed to have some confidence in its future. At present only receivers of pensions under Social Security and other guarantee systems can have this confidence and stability, but providing such guarantees to most of the poor could make a vast improvement not only in the income structure of poor Americans but in the opportunity structure also.

Benefits from a decent federal income-maintenance system, however,

6. James S. Coleman and others, "Equality of Educational Opportunity," Report submitted to the President in response to Section 402 of The Civil Rights Act of 1964 (Washington, D.C.: U.S. Department of Health, Education and Welfare, July 1966).

would go not only to the poor but also to states and localities. States and localities now spend more than $5 billion of their own funds on public assistance in addition to the federal contribution. This is slightly less than 5 percent of state and local revenues. A federal system that relieved all or part of this burden by treating low-income poverty as the national problem that it is and financing public assistance entirely from federal revenues would be the fiscal equivalent of federal grants-in-aid of the same amount, freeing local tax resources to that extent.

Finally, one argument that may be slightly more dubious concerns the effect of a federal income-maintenance system on the rural-to-urban migration flow. It is sometimes contended that people move from low-welfare states like Mississippi to high ones like New York and California in order to receive public assistance. Aside from occasional anecdotes this has never been demonstrated; most migrants are those who move reluctantly in search of jobs, not relief, and the "boxed-in" poor who cannot help themselves anywhere are typically those who remain in rural areas. Nonetheless, the differences between the low- and the high- welfare-payment states are striking and perhaps "ought" (in the economist's amoral usage of the word) to induce movement. A federal system with equal, or at least more nearly equal, payments would remove whatever inducement does exist.

What kind of Income Maintenance system then? The previous chapter outlined the defects of the current AFDC system; the desired characteristics of a new Income Maintenance system are almost the precise opposite of these:

1. It should from the very beginning provide a decent level of support for all recipients in all parts of the country.
2. Need alone, rather than "deservedness," should be the requirement for eligibility. Such need should be defined simply in terms of income of the family unit in need and should be based on a simple affidavit of family income. Enforcement would be by simple spot check as it is in the federal income tax system rather than by detailed universal investigation.
3. In order to preserve the incentive to work and get off the rolls, recipients should be allowed to retain a large portion of income main-

tenance payments as their earnings increase up to some break-even level.

4. In order to preserve the incentive for a family to stay together, payments should be made on the same basis to intact families as they are to broken families. They should be made to poor families with employed as well as unemployed male heads.

5. The Income Maintenance system should be uncoupled from the services provided by social workers. Family receipt of such services should be voluntary and should not be a condition of eligibility for Income Maintenance.

6. The application of the system as well as its basic rules should be national and not determined by states or localities.

In addition to these criteria, each of which corrects a defect of AFDC, one additional criterion would correct a defect of the overall welfare system in which AFDC is embedded:

7. Insofar as possible, this system should be noncategorical. A single national Income Maintenance system going to all needy Americans simply because they are in need is the requirement. To the extent that categories of need must be established, they should avoid both the morally dubious calculus of deservedness and the accidental creation of perverse incentives. A categorization that separates the aged from others, for example, is less harmful than most because it sets up no implementable incentive to age more rapidly. On the other hand, a categorization that favors female-headed families over male-headed families creates an incentive for family breakup, and a categorization that attempts to separate the "employable" from the "unemployable" sets up an incentive to become unemployable or at least to look that way. In between is a categorization that favors families with children. This does create some financial incentive to have children, and if it is believed that this incentive would be a strong one, such a categorization too should be rejected. However, some slight evidence from countries with Children's Allowances indicates that this incentive is quite weak.

Running through all these criteria is the theme of simplicity, both in concept and in application. A basic difficulty with the Public Assistance system of the United States, perhaps the basic difficulty, is that it is so intricate it must necessarily be arbitrary and inefficient. It is a system of rules within rules in which national policy is expressed in detail by congressional statute and federal regulation, interpreted by state and county regulation, and applied by individual social workers. And although there is a great incentive for bureaucrats at each level to follow the rules, there is no incentive to carry out the *intent* of the system, and, somehow, following the rules too frequently ends up with brutal applications that are the reverse of charitable intents. Perhaps this result could be changed by thinking up a better system of rules, but rule-changing in such a situation almost always tends to make things worse not better.

Behind the unworkable intricacies lies the attempt to separate the deserving sheep from the undeserving goats, the attempt to make sure that no one will get more than he needs or warrants. In order that a family with some of its own resources will not get welfare, every family must be investigated; in order that a woman will not get money from both a man and the government, the bed must be checked; in order that a poor Georgian will not get a sum of money determined by the need to cover the higher living cost in Pennsylvania, an intricate system of interstate discrimination must be created. The only alternative to an intricately detailed unworkable Public Assistance system of the sort we have now is a general system with levels set for a few classes of cases (primarily according to family size alone), applied equally to those who are in generally equal circumstances.

What is needed is a relatively simple system that meets all or most of the preceding criteria. Three alternatives to the current Public Assistance system might do the job: a Negative Income Tax, a renewed federal-state welfare system based on improved federal standards, or a Children's Allowance.

I have made clear my preference for the first of these, the Negative Income Tax. Such a system would be designed to meet criteria 1 through 7, but it is *defined* by the way it meets the third criterion, preservation of the incentive to work. The key to the system is the "taxing" away of only a fraction of an income maintenance dollar for every increased dollar of family earnings. The tax fraction usually discussed is 50 percent or less, on the not very well established ground that work incentives disappear rapidly if one cannot retain at least half of his earnings.

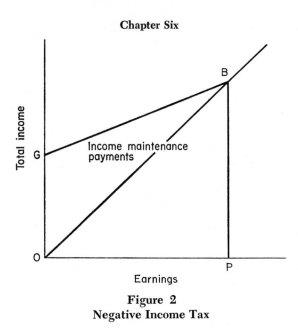

Figure 2
Negative Income Tax

Figure 2 illustrates the Negative Income Tax mechanism. For any size of family, a minimum income guarantee level would be established, and if the family had no earnings, the guarantee would be met entirely with income maintenance payments, *OG* in the figure. As earnings increased, total family income would increase along line *GB* (with no income maintenance, earnings would have increased total income along line *OB*), and income maintenance payments would thus be the vertical distance between lines *GB* and *OB*. At *B*, the break-even point, income maintenance payments become zero. The tax rate, then, is given by the ratio of *OG* to *PB*, and the retention rate is one minus this ratio. If a dollar of welfare payments were taken away for a dollar of earnings, as has been the case until recently, *OG* would equal *PB*, the tax would be 100 percent, retention zero, and total income completely insensitive to earnings up to the break-even point. A Negative Income Tax, however, keeps *OG* smaller than *PB*, so that total income increases as earnings increase, and thus there is an incentive to work. The lower the tax rate (*OG* divided by *PB*) and the greater the retention, the greater the incentive. This retention-induced incentive is precisely the object of the ingenious mechanism of the Negative Income Tax.

Future Directions

My preference for the Negative Income Tax is not based on the ingenuity of its mechanism, however; it is based on the fact that among the three broad alternatives for Income Maintenance, it both meets criteria 1 through 7, which the improved federal-state welfare system alternative does not, and it gets most of the money to those with the lowest incomes, which the Children's Allowance alternative does not.

There are then two alternatives:

1. A welfare system based on improved federal standards *could* fill all the criteria previously listed with the major exception of number 6, federal administration. Federal payment standards *could* provide a floor for all beneficiaries; rules *could* be changed to simplify both the requirements for eligibility and the applications of these requirements; partial retention of payments *could* encourage earnings incentives, as indeed has already been done to some extent within the Public Assistance system; the incentive to family breakup *could* be removed as the AFDC-UP program has done to some extent; the requirement to receive social services *could* be lifted; the system *could* even be made noncategorical.

   In principle, then, the system could look like the Negative Income Tax diagramed in Figure 2. But one crucial factor would not have been changed, and this failure would mean a failure to make a real change in many of the others. Such a system would still be administered by state and county welfare authorities, and such administration would in far too many places continue the arbitrary nature of the current system. To take an admittedly extreme example, it would still be possible in some states to exclude people from welfare rolls in order to maintain a supply of cheap labor — exclude people because they "refuse to take available jobs" — but if that reason were gone, another pretext could certainly be found. Presumably such exclusion would not take place under the new system, but it is not presumed to take place now yet it does. For reasons like this, it seems likely that in far too many places continued state and local administration would mean continued capricious determination of eligibility, continued family breakup (state administration has made AFDC-UP far less effective than it should be), continued welfare investigation, and so on. Thus, although the current system can certainly be improved, such improvement will fail to make the basic changes necessary.

2. The Children's Allowance system has a number of arguments going for it. It is the only system with no income test at all and thus no need for even an affidavit of eligibility, never mind an investigation. Income would simply be by right of being an American child, and this is attractive. Furthermore if as contended by perhaps the strongest advocate of Children's Allowances, Alvin Schorr, that phase of family life when young children are present is the most crucial in breaking the family cycle of poverty, income support at that time is most important. Schorr's argument is weakened, however, by the fact that his reasoning leads him to favor Children's Allowances primarily for children below the age of six, while almost all other advocates favor them for children of school age.

Finally in favor of Children's Allowances is the political argument discussed earlier. If it were true that the only national Income Maintenance system that could be sold to the American people were one that provided payments to all income levels — if, in other words, a Children's Allowance were the only alternative to the current Public Assistance system — this would be a very strong point in favor of the Children's Allowance. But this has been asserted, not demonstrated, and it is probably not true. Countries like the United Kingdom and Canada with very low level Children's Allowances in effect are moving now toward income-tested maintenance programs like the Negative Income Tax rather than increasing their Children's Allowances. They are doing so because they have realized that for a Children's Allowance, the ratio of payments to recipients at the lower income levels where they are most needed to total costs is so very very low.

And that finally is why I reject the Children's Allowance in favor of the Negative Income Tax. The theme of this book has been that Income Maintenance should go where the need for income is greatest, opportunity programs where they can be most effective in improving people's future chances. The Children's Allowance, however, distributes income maintenance payments regardless of need for additional income. (In Figure 2, lines *GB* and *OB* would never meet;

every family with children would receive some income maintenance payment regardless of other income.) If resources were unlimited and every family with children in the country could be provided a really substantial sum of money, say $500 per child per year, then the Children's Allowance would be a lovely program. But resources are not unlimited, and such a lovely program would cost somewhat more than $30 billion a year for children under 16. Some of this might be recaptured by positive taxation in the upper brackets, but if much of it were, it would merely become the equivalent of an income-tested Negative Income Tax for children under another name, and it would take a complete revision of the federal tax system to achieve this change of name. And at sums anywhere near $30 billion we are obviously in a different world from the current one. At $5 billion, which would buy a generous Negative Income Tax for all families, with or without children, a Children's Allowance would give each child perhaps $80 a year. And this becomes a trivial program in terms of social effects at what is still a very high cost. It is for reasons like this that most analysts who look at costs end up with some variety of Negative Income Tax.

If a Negative Income Tax, then what kind of Negative Income Tax at what cost? My preference would be to start with a "universal" Negative Income Tax, one going to *all* poor people. One example of such a tax could utilize a simplified and rounded version of the Orshansky poverty line with a break-even point (*B* in Figure 2) at the poverty line and an income guarantee (*OG* in Figure 2) at half the line. This would mean a tax rate and a retention rate of 50 percent. It would work as follows, using a simplified $3,000 poverty line for a family of four as an example. If such a family had no other income, it would receive $1,500 of Negative Income Tax payments. For every dollar of earnings, 50 cents would be taken off this $1,500; as a result if the family were to reach $2,500 of earnings, $1,250 would be subtracted from the $1,500, leaving $250 of Negative Income Tax payments for a total income of $2,750. When earnings reached $3,000 (*P* in Figure 2), Income Maintenance payments would drop to zero.

This is a simplified explanation of a rather complex system, but far less complex in application than the current Public Assistance system. A substantial literature on the precise structure and application of such a system is available,[7] but the general description suffices here. Such a system would cost on the order of $5 billion a year over current federal Public Assistance costs. A lower cost alternative mentioned earlier would be to start a system with similar rates, but only for families with children under 18. The advantage of this alternative would simply be that it would cost $2 billion instead of $5 billion and it could still end AFDC as it operates today. The disadvantage of the $2 billion Negative Income Tax for families with children is that it leaves out a lot of poor people. It leaves out most of the aged. (But they could be taken care of by blanketing into Social Security those not now covered and instituting an income-related minimum payment under Social Security. This cost, then, would have to be added to the $2 billion.) It also omits the unmarried over 18 and childless couples. If such people are below the poverty line ($1,600 a year for an individual, $2,100 for a childless couple), they are poor indeed, and if we are serious about ending poverty, they too need income supplementation. Furthermore, a children's Negative Income Tax would introduce the categorization that this system is designed to avoid, introduce it to be sure in a way that at least does not invidiously discriminate between the "moral" and the "immoral" or the "deserving" and "undeserving" but introduce it nonetheless. Some members of the groups left uncovered by a children-only plan are going to be politically the most difficult to touch — hippies, for example (those hippies who neither are nor have children) — but some, such as the young unmarried black man or woman in a city slum, may be the most crucial to reach. I would not let a Negative Income Tax stand or fall on its inability to reach hippies, but I would argue that if it is possible, fiscally and politically, to start noncategorically, it should be started that way. In any case, the steady-state goal would be to cover all those in need with a Negative Income Tax that had a guarantee at the poverty line. The ultimate annual cost of this program would be about $12 billion.

Two other policy questions concerning the Negative Income Tax are (1) should geographical cost of living differentials be built in, and (2) who

7. E.g., James Tobin, Joseph A. Pechman, and Peter M. Mieszkowski, "Is the Negative Income Tax Practical?" *Yale Law Review*, Vol. 77, No. 1, November 1967, pp. 1–27.

should administer it? On the first, ideally it should be uniform nationally, although again we should avoid letting the achievement of a Negative Income Tax stand or fall on the issue of uniformity. The reasoning for avoiding geographical differentiation if possible is based on the complexity added to the system by such differentiation. Certainly the cost of living in rural Alabama is less than the cost of living in San Francisco, but a system that tried to adjust to every variation in cost of living would again move back toward the detailed differential Public Assistance system and away from the desirable simplicity of the Negative Income Tax. In 1968 representatives of relevant federal agencies met on the question of whether to regionalize the poverty line in its uses as a program standard as well as a statistical device; it was unanimously decided not to. The statistical basis is too meager and the infinite variation of applicability too great. Allowing for variations in the cost of living is very tempting, but it is the same kind of temptation that begins to allow for variations in need and ends up as Public Assistance. It is not irrelevant that the progressive rates of the positive income tax are uniform throughout the United States. If $10,000 in rural Alabama is equivalent to $10,000 in San Francisco, perhaps $2,000 in each place should also be considered equivalent. In any case, if state or local authorities in the wealthier states wanted to supplement the federal payments, they could. Presumably those states now paying higher than the suggested federal payments would want to continue to do so; such supplements would cost the states and localities no more than their current contributions to Public Assistance.

So far as the administration of a Negative Income Tax is concerned, the basic requirement is that it be national and not state or local. In 1968, the Internal Revenue Service reluctantly admitted that it was capable of administering a Negative Income Tax as well as a positive one — which may not have been unrelated to the fact that Bertrand Harding, the Acting Director of OEO in 1968 and an advocate of the Negative Income Tax, had for many years previous been Deputy Director of the Internal Revenue Service. Having had some experience with the administration of OEO, Harding felt strongly that the administration of the Internal Revenue Service was very efficient. In any case, IRS can do the job, and I would recommend IRS. An alternative would be the Social Security Administration; the third alternative would be a new federal organization devoted to this purpose only, but there seems little reason for such pro-liferation.

Manpower: JOBS and Public Employment. The single most crucial re-quirement for a successful Manpower program, indeed, for a successful equal opportunity and antipoverty program, is a prosperous economy. As suggested in Chapter 5, there can be no doubt that the prosperous economic growth and low unemployment rate of recent years has been the most powerful factor in achieving the sharp reduction in poverty since 1964. As the less employable portion of the poor is reached, pros-perity alone will not suffice, but in order to continue any progress toward the poverty and opportunity goals, high prosperity and low unemploy-ment will have to be maintained.

Beyond the necessity for continued prosperity to avoid pauses in progress, any sharp reduction in real growth or increase in unemployment would be a setback to the War on Poverty and perhaps a fatal one. We can't go back again. Since late 1965, a year after the beginning of the War on Poverty, unemployment has been below 4 percent except for a few random months; since mid-1967, it has been hovering around 3.5 percent. These are the conditions under which Manpower programs such as JOBS have achieved what they have. The demand for jobs was grow-ing in many areas and industries, labor was short, and it was possible to provide a substantial portion of the new jobs to those most in need, the poor and members of minority groups. Reversion to the greater than 5 percent unemployment rates of the late 1950s and early 1960s would not merely mean a pause in providing new jobs to the underprivileged. Rather, it would mean one of two things: Either the new jobholders would be laid off first because of their low seniority and thus would en-joy again the last-hired first-fired experience that has been the lot of the poor and the black in the United States, or seniority would be bent and newer, largely black, employees would be retained whereas older, largely white, employees would be laid off. Minor fluctuations may be amelio-rated: cuts in overtime and short work weeks can spread the misery a bit, and the fallbacks of Public Employment and Negative Income Tax suggested here can provide cushions to supplement the unemployment insurance system. But we should make no sanguine mistake about it; if the unemployment rate breaks through 4 percent and rises to or beyond 5 percent, melioration will not be enough. The poor and the black will be set back to where they were in 1964, or the lower middle class and the white will see the newcomers taking "their" jobs. The remaining choice left to the government will be whom it wants to lead a revolt, Eldridge Cleaver or George Wallace?

Avoiding such unemployment rates is something we know how to do very well. We don't know how to do it without more inflation than we might like, but so far as the poor are concerned, inflation helps rather than hurts them. Not only does the high employment of an inflationary period help but so does the contraction of differentials between low and high wages. Social Security and even Public Assistance payments also tend to go up with the cost of living, so that even the transfer-payment poor are hurt little, if at all.[8] A good deal of inflation and even balance-of-payments difficulties are thus prices that should be paid, if necessary, to avoid higher unemployment.

The Manpower programs to be suggested are not dependent upon the existence of a Negative Income Tax for their workability. Without a good income maintenance program, however, we shall continue to face the equity-effectiveness dilemma. Without such a program, the approach will have to be a continuation of the current one, concentrating federal expenditures primarily upon the poor with the expectation that this guideline will not be observed strictly and that the privately funded portion of the JOBS program will hit above the poverty line. The Public Employment program also should be allowed to go to those above the poverty line. It should be available to anyone willing to accept the relatively low pay associated with such a low-skill residual Public Employment program. Public Employment incomes are likely to stay too low to attract huge numbers of people that are not really in need of federal help.

With a Negative Income Tax things become easier. Both JOBS and the Public Employment program can be freed from poverty line constraints to seek those who need them most. To prevent real abuse — pri-

8. See, in particular, Robinson G. Hollister and John L. Palmer, *The Impact of Inflation on the Poor,* University of Wisconsin Institute for Research on Poverty Discussion Paper 40–69, 1969.

vate industry using federal funds merely to carry on the ordinary training for regular trainees always considered a normal part of the business, and public bodies using federal employment subsidies to finance their regular efforts with their regular employees — certain maintenance-of-effort regulations and spot checks would be necessary. But in the economics of the marketplace, a price increase to increase the supply of a commodity necessarily means that some suppliers will receive prices above those at which they would have been willing to make their supply available anyhow. If we are to apply the efficiency of the marketplace to manpower programs — and such an application of market efficiency is the most attractive thing about a program like JOBS — then we must recognize that to increase the quantity of training and jobs available to those in need it will be necessary to pay for some of the training and jobs that would have existed anyhow.

It does seem possible through regulation to control abuse by business and by government. What about "abuse" by program recipients? What will prevent a person from retiring on Negative Income Tax payments rather than getting a job or entering a manpower program when he is able-bodied and capable of working? The answer to this lies in the positive incentive. The $1,500 guarantee under a Negative Income Tax is just not going to be terribly attractive to someone who can get a job at $1.60 to $2 an hour ($3,200 to $4,000 a year) with an open future. For those whose productivity is so low that the Negative Income Tax is really competitive to a job, there is a real question as to how strong the social interest is in their working anyhow. Similarly, the $3,200 to $4,000 a year for a Public Employment job is not going to be very attractive to someone who can do a semiskilled or skilled job that pays more and has an open future.

JOBS (Job Opportunities in the Business Sector). The JOBS program as it exists has been described in the previous chapter, and the description need not be repeated here. As suggested in that chapter, it seems to be working pretty well, but we are not sure; in particular, we are not sure about the federally funded portion of the program. What we are most unsure about, however, is less the quality of the programs that exist than their ability to expand substantially. It may be that business simply won't buy. What is suggested here, then, is that the JOBS program be planned initially for levels not above the current ones for the fifty cities in which it was first instituted. Expansion should take place, as has been begun by the Nixon Administration, in the smaller areas. In both old and new areas, we should be feeling our way toward proper levels.

It is not clear at this point whether the current slow growth of federally funded slots is due to recruiting difficulty or business unwillingness. In a sense it must be both, with business unwilling to take on the recruits who are coming forth. This situation may be improved substantially by more experience and simpler contracts, if we assume that current experience is favorable enough to encourage further business participation, that the Labor Department is willing to simplify contracts sufficiently, and that the economy remains prosperous. In addition, if a Negative Income Tax is forthcoming soon, a breakthrough on the size of the JOBS program might be achieved by removal of the poverty line criterion. If industry can honestly use the federal funds to train individuals more to their taste than the hard-core poor (but individuals in need of opportunity-equalizing assistance nonetheless), the possibility for expansion might be substantial. At present, however, the estimated cost of the JOBS program expanded along the current lines might be on the order of $400 million a year (100,000 federally funded trainees at a $4,000 man-year cost, which is higher than the current $3,000, in order to sweeten the pot for business to come in). This figure is twice the $200 million estimated for fiscal 1969. A peak cost might be $800 million a year for over 200,000 trainees.

The JOBS program is certainly not working so well, however, that experimentation with new techniques is unnecessary. A number of approaches should be tried out. One would be simply to raise the ante drastically. The economist's cant phrase is "There is some price at which" anyone can be induced to do anything. If $3,000 has proved insufficient for JOBS, and if the $4,000 suggested here still doesn't work, what about $10,000? A price like this might be worthwhile, particularly if paid for a finished product — a jobholder guaranteed to be able to earn good wages. A second form of experimentation relates to a major reason for business failure to come in en masse — fear of risks — what will really incompetent new workers do to machinery, production schedules, the rest of the labor force? Risks can be insured against, and experimentation with various forms of insurance might well pay off. Experimentation may also be worthwhile with various condominum arrangements to educate and train the hard core up to minimum standards before bringing them onto production lines; this too might help calm employer fears, and it might work better than current preliminary treatment through the Concentrated Employment Program.

In addition to experimentation within JOBS and the use of a low-skilled Public Employment program to be discussed as a supplement to JOBS, two alternatives to JOBS should be mentioned. One of these, which seems a useful variation on JOBS, is JOPS (Job Opportunities in the Public Sector). This is intended to be almost the precise analogue of the JOBS program except that the organizations receiving payments for the entry level training are public rather than private and the trainees are training for Civil Service jobs rather than private industry jobs. The JOPS program is different from the residual Public Employment program to be suggested later because the residual program is primarily for low-skilled work that probably would not be done at all were it not for the federally funded public employees, whereas the JOPS program is designed to integrate poor and minority group workers into the ongoing public economy, just as JOBS is designed to integrate them into the private economy. In this respect, JOPS has more resemblance to the Scheuer New Careers program than it does to residual Public Employment. As suggested in the previous chapter, the New Careers program has not achieved much in the way of changing the structure of public organizations by extending subprofessionalism; it has trained poor people to do good jobs of an ongoing type in the public (and nonprofit) sectors. This is what JOPS would do. In this context, JOPS is almost a pure alternative to JOBS, and the stress and funding that should go into each should be a function of two factors: first, which sector — public or private — is more ready to absorb new trainees at a given subsidy cost; and second, which needs — public or private — are considered more crucial for federal assistance. My own feeling is that public needs are more pressing than private and that JOPS might thus be a worthy rival for part of the JOBS funds, but public versus private decisions seem to depend very much upon the mood of the American people at any given moment, so JOPS may never get as big as JOBS as long as business is "in" and government is "out." At any rate, for purposes of this program, the JOPS alternative may be considered part of the JOBS program without changing the basic arguments or figures already given.

Another alternative, but one I would consider at best to be premature, is tax incentives for training. Stripped of a certain number of political irrelevancies surrounding the question of tax incentives for training, such as the analogy to tax incentives for investment (the investment tax credit was designed to increase the *aggregate* of investment in the American economy whereas the training objective is to direct training to certain specified groups), the argument for using tax incentives is not a complex one. It is the same as the argument for the subsidized JOBS program plus the contention that it will work better with tax incentives than with subsidy payments.

Indeed, it might well work better with tax incentives. Business generally considers tax deductions or credits simpler and more routine than federal subsidies. The bureaucratic difficulties of haggling with government contract officers over the details of a training program are removed. Business fills out its own tax returns; business accountants figure out the deductions and credits allowable and submit them, and they are reviewed by Internal Revenue Service accountants. This has become the normal way of doing business in the United States. Given a new tax provision with a special deduction for training programs for the poor, a firm could institute the program without ever talking to a bureaucrat until the end of the tax year for which the credit is claimed. Perhaps it would be disallowed — such things have happened — but most likely, if the accountants are careful, it would be allowed. This kind of operation has become routine in the era of 50 percent corporation taxes.

The result of such a tax-incentive program as compared to JOBS-JOPS would undoubtedly be a larger-scale program but one with more "wastage," defined as government payment (i.e., noncollection of taxes) for things that would have been done anyhow. We do not know what the margins would be: how much larger the tax-incentive effort would turn out to be or how much more payment for things that would have been done anyhow. My reason for recommending postponement of tax incentives is that more time is needed to explore the limits of JOBS and JOPS to see whether such programs can be made relatively routine and large scale. If it turns out that JOBS is not expanding much and that there remains a substantial number of individuals in need who look as though they ought to be eligible for federally subsidized on-the-job training, then it will be time to start a tax-incentive program. In the meantime, tax incentives too need experimental treatment. But in my view, it is too early for a full-blown training incentive to be incorporated into the tax system.

Public Employment Program. As has been suggested, the Public Employment program recommended here is different from most programs in being. It is not a New Careers program, nor is it primarily a training program. Certainly some of the individuals receiving work experience in public employment will come to be considered trainable whereas before they were considered untrainable, but that is not the primary objective. The objective is to provide jobs for those who are at least marginally employable but cannot get any other jobs and cannot succeed in training. "Operation Mainstream," an employment program carried out under Senator Nelson's 1965 amendment to the Economic Opportunity Act, may be considered a small-scale prototype, although Mainstream emphasis is on beautification work carried out by aging rural people, and the new program would be broader. Another prototype is the so-called Happy Pappy program for public employment of family heads, begun in depressed eastern Kentucky under the Work Experience program delegated by OEO to HEW and continued with Labor Department funding. But the Public Employment program really harks back to the WPA of the 1930s.

The point is that for various reasons many poor people in the United States cannot get or cannot use the training to integrate into the private or the "regular" public sectors of the economy but nontheless want and need the relative dignity of a job as compared to Income Maintenance. If the Public Employment pay rate were set at $1.60 to $2 an hour ($3,200 to $4,000 a year), it would be high enough to carry some inducement to get off Income Maintenance but still low enough to make JOBS or JOPS look better in those firms and institutions using it as intended, as entry level training for the $3, $4, and $5 an hour semiskilled and skilled jobs.

Who then would enter a Public Employment program? One primary group would be those in need of jobs in rural areas like eastern Kentucky and in small towns where the industrial base is insufficient to support a private business JOBS program, where there are few entry level jobs for anyone. Indeed, Public Employment would probably initially be fairly heavily rural. In cities, the program would be one of jobs for those who simply can't get into training programs or for those who have gotten in but dropped or flunked out. No training program has a 100 percent success rate; 75 percent is ordinarily considered good, and 50 percent is more usual. Some analysts are optimistic enough to believe every person is trainable and that anyone who flunks or drops out should be started again. Perhaps they are right philosophically. It is difficult for a liberal ideology to admit that some people are simply not trainable, but because of slum education and the pressures of slum life, it is not surprising. While waiting for the optimistic liberal ideology to be confirmed, however, it does seem preferable to help people with jobs in the meantime.

The final group who might enter a Public Employment program are those who now have jobs at a 3.5 percent unemployment rate but who will lose them in even minor fluctuations. As suggested earlier, neither Public Employment nor anything else is going to solve the problems of 5 percent unemployment, but certainly such a program can help cushion minor cyclical fluctuations.

Implicit in the description of those in need is the fact that the jobs provided would not be of top quality. It would be nice to avoid leaf-raking simply because of symbolism, but outdoor maintenance — snow shoveling, digging and planting, cleanup, removal or rearrangement of accumulations of natural debris including arboreal — would undoubtedly be a large part of any Public Employment program. So might other heavier work. Roger Starr and James Carlson have suggested that water pollution problems might be alleviated by increasing the amount of manual labor going into such tasks as separating sewers and storm drains.[9] Undoubtedly, many similar tasks could be uncovered. It seems likely that post offices could extend needed services, and so could other public institutions. Current needs are somewhat different from the WPA days, when the people in need of "residual" jobs were so many and so varied that jobs

9. Rogers, Starr, and James Carlson, "Pollution and Poverty: The Strategy of Cross-Commitment," *The Public Interest*, No. 10, Winter 1968, pp. 104–131.

ranged from leaf-raking up to writing guides to the states and localities of the United States. The residual today is a lot more residual.

The proposed Public Employment program differs also from the 5 to 6 million job program of the 1966 Report of the National Commission on Technology, Automation, and Economic Progress,[10] which was based in large part on a report done for OEO by Greenleigh Associates.[11] The 5 to 6 million job estimate was of virtually *all* the public jobs that needed filling for which little or nothing was being done. The jobs ranged almost as widely as the WPA jobs and included a very healthy proportion of subprofessionals. Within the overall manpower program recommended here, however, people qualified to become subprofessionals would be qualified for JOBS or JOPS, and, except perhaps in rural areas, they would not be likely to be attracted to a $3,200 to $4,000 residual Public Employment program.

On the other hand, the emphasis on Public Employment as a truly residual residual for the least employable of the unemployed does not yet imply that it is an "employer of last resort" program. Ultimately the difference may not be an important one, but the use of the term "employer of the last resort" implies that anyone coming to register at the Employment Service or wherever would immediately be put on a payroll, and it is difficult to see how this could be handled. What is suggested here is that the program be begun and funded at an initial level on the order of 150,000 jobs costing up to $600 million. At first these jobs would be mostly in the rural areas as we feel our way to the limit of need in both rural and urban areas. The first operational step would be to develop the jobs, that is, to make sure that when 150,000 people come down to register, there will be someone to receive them and put them to work. As we approach the steady state over a period of time and become more knowledgeable about what we are doing and how much of it we have to do, this concept will converge with the employer of last resort because the number of jobs will match the number of applicants.

10. "Technology and the American Economy" (Report to the President and the Congress by the National Commission on Technology, and Economic Progress, February 1966).

11. "A Public Employment Program for the Unemployed Poor" (a study done for the Office of Economic Opportunity by Greenleigh Associates and Company of New York, November 1965).

The peak estimate for this program — a guess based on the general concept of job needs given the other programs in existence — is one million jobs at $4 billion. This is more than four times as much as the dollar estimate for JOBS-JOPS even though JOBS-JOPS is a higher quality program. The reason is that the estimated $3,000 per slot cost of JOBS-JOPS is a one-time training cost with no further subsidy for the trainee; Public Employment payments go on year after year for the same people. That is why the *social* benefit as well as the individual benefit is much higher for JOBS-JOPS, those with whom it works. It is also why $10,000 might not be an unreasonable cost for a successful JOBS trainee.

Community Action — or Reasonable Facsimile. The need for some variety of community action effort has already been detailed. A Negative Income Tax growing to a high enough level will end low-income poverty as defined by the Orshansky line, and good Manpower programs will go a long way toward equalizing earning opportunity for those poor and near-poor who can work. Nonetheless, if we are serious about equalizing opportunity for groups now treated unequally and for the individual members of each group from top to bottom of the income distribution, the institution-building and institution-changing effects of community action are necessary. Without such equalization of opportunity, a continuing high level of Income Maintenance and a continuation of remedial Manpower programs will remain necessary to maintain the victory over low-income poverty because too many of the poverty-causing conditions will still remain.

Community Action or something like Community Action thus remains necessary to continue building the institutions of the slums and to continue pressing on the institutions of the larger community to perform on behalf of the poor and the unequally treated. The continuation of the Community Action type of effort need not be defined into any single precise shape. What is needed is to keep *something* going to continue slum and ghetto community interest in building institutions and to continue pressure on surrounding institutions.

This something can take any of several shapes. One that was tried in the early days of Community Action (see Chapter 4) and found wanting is likely still to be wanting, but fortunately it is not likely to be tried again anyhow, at least not with federal funds. This is disembodied community organization, not connected with any ongoing service programs or attempts to build service programs. Such political and quasi-political action for the sake of the action quickly comes down to what Moynihan calls "systematic agitation," and such agitation is the most likely form of action to unite the majority of the community against the minority to their mutual detriment. Indeed, a highly agitational mode even if connected with services is likely to lead to the CAP model described by Sundquist and Davis as quoted earlier: "The outcasts — those that had not been able to match their militancy with a leadership and competence that compelled respect. They were effectively contained, left to administer the programs financed from Washington but otherwise ignored or even shunned."[12]

The effort then must be for an independent community action type of program to organize institutions around services — whether neighborhood centers, education, economic development, or what — and to use both the services and institutions to influence the services and institutions of the larger community. Again, we are concerned with the issue of pressures of various sorts to build political coalitions.

The "systematic agitation" model is in a sense, then, an extreme and one to be avoided. It is not quite the most extreme of extremes. Such a compounded extreme is the model that would be likely to be formed independently in many ghetto communities if the attempt were made to suppress independent community action entirely. When Vice-Presidential candidate Spiro Agnew suggested during the 1968 political campaign that residents of poverty communities should defer to the experts, who know best, he seemed to imply a movement away from official sponsorship and toleration of the Community Action type of organization. It is certainly possible to move away from such official sponsorship, but the genie of grass roots organization will not go back into the bottle. If existing organization is suppressed or put in its place by official action, then future organization will be strongly antiofficial and far more revolutionary and divisive than it ought to be. The dialectic of "establishment" and "antiestablishment" has begun, and a wise establishment will begin to look for

12. James L. Sundquist with the collaboration of David W. Davis, *Making Federalism Work* (Washington, D.C.: The Brookings Institution, 1969), p. 47.

a synthesis, again, a politics of coalition. A less-wise establishment will try to suppress the antithesis and by doing so actually promote antithesis in a traumatic way certain to make later peaceful synthesis more difficult to achieve.

If we dismiss the agitational extreme, a variety of models still remains. It has already been suggested that the present state of political/institutional life in the ghetto is Hobbesian, a relatively uncontrolled state of natural conflict in which many institutions vie to see which is the fittest. One alternative — and it may actually be the only one realistically available — is to continue the Hobbesian state. This would mean continuation of independent federal funding of Community Action (or a successor) and a number of other programs (e.g., economic development and manpower).

Such a Hobbesian solution would not preclude giving more of the action to one or another of the organizations; it seems extremely likely that an increasing portion of federal funds for poverty target areas will go through the Model Cities program. This may imply close control by the elected city government, or it may include a real degree of target-area participation by neighborhood councils within the Model Cities structure. But even with participation, if Model Cities were the *only* funding channel, the real impact of target-area organization would be greatly limited by the fact that the main bargaining sanction of the neighborhood councils would be to say in effect, "We don't want your damned money." Cutting off one's nose is not a strong basis for effective bargaining power, and a neighborhood organization's ability to go to another source of funding remains necessary to provide real bargaining power and a safety valve for community residents.

In any case, if all funds were channeled through elected officialdom, we would be out of the Hobbesian state and into the second possible model. This second model, one of imposed control, is similar to Thomas Hobbes's own solution for the state of nature, which he abhorred. Changing the metaphor, we might call it the Gaullist model, after the recent French system that derived all power from a single source, a democratically elected one to be sure but a single source nonetheless. Not only is this centrally controlled model the most satisfactory on its face to the politician who would like to maintain his own control, but it also looks good to the bureaucrat who is more interested in smooth working efficiency than in effectiveness in achieving program goals. It looks very neat on an organization chart. It resolves all conflicts in advance by making clear with whom the decision-making power lies. Secretary of Housing and Urban Development George Romney, for example, has made it clear that in his view of the Model Cities program, "adequate citizen involvement" would be retained but that "the final authority must be the local officials."[13]

Unfortunately, however, conflicts in poverty target areas (and in cities as a whole for that matter) are based on clashes of real interest and are just not easily suppressed by giving authority to local officials or anyone else. The Gaullist analogy applies again here. General de Gaulle kept conflict in France well bottled up until May 1968, when it exploded violently because the central control controlled tightly without satisfying very many Frenchmen. A similar explosion took place for similar reasons in May 1969 under the Ongania government of Argentina. Such analogies should provide a warning to American urban officials. Sweeping conflict under the rug does not make it go away. Disregard of black communities by urban officialdom, by the press, and by virtually everyone else through the early 1960s led as much as anything else to the riots of 1965 through 1967. And the lesson that should be learned by urban officials and by federal officials making urban policy is that an effort to create a single "coordinated" federal program for each city (presumably under the Model Cities label) is extremely dangerous. Wise local political establishments can presumably allow and channel conflict within such a program, but not all local establishments are as wise as that, and holding the cork firmly in a bottle with increasing pressure is going to blow up the bottle.

Finally, on a less dramatic level, the effectiveness of antipoverty programs controlled through traditional channels is increased by the threat of rivalry from independently funded competitors. This idea does not appeal to bureaucrats because it does not fit well with who-reports-to-whom organization chart efficiency, but it should have an intuitive appeal to those who take seriously the ethos of competition as a means of inducing improvement in products.

For reasons like this, the Gaullist model does not seem highly desirable. The third model looks more attractive. John Locke, unlike

13. Quoted in *The New York Times*, April 29, 1969.

Hobbes, refused to be panicked into totalitarianism by the horrors of the state of nature. Instead he proposed the principles of representative democracy that led through James Madison to the American republican system. In theory it is possible to organize ghetto political/institutional life on the basis of republican principles. What would be needed is a rather formally elected slum legislature with the right to sign off for the target community on any action within the community, subject to Bill of Rights type limitations to protect the rights of individuals within the community. This sign-off power together with the city government's power to do likewise on most programs would mean a double-veto system although of course outside the target areas the city government would need no such acceptance, and on some programs capable of independent funding, the slum legislature might need no clearance from the city government. Election of the legislature could take place under a system similar to that used for labor union organization: A national body analogous to the National Labor Relations Board would certify geographic areas as election units and then supervise the elections. Unlike union elections, the election in the ghetto would not be of a single organization but of a group of representatives who would comprise the legislature. To make the system work, existing organizations in the ghettos would have to work within the system as quasi-political parties rather than remaining completely independent, as in the Hobbesian model, or being effectively suppressed as individual power centers, as in the Gaullist model. Frankly I do not think that this plan is realistically possible, that we are ready for such a formalized structure, or perhaps that we will ever be. The implications for the structure of city government are radical, the resistance will be strong, and it is not particularly clear that most target areas are ready for it either. For the system to work, existing organizations will have to accept the will of the majority, and their willingness to do so is in substantial doubt.

But if the republican legislative model is premature and the Gaullist model is likely to build up pressures explosively, then continuation of the Hobbesian state of nature is all that is left. We should not delude ourselves into thinking that any new additional body or program put into target areas is somehow mysteriously going to overcome all existing interests and become the program that coordinates all others, happily and voluntarily. This

223

was expected of CAP, and it did not materialize; it had been expected of organizations formed under the Kennedy-Javits Urban Impact amendments to the Economic Opportunity Act, and it has not materialized; it is now expected under Model City neighborhood councils and shows little sign of materializing. Some advocates of ghetto economic development programs argue that legislation will enable local development structures to become the target-area coordinators coordinating all the other coordinators; it seems unlikely. So long as the many existing organizations and interests continue to exist, their existence will prevent a monopoly and continue something akin to the Hobbesian state. They can be put out of existence in two ways only: by the Gaullist model, which puts all the power in one center, presumably the city government, and which is likely to build up the pressure for its own destructive explosion, and by more or less formal legislative organization that seems too idealistic to be possible, at least at this time. I am not arguing that *more* and *better* coordination is impossible, that *more* channeling of funds through programs like Model Cities is impossible or undesirable, or that Model Cities as a *voluntary* coordinating mechanism is a bad idea. Improvement is possible; better coordination and voluntary cooperative planning are possible. But the emphasis must be on the voluntary nature and on bargaining among groups that if not equal at least have some independent power of their own.

At present, much of the independent activity in poverty target areas is carried out through Community Action agencies and their delegate programs. Any precipitate ending of Community Action would gore too many oxen to be viable, but it may be that it is time to phase out Community Action as being too scarred by past battles and to bring in a fresh young substitute to carry on independent local action. If this is the case, simple name-changing, which starts out with CAP and through something akin to the shell game ends up with CAP renamed, may suffice, but a new organizing principle may be needed. Organization of the poor, institution building, and institution changing are not politically sexy enough to be acceptable principles for local action. For this reason as much as any other, the stated purpose of CAP in its early years was coordination and planning. Coordination and planning are good and acceptable principles of organization, but organization against the establishment is bad and unacceptable. As much as anything the failure of CAP to coordinate and plan has led to its political unpopularity; in any case, Model Cities has taken over the coordination and planning task. So what may be needed is a new acceptable principle, a new "social myth," to justify the independent local funding that is the essence of Community Action. One such principle may be ghetto economic development. Ghetto economic development leaves a lot of economic questions unanswered and in leaving them unanswered throws doubt on its utility for building social and political institutions, but in this game of keeping a few years ahead, ghetto economic development may be the successor to coordination and planning as the viable social myth on which we can base the new community organization that succeeds the Community Action Program.

The discussion thus far has been of urban Community Action. The policies suggested here are not necessarily purely urban, however. Much of what has been discussed can be applied to rural target areas: concentrated poverty communities in Appalachia, in the flatland South, and scattered more lightly through other parts of the country. The need for institution building is at least as strong; the need for institution changing in some of the feudal counties of poverty is much stronger. Realistically, however, the rural job is more difficult. The institutions of the urban slums have been built largely upon preexisting nuclei like civil rights organizations and groups of activists. In many rural areas, these nuclei do not exist. If anything they exist less in the rural white communities of poverty than in the black ones. And the feudal political structures that exist in many poor rural counties are difficult to bring down. For reasons like this, although we must try, it will necessarily be a long hard task. The end of low-income poverty will have to depend more heavily in rural areas than in cities on the Negative Income Tax and the Public Employment program. The equalization of opportunity for groups in rural areas may have to depend on future migration into urban areas by members of the groups.

The current annual cost of "mainstream" Community Action programs (outside of Head Start, health centers, etc.) is roughly $450 million. Some modest expansion would be useful in the first year of a renewed antipoverty program, primarily because of the difficulty of dismantling the old in order to get funds for the new. The first-year cost thus might be $600 million, compared with the current $450 million. A peak cost for mainstream Community Action programs might be as high as a billion dollars a year if rural areas can be penetrated. As compared with the funds needed for Income Maintenance and Manpower programs, these increases are modest.

In addition to mainstream Community Action, the previous chapter suggested that the OEO Legal Services Program was in itself a highly effective institution changer. This program, now funded at $42 million, could be increased modestly to $60 million the first year of the new program and doubled at the peak.

OTHER PROGRAMS

The basic recommendations here are within the Negative Income Tax–Manpower–Community Action triad. To repeat, this does not mean that these are the only programs desirable or the only ones necessary. What it does mean is that, as new funds become available to the War on Poverty, Income Maintenance and Manpower are the most important candidates for substantially increased budgets; in the case of Community Action, it means that political stress should be continued although major funding increases are less important.

But nothing is ever simple, nor should it be oversimplified, and other programs are also necessary on a smaller and more experimental basis. Actually, educational experimentation and evaluation might be considered as crucial as the three major thrusts. Although it is not suggested that major monies be put into antipoverty education programs now, that is because we do not know how to spend them effectively, not because education is unimportant. Indeed, opportunity will never be truly equal until the educational achievements of disadvantaged groups are made effectively equal to those of the majority. For this reason, a very high priority should be put on rigorously controlled experimentation in order finally to obtain answers to the unanswered questions listed in the previous chapter: What are the best ages of educational intervention, the relationships of educational achievement to social and economic effectiveness, the interactions among the various aspects of learning, the needed kinds of educational inputs such as curricula and teacher training, and so forth? Each of these questions suggests controlled experimentation to find answers. In addition, far better evaluation is needed of programs that group together in different organizational patterns various sets of techniques, intervention ages, and so on. The Head Start evaluations discussed earlier are not all negative; there is a suggestion that some techniques within Head Start may work well. It may be that better evaluation of More Effective Schools, evaluation of community control experiments, and evaluation of other programs will demonstrate previously undiscovered, sustainable gains.

Certainly one other kind of program that should be experimented with, even though it will take fifteen to twenty years, is one which provides compensatory education to slum children from near infancy through high school or beyond. Intuitively, I believe that such a controlled experiment would in fact discover a high degree of success for the experimental children. Such a success may be due to particular techniques or it may be due to a Hawthorne effect in which the years of attention paid to the children will pay off. Either way, we simply do not know, and the American commonweal is not going to do the proper things until it does know.

Other possible techniques for inducing successful education that ought to be experimented with include the provision of special grants to families to buy for their children the best education they think they can find, and contracts with profit-making organizations to take slum children as inputs and produce better-educated citizens as outputs; payment should be contingent upon results. In addition, relatively successful programs like Upward Bound should be continued, expanded, and evaluated more thoroughly.

In discussing program categories like Education in which the poor partake but which, unlike Income Maintenance for example, they do not dominate, the additional question must always be asked: Which budget are we talking about? Within a given *antipoverty* budget, education does not take priority. But the *antipoverty* budget overlaps with the total national *education* budget, an increasing portion of which is federally funded. If we should avoid putting too large a chunk of the antipoverty budget into education, I would nonetheless contend, on grounds of equity if no other, that as much as possible of the national education budget should go to the poor and minority groups. If we know little about what works in education, we can still be pretty sure of two negative points: first, that more money is at least no worse than less money, so that more money will certainly do the poor no harm; and second, that substantially smaller sums are spent for the education of the poor than for the better-off, and that is just plain unfair. It may well be, because of the current state of our knowledge, that spending more on the poor will help little if at all and that equalized expenditures between the poor and the better-off will do little to equalize educational achievement. Nonetheless, simple justice seems to dictate movement toward such equalization. More specifically, this would mean that in the national education budget, federal funds should be shifted from a program such as "impacted areas," which provides funds to areas with large numbers of federal employees, like wealthy Montgomery and Arlington counties in the Washington area, and into alternative programs like Title I of the Elementary and Secondary Education Act, which provides funds to slum schools with large numbers of poor children. But to be realistically pessimistic, precisely such a shift from federally impacted areas to slum areas has been recommended by both the Johnson and Nixon administrations and has been turned down by Congress several times.

Nutrition programs also need to be both expanded and improved. As already suggested, in the ideal commonwealth of the informed consumer, a free choice of purchases should be left up to the individual, and money provides more choice than food stamps or commodities. Free consumer choice is an important principle, but the connection leading directly from malnutrition in pregnancy and early childhood to irreversible brain damage is becoming too well established, and the route from the ignorance of destitute parents to the hunger of their children is too dangerous to allow consumer choice to be the only consideration.

As much as possible, nutrition programs should be directed first to those for whom food will make a real difference in performance, mothers and young children, but it is not possible to confine food programs as narrowly as this. What is recommended, then, is the increase of the food stamp program to cover all poor families with children (a Negative Income Tax for families with children would make such a stress easier), an increase in school lunch programs, and continued experimentation with new ideas like school breakfasts. The cost of such efforts would raise federal nutritional expenditures from about $700 million in fiscal 1969 to $1 billion the first year and perhaps a $1.25 billion at the peak, assuming that these programs were add-ons to a negative income tax, which in it-self would help the nutrition of the poor greatly. A negative tax would also solve the problem of those with too little money even to buy food stamps. Nevertheless, administration of food programs should be moved from the Department of Agriculture to Health, Education and Welfare or, even better, to OEO.

In addition, certain other programs at least deserve mention as being worth continuing. The Neighborhood Health Center program, begun under OEO, should be continued, but, if the program is to be effective in guiding the expenditures of the vast sums of federal money going into other federal antipoverty health programs, much better experimentation and evaluation is needed. Family Planning programs should be increased, but evaluation ought to progress from estimation of benefits *if* the pro-grams work to measurement of *whether* they work. Housing programs are going to continue, and the need for experimentation and evaluation here too will continue. The VISTA program too deserves to be continued. It is so difficult to evaluate as an antipoverty program that perhaps it should be considered as part of a national youth program encompassing VISTA, Peace Corps, Teacher Corps, and military service as well as remedial programs for youth needing remediation. That, however, must be somebody else's book.

Finally, some programs that have been recommended as major anti-poverty efforts simply appear unlikely to be fruitful, at least above the experimental level. These include Children's Allowances and major Eco-nomic Development programs, whether rural, urban industrial, or black capitalism. Others may fall into the same questionable category. New Cities, for example, seems a long way from success even as a residential program for the middle class, and for the poor it is indeed a long way off. Yet if taken seriously, it could sop up an awful lot of money very quickly so that as a budgetary alternative it becomes a danger.

I have no intention, however, of trying to dismiss bright new ideas with a word even if I could. In none of the categories and programs dis-cussed here — Income Maintenance, Manpower, Community Action, Edu-cation, and the rest — do we have the ultimate answers to solve all problems. This is the final program recommendation: Experimentation, demonstration, and evaluation should continue and be expanded. This statement does not mean that experimental programs should be substituted for action programs. There are those who feel that the basic error of OEO was and continues to be the opening up of large-scale activities without a good deal of previous experimentation, but I share Sargent Shriver's belief that the only way to move ahead is to move ahead. Indeed, looking at the range of interpretations that can be put on the results of almost any social experiment, I think it is obvious that waiting for unambiguous results from any experiment is going to take a long time, perhaps infinitely long.

But powerful use can be made of guided innovation that starts with a hypothesis, uses rigorous experimentation to gain specific information needed to complete the hypothesis (e.g., the use of the New Jersey Graduated Work Incentives experiment to gain information about the effect of income maintenance on work incentives), sets up programs of operational demonstration (without necessarily waiting for all the experimental information) to find major operating flaws, and moves to the major program through a large-scale pilot phase (the first year of Head Start). In education, in health, even in manpower and housing, we do not know all the answers, and the War on Poverty must preserve and improve the process that will help produce new ones.

ADMINISTRATION OF THE WAR ON POVERTY

Most of the arguments indicating the need for continuing independent local Community Action apply also to an independent antipoverty agency at the federal level. The institution-building concept is not really relevant to the national level, but the idea of institution changing — using new institutions to change the attitudes and working methods of old ones — is very relevant indeed. The temptation exists in the federal government as well as elsewhere to build an organizational structure that is readily explainable by a simple organization chart. Such a federal structure would probably group programs functionally — all manpower programs in one place, all educational programs in another — with a flow of authority that ran from the President and his staff organizations, including the Budget Bureau, to functional chiefs like the Secretary of Labor and the Secretary of Health, Education and Welfare.

Such a structure would leave no independent agency such as OEO crossing functional lines. It would certainly be possible to restructure administration of the antipoverty program in this way; indeed it was possible to have structured it functionally from the start, and, as discussed in Chapter 4 on the history of the War on Poverty, such a functional structure was advocated in 1965 by several cabinet members. Instead, however, a complex, not easily diagrammed, form of administration was created in which the independent OEO: managed some programs directly; "delegated" others to various executive departments for administration while keeping budgetary and other strings on these programs; was supposed to have coordinated all the directly managed programs, the delegated programs, and the other antipoverty programs not under the Economic Opportunity Act; and indeed did stick its nose into almost everything relevant.

This looks very messy and it is. But it was created this way for a reason and the reason still exists. Public decisions in the United States are not made by simple lines of authority on a simple organization chart. Rather, decisions — whether federal, state, or local — are arrived at in large measure by a political bargaining process. He who has the ability to apply pressure has the ability to affect a decision. And one reason for the past lack of services of all sorts to the poor has been their weakness in this bargaining process. The poor have not been felt in the education process; therefore poverty-area schools have been treated poorly. The poor have not been felt in legal circles; therefore justice for the poor has been unequal, and so forth. Typically until recently, the bargaining constituencies of any government agency consisted of its clientele and its own bureaucracy — the clientele with its own interests, the bureaucracy with its interests and its professional ideology — an ideology that, in the case of an old bureaucracy like that in education, for example, is encrusted with inherited lore. The poor have not been the major clientele of any agency except Welfare, and the Welfare clientele has been weak because of its hat-in-hand petitioner status while the bureaucratic ideology of the Welfare profession has been paternalistic and superior.

The creation of the Office of Economic Opportunity has begun to change this situation; the bureaucratic ideology has centered on "participation," and this in turn has provided bargaining power to the clientele. Indeed Secretary of Labor Wirtz himself testified to the existence of this situation during the 1967 hearings of the House Education and Labor committee:

> I know the argument that some of these programs are now at a point that we should shift them someplace else. I am in a pretty good position to say to you, Mr. Chairman, that it takes more than three years to upset the inertial forces that characterize some of the established departments of government, including the Department of Labor. Three years is not enough to serve as a basis for any assumption that the established departments are now going to do right what they didn't do at all before. I would urge very, very strongly the continued development of this program for the time being through somebody whose job and whose sole job is to recognize the effects of poverty and to develop those institutions and procedures which will meet that problem. There will be a time for turning it over, but it is not now.[14]

There was a need for an independent antipoverty agency in 1964, when the Economic Opportunity Act was first passed, there was a need in 1967 when Secretary Wirtz testified, and — while it will not be true forever — the ideology of the poverty bureaucracy will inevitably age — there is still a need today. An independent antipoverty agency managing some programs is still necessary to keep the older-line agencies that will continue to manage the bulk of the effort on their toes; and the delegation instrument, which looks messy indeed on an organization chart because it splits responsibilities between agencies, is also still necessary.

The split responsibility of delegation is a means of maintaining the independent antipoverty agency as a watchdog, a watchdog with some teeth, while refraining from making the independent agency a direct program operator on a scale so large that it matches the other agencies. The description in Chapter 4 of the delegation agreements between OEO and the Department of Labor illustrates both the difficulties of delegation and the need. The result of the manpower delegation has by no means been a perfect system. There has been conflict aplenty, but the

14. Economic Opportunity Act amendments of 1967, Hearings before the Committee on Education and Labor, House of Representatives, 90th Congress, First Session on HR 8311, Part 2, pp. 1193–1194.

programs are different from and better than what they would have been if the single authority of the old manpower bureaucracy (the Labor Department staff and the U.S.-State Employment Service and their clienteles) had the right to decide all policy matters unilaterally. The programs are still not very efficient in the narrow sense, but that is because the real world is not neat.

What the delegation has accomplished, however, is that OEO has shaken up the old way of doing things. It has brought Community Action programs into local manpower policy making through the regulation that Community Action agencies should have first refusal as prime sponsor of such local manpower programs. As a result there is at least some degree of participation in policy determination by the poor who are represented in Community Action programs. It is important that OEO participation has kept the focus of the programs on the hard-core poor. Moreover, OEO participation has forced an outreach system that not only takes the Employment Offices out of downtown and puts them into the ghettos but also takes some employment officers out of their offices and puts them into the streets and tenements. Finally, OEO participation has also provided an intellectual stimulus to finding new kinds of programs; in large measure the JOBS program stems from ideas put forth by an OEO staff that was unhampered by received doctrine.

Delegation has thus proved operable, because of the capability and will to operate it. It has proved a powerful and flexible tool and has made major differences in the central thrust of the manpower program. It has made these changes by bringing groups into the political bargaining process, groups such as the poverty clientele and the antipoverty bureaucracy, that would not otherwise have been represented. It has done so at the cost of a good deal of untidiness and with somewhat less efficiency than might have been the case under centralization.

Of course neither the initial set of programs managed by OEO nor the existing delegation agreements are sacrosanct. The "guided innovation" process already suggested provides a natural mode of operation for programs in an independent antipoverty agency. The principle for most programs should be temporary management by OEO. As a program moves through the pilot stage to continuing operations, it should also move through delegation to ultimate spin-off to an old-line agency. The only exceptions are certain core programs that are as much ways of doing business designed to affect the whole range of antipoverty efforts as they are direct antipoverty service programs themselves. This core to be retained by the antipoverty agency includes independent Community Action or its successor program, and it includes the institution-changing Legal Services Program. In addition, VISTA should remain in OEO, at least until the establishment of a national youth service corps. The independent antipoverty agency should also retain a substantial chunk of research and demonstration for the early phases of the guided innovation process.

Outside this core, most of the original OEO functional programs are probably candidates for delegation and spin-off or both, and they have been moving in this direction. Head Start has moved to the Department of Health, Education and Welfare, and this is probably as it should be (although Congressman Carl Perkins argues well that stripping the popular programs like Head Start out of OEO and leaving the less popular Community Action core naked writes a prescription for the death of an independent antipoverty agency). Head Start, however, should continue to be delegated rather than being transferred outright to Health, Education and Welfare. Such delegation should make it easier to maintain experimentation in the program, and since its success thus far has not been strong, experimentation is necessary. In addition, the very popularity of Head Start has led to demands that it be expanded to a preschool program for all children, rich and poor alike; continued strings to OEO will help prevent this dilution of function and funds. The Neighborhood Health Center program, however, might just as well go all the way to the Department of Health, Education and Welfare without delegation. If, as suggested earlier, the major function of this program is to act as a pilot influence on the vast sum of federal health expenditures, such a purpose can be promoted as well from outside OEO as within.

Job Corps has gone from OEO to the Department of Labor, to be integrated with other Manpower programs. In itself this seems a good move, but it brings up the question of whether the overall antipoverty manpower effort should continue to operate in large part under delegation from OEO to the Labor Department or whether the Labor Department should get full authority in the name of a "comprehensive" manpower program. Pressure for such a comprehensive program under a single legislative authority is strong and has been for a number of years. In 1967, Garth Mangum and Sar Levitan suggested it in a pamphlet,[15] and in 1969 the National Manpower Policy Task Force of which Mangum and Levitan are members recommended it again.[16] But the wisdom of the recommendation is questionable. Manpower programs are so central to the antipoverty effort and the ease with which needed future progress can be stymied and perhaps past progress reversed is so great that delegation remains an important control. The U.S.-State Employment Services in particular maintain a constant pressure on the Labor Department to move away from the poor and those hard to deal with toward their old mode, satisfying their employer clientele by providing "attractive" people to fill job openings. It seems important to continue the countervailing pressures of an independent antipoverty agency at the federal level and Community Action agencies at the local level.

Other programs might well profit from moving into the OEO orbit, perhaps for a period as OEO-managed programs but more likely under delegation arrangements. Some of these are relatively new efforts such as Ghetto Economic Development. The major viable objective, if any, of such development is the building of social and political institutions around economic ones, and thus far the innovative staff of the Community Action Program has proved best able to set up programs that show promise in that direction; the development program in the Hough area of Cleveland, for example. (It should be made clear that, unlike me, Economic Development staff of CAP are enthusiasts for such development.) If OEO were given the central role in building such programs, the track record indicates that economic development would be most likely to develop initially in a way that would fulfill whatever potential it has. In addition, if economic development is to become a new social myth for organizing ghetto institutions, it is important to keep such development within the antipoverty agency.

15. Garth, Mangum, and Sar Levitan, "Making Sense of Federal Manpower Policy" (A Joint Publication of the Institute of Labor and Industrial Relations, The University of Michigan-Wayne State University, and the National Manpower Policy Task Force, Washington, D.C., March 1967).
16. National Manpower Policy Task Force Report, "The Nation's Manpower Programs."

Were it possible, the nutrition programs now managed by the Department of Agriculture would also benefit from an OEO connection. Thus far most of the debate on the administration of such programs has been over whether they should remain within Agriculture or should be shifted to Health, Education and Welfare. Certainly, in light of the record, HEW would be better than Agriculture, but too little attention has been paid to the fact that the welfare workers themselves in the Southern areas of greatest malnutrition have been responsible for determining eligibility for federal food programs and have been carrying out their job narrowly and ineffectively. Indeed, this is true not only in the rural South. In 1969 the staff of Senator George McGovern's select Committee on Nutrition and Human needs reported that in the District of Columbia, "Welfare Department officials admitted to Committee staff members that caseworkers were not informing new recipients on a regular basis about the program and were tardy about completing the paper work necessary to enroll recipients," and that in the District of Columbia food stamp certification center, "potential applicants were turned away because they arrived too late or walked away because they were kept waiting too long."[17] It seems likely that the influence of OEO and local Community Action would be very useful here.

Thus the continuation of OEO or a successor independent antipoverty agency seems important for maintaining the effectiveness of the entire range of programs. But one task that OEO has not carried out well — practically not carried out at all — is coordination of antipoverty programs. Coordination includes such activities as (1) forward-looking planning and budgeting; (2) day-to-day operational meshing of programs so that conflicts are minimized, orders are clear, and needs are filled rather than being left in a limbo between two programs that don't quite match; and (3) evaluation of what happened in the past so that future planning may benefit. Only in part has OEO succeeded in doing these things.

It is clear that OEO has planned comprehensively and carefully, and these plans have illuminated and helped direct some actions; but as comprehensive plans to guide the entire pattern of action they have never been taken seriously. My contention is that it would be unrealistic ever

17. Quoted in *The Washington Post*, April 16, 1969.

to expect long-range plans to be any kind of precise guide; in any case, OEO's plans were not used as this kind of guide.

At the other end of the spectrum, OEO in recent years has carefully evaluated its programs and many of these evaluations are reflected in the previous chapter. Probably OEO has done better in evaluation than any other federal agency, but the result still looks to an outsider like biased OEO self-evaluation and can never be completely satisfactory. (Those of us who were doing the evaluation for the Job Corps, say, felt that we were outside Job Corps and thus could be objective; but from the viewpoint of those outside OEO, we were insiders and therefore suspect.)

And as for the middle category of coordination, the day-to-day meshing of programs and minimizing of conflicts among agencies and among persons, OEO has hardly ever tried.

One lesson that has been learned by all concerned is that a single agency cannot be both a coordinator above the battle and an operator within the thick of it. For reasons like this it is generally agreed that antipoverty coordination — particularly day-to-day operational coordination, but also planning of the range of antipoverty programs, and "outsider" evaluation — should be taken out of the independent antipoverty operating agency and placed in a new small elite body at or near the White House level. Separation of coordination from operations was the recommendation of the General Accounting Office.[18] It was the recommendation of various formal and informal advisory groups to the Johnson and Nixon administrations, and indeed it was OEO's own recommendation. A new coordinating body might be a council of cabinet-level government officials like the Urban Affairs Council set up by President Nixon with Moynihan as its executive secretary, or it might be structured in another way. But more important than the structure of any council is its staff, which would be the day-to-day planning and coordinating group. Such a group could be staff to a council like the Urban Affairs Council, it could be placed within the Budget Bureau to augment the Human Resources staff of the Bureau, or it could be put into some other organization. Its size would depend upon its location. A true White House staff is necessarily small, and two alternative models thus are a small high-level

18. Comptroller General of the United States, *Review of Economic Opportunity Programs,* March 18, 1969.

group depending upon detailed staff work done by agencies such as OEO, HEW, and Labor; or a larger group doing more of its own staff work but further from the seats of power than in the first model. Combinations of these various pieces may be put together to build an array of alternatives. The single crucial factor is that the planning-coordination-evaluation job needs doing somewhere at a level where it will be taken seriously, and to be taken seriously it must be divorced from the operations of the independent antipoverty agency and other federal departments.

Table 14 lays out the rough cost implications of the recommendations discussed throughout this chapter. It should be stressed that the numbers *are* rough, particularly in the last column. The cost of a Negative Income Tax with a guarantee at the poverty line is estimated at $12 billion above current Public Assistance costs, for example; but if manpower and other opportunity programs work less effectively to reduce poverty through increased earnings than is assumed, the cost could easily be $3 billion higher, or vice versa.

Nonetheless, the table does indicate two things. First, the best estimate for the additional cost of the recommendations here is $6 billion more than current costs in the first year for which all recommendations are implemented, and $18 billion more at the top. As suggested at the beginning of this chapter, these numbers are not large compared with expected increases in federal revenues over the relevant time periods. But second, the table also brings out the fact that the recommendations here cover only about 20 percent of the total monies now going into the antipoverty budget, although if Social Security were included in the portion of the budget covered by the recommendations here this would raise coverage to about $13.5 billion, more than half of the total. Inclusion of Social Security may be appropriate because the Negative Income Tax cost estimate assumes that the negative tax will carry the burden of ending poverty among the aged, but running this portion of the Income Maintenance through Social Security would be an acceptable alternative.

In any case, the portion of the budget not covered by my recommendations is going to have its automatic and less automatic demands for increases also, so that the $6 billion and $18 billion increment figures tabulated here are somewhat illusory.

Table 14
Costs
Recommended Increments to the Antipoverty Budget
(billions of dollars)

	Fiscal Year 1969	Program Year 1	Peak Year
Manpower			
JOBS-JOPS	.200	.400	.800
Public Employment	—	.600	4.000
Individual Improvement			
Educational Research	.017	.030	.050
Nutrition	.702	1.000	1.250
Family Planning	.045	.075	.150
Community Betterment			
Independent			
Community Action	.450	.600	1.000
Legal Services	.042	.060	.120
Income Maintenance			
Public Assistance	3.500	—	—
Negative Income Tax	—	8.500	15.500
Total covered	4.956	11.265	22.870
Total not covered	20.856		
Grand total	25.812		

Nonetheless, $6 and $18 billion do roughly approach the costs for implementing these recommendations. To repeat at the end of the chapter what was said at the beginning, I am not contending here either that the recommended programs will solve all the social problems of the United States or that the increased costs are trivial and will be easy to finance. But costs on the order of magnitude of these are at least substantially less than the $100 billion figures sometimes cited, and this is worth pointing out. Indeed, it is doubtful that we would know how to spend $100 billion increases for the War on Poverty even if we knew how to get them.

7
Conclusion

The programs recommended in Chapter 6 will not cure all the social ills of the United States. Nor are they a rigid immutable set that will not work at all unless implemented in full. The recommendations are for a set of programs that in the light of experience, analysis, intuition, and guesswork looks to me to be the most likely to solve the problems to which they are addressed, that will end poverty within the United States and make a substantial step forward toward equalizing opportunity.

But alternatives are certainly available all along the line, and many were discussed in the previous chapter. Perhaps, after all, a family allowance unrelated to income is the only kind of Income Maintenance system acceptable to the American people. Perhaps private business will simply not be willing to work effectively in the manpower training areas, and the entire task of training and of providing jobs will have to be done by government. Perhaps somebody somewhere really has the magic key to improving the education of the deprived. If this were the case, my priority set of recommendations would change drastically. Perhaps Community Action is less than the crucial complement to service delivery programs that I made it out to be, or on the other hand, maybe it is the key to everything else that the early OEO ideologues thought it to be. All these things are possible, and following the flexibility criterion of the previous chapter, the overall program recommended here is designed as a whole in which parts can be replaced without starting over again from the beginning.

As has been obvious throughout, there are certain programs and concepts that I feel strongly about: Negative Income Tax, Community Action, the need for understanding the relationship between the low-income poverty objective and the equal opportunity objective. But just as the program recommendations are less than sacred, so is the frame of reference within which they are derived. Respectable arguments can be built up for abandoning the elimination of low-income poverty as an immediate objective and substituting completely a war for equal opportunity. I do not believe this would be workable. The humanitarian pressure to aid the truly poor and hungry would continue to focus on them programs better designed to equalize opportunity for a somewhat better-off clientele more likely to succeed in such programs; that is why the Negative Income Tax or some form of Income Maintenance aimed at those whose primary need is income is so central to the success of anything else.

On the other hand, the explicit statements of the War on Poverty since 1965 have stressed elimination of low-income poverty almost to the exclusion of the equal opportunity objective. (If this has been an error, I must admit that I am as responsible for the error as anyone else.) We may continue along these lines for a while, but sooner or later I think we will come to the recognition that if eradicating low-income poverty is really our objective, Income Maintenance is the easiest way to achieve it. If we confine ourselves to combatting low-income poverty, we will then adopt a general Income Maintenance program and toss everything else out, as is recommended by some very conservative (i.e., very nineteenth-century liberal) economists like Milton Friedman. For my taste, this comes far too close to ending the problem by redefining it. In fact, for better or for worse, the intentions of the founders of the poverty program, many of the congressmen who passed it, and the American people (at least at that time) did go substantially beyond ending low-income poverty and toward equalization of opportunity. To give up programs like Manpower and Community Action, which are most effective for the equal opportunity objectives, simply because we have made a semantic decision that poverty will mean only low income is neither socially acceptable nor politically viable. We are saddled with the equal opportunity objective — or blessed with it — and in the name of social progress in this country we ought to go ahead with it. The programs suggested here would take us a long way.

We should be clear, however, that if ending low-income poverty is very easy, at least conceptually, equalizing opportunity is much more difficult. One theme that has been implicit on practically every page of this book but has seldom been brought in explicitly is that of racial discrimination and segregation. Clearly, bluntly, and obviously, equality of opportunity in the United States is not possible without an end to racial discrimination and without a relegation of enforced segregation to country club strongholds, where it makes little difference anyhow. If racial discrimination and segregation in the United States were to reach the current low level of religious discrimination and segregation, the problem could be considered for practical purposes solved.

But exhortation will not make discrimination go away, nor will a mass examination of individual consciences. That is why the "white racism" accusation of the Kerner Report, although true, is irrelevant at least as it has been interpreted. The problem-solving style dictates that doing something about ending discrimination and segregation means not just talking about them but having programs that attack them in detail. That is why discrimination has seldom been mentioned here: because in fact almost every program mentioned — from JOBS to give workers and groups discriminated against an equal opportunity to Community Action designed to give groups themselves an equal chance at institutionally based political power — has been an antidiscrimination, antisegregation, and antiracism program.

But the problem-solving style also dictates that we be honest with ourselves and admit that discrimination and racism will not be done away with easily. We may in the not too distant future get a Negative Income Tax of some variety — Income Maintenance just costs money, and the American people are not too ungenerous with money — particularly if the money can be taken out of annual increments of growth so that nobody ends up worse than he was before. It also seems likely that most Americans honestly feel that they are willing to give up racial discrimination.

Conclusion

The ordinary answer to an accusation of discrimination is increasingly becoming "Who, me?" and it is meant sincerely. What will really be hard to give up, however, are habitual patterns that lead to discrimination without that intention: the pattern of the man who honestly doesn't mind living in an integrated neighborhood but doesn't want property values lowered; the pattern of the man who honestly doesn't mind working in an integrated situation but doesn't want seniority bent; the pattern of the man who honestly wants to see people of all races in managerial positions but won't turn down a Harvard graduate in favor of one from Howard. Even more subtle are the patterns that show a willingness to change but fear of changing too far; Thomas Schelling's models have suggested, for example, that if all the whites in a neighborhood are willing to live with 30 percent of Negro neighbors, the neighborhood will not stabilize at 30 percent but will tend to become all black.[1]

Other people may have other descriptions of unintended institutional racism, but anyone who has looked at the problem agrees that it exists. In a way, the programs recommended here try to get around it rather than attacking it directly: providing jobs for blacks and depending on continued high-level economic prosperity to do so without taking them away from whites; downgrading housing programs because real integration is the one equal opportunity effect we might want to get from housing programs, and real housing integration seems simply beyond current reach, so we hope it will follow on equalization of earnings opportunity as it has for earlier minority groups.

Ultimately, however, unintentional as well as intentional patterns of discrimination and segregation will have to break if success is to be achieved. If the programs suggested here tend to live with such problems rather than changing them, it is because they may be easier to change ultimately by getting around them initially than by colliding with them head on.

The concluding paragraph of a book on poverty and equal opportunity written in the 1960s ought by all rights to contain the exhortation that the alternative to victory in these better wars is either chaos or the end of our democratic system. As a matter of fact, I have a strong feeling

1. Thomas C. Schelling, *Models of Segregation,* RAND Corporation Memorandum RM-6014-RC, May 1969.

that these indeed are the alternatives: *either* an end to poverty and the establishment of far greater equality of opportunity; *or* a revolutionary degree of chaos; *or* a system much closer to totalitarianism than we would like to contemplate. But it is not the problem-solving style to point this out and cry doom. This book has been an effort to suggest a course between Scylla and Charybdis.

8
Epilogue:
The Beginning of the Nixon Administration

Two themes run through the beginning of the new story, the story of the Nixon administration and the War on Poverty. The first of these is that the new Administration in its first year showed a degree of liberalism and openmindedness to new and progressive ideas surprising to those who had developed an intense dislike and fear of Richard Nixon throughout his first twenty years of public life. The second theme is that the new Administration showed a degree of indecision and uncertainty surprising to those who believed that Nixon had been training for the Presidency for sixteen years and running for ten.

The feeling that there was indecision and all too deliberate speed was common among bureaucrats, journalists, and other Washington hangers-ons who compared it to the first-year hyperactivity of the Kennedy and Johnson administrations. It might be objected that the artificial Washington community was unrepresentative of anything but itself, that the nation at large really wanted the relative relaxation shown in the first year, and that the President was going as fast as he possibly could in this atmosphere of antiactivity. The argument would be, and was, that the "Bring us together" and "Let us lower our voices" slogans of the new Administration were simply incompatible with too many bold new initiatives in social fields.

Perhaps then the Administration's slowness to act was a deliberate stratagem well suited to the political atmosphere. Unfortunately, such a stratagem may carry with it severe drawbacks in terms of the very "bring us together" objective; the reunifying of the nation required more than the calming of the voices of the middle class. At least until the campus disturbances of 1969, the main immediate source of harsh civil strife was not the middle class but the poor, particularly the black urban ghetto poor but also the Spanish-speaking poor of the Western cities and valleys. Leaving these groups with the feeling that the Administration to be in office for at least four years and perhaps more was simply not concerned with them could lead to a renewal of urban disorder and to a harsh and militant separatism that for the first time could affect the majorities of these groups, not merely militant minorities on the fringe.

In any case, the first year was too early to be certain of the long-run attitudes of the poverty groups toward the new Administration or of the effects of these attitudes on civil harmony or disorder. The summer of 1969 was a cool one; perhaps that was misleading as to the long run.

What was more discernible in the first year was the policy direction of the Nixon administration. And, as already suggested, this policy direction was both surprisingly liberal and surprisingly uncertain. Action in the four major antipoverty program categories discussed here may be summarized as follows:

1. In Income Maintenance, Administration proposals made a major breakthrough toward a Negative Income Tax. The very fact of these proposals and the emphasis this study puts on the centrality of such an income maintenance scheme means that my overall evaluation of the new policies must be substantially favorable. But the pain with which the position was arrived at, the initial degree of dilution between general proposal and legislation sent to the Hill, and the inevitably slow legislative and public opinion formation process (while other, much worse Administration proposals were likely to make their way much faster) all meant that the new liberalism of the Negative Tax proposal would be badly diluted by the new uncertainty of policy making.

2. With respect to Manpower, however, Administration proposals were not uncertain; they were instead very unwise. For the Administration proposed so-called Comprehensive Manpower legislation that would

shift the laboriously constructed balance of bargaining power away from the OEO, away from the poor, and toward the old-line federal-state manpower bureaucracies, and toward the worst portion of these bureaucracies, the State Employment Services, at that.

3. In Community Betterment, the Administration attitude toward CAP remained undefined, particularly in the crucial aspect of CAP relationships toward elected city governments.

4. And in Individual Betterment — education and health — little new seemed to be happening.

Outside these four functional areas, Administration policy was uncertain or worse on two major issues. First, the future of OEO as an organization, although improved by the appointment of a young and dynamic new Director from the liberal end of the Republican spectrum, was clouded by the slowness of the Administration, including the new Director, to make their moves on organization and personnel and get on with the antipoverty job. And second, in the fight against racial discrimination, the new Administration seemed to be in full retreat along much of the front: particularly on education, and even voting rights.

The total picture, then, was one in which the dominant direction was perhaps still no direction at all but in which the Income Maintenance proposals in particular still held out hope for progress through the four or eight Nixon years.

In Income Maintenance, the breakthrough was crucial and perhaps even spectacular. Speaking to the nation on August 8, 1969, President Nixon proposed a Negative Income Tax for families with children. He did not call it that — for sound political reasons — but that is what it was. The Nixon proposal fulfilled the six basic criteria for an income maintenance scheme listed in Chapter 6: It started out at a decent level of support; it was based on need of the recipients rather than "deservedness"; it allowed retention of more than half of earnings over and above income maintenance payments; it went to intact families as well as broken ones; it was not coupled with social workers' services; and, most important, it was to be federally administered rather than being carried out under the existing welfare system, which the President called "wrong and indefensible." The proposal was not noncategorical (the seventh criterion), but by going to families with children it at least set up a categorization that avoided both the moral calculus of deservedness and the perverse anti-family incentives of the Aid to Families with Dependent Children program. AFDC was to be abolished.

The Nixon Negative Income Tax proposal was not greatly dissimilar from the proposal made in Chapter 6. For families with children it had the same 50 percent tax-away rate on assistance payments; it had a $1,600 income guarantee for a family of four (Chapter 6 proposed $1,500); it went up or down by increments of $300 for additional or fewer children (Chapter 6 proposed $500). In Chapter 6, assistance payments were to be reduced by fifty cents for each dollar earned from the very first dollar of earnings. The Administration proposal allowed $720 of earnings — justified as the cost of carfare, work clothes, lunches, and so on, once a person went to work — before reducing payments at all. This seems reasonable.

On the two key issues that mark the difference between one more futile reform of the current system and a shift to a new system, the Nixon proposal made the shift. Payments were to go to the working poor as well as to those not working, and the system was to be administered by the federal government (some unspecified combination of the Social Security Administration and the Internal Revenue Service) and taken out of the hands of state welfare authorities. States were to be required to maintain their level of fiscal effort, and those states that had been paying more than the $1,600 for a family of four were to maintain payments, but state costs would be below previous costs in all cases, and states could contract out the administration of the additional payments to the federal government. The estimated federal cost was slightly more than $2 billion for the first year.

On many of the vital issues, the Nixon plan was almost all that could be desired by the most ardent advocate of a Negative Income Tax. But one key point was left ambiguous. In the specific details of the scheme and in the public rhetoric surrounding the announcement of the proposal, it was stressed by the President and others that income maintenance payments would *not* go to those who could work but would not, that this was not a plan for the deliberately idle. This stress is obviously good politics in selling the scheme to the Congress and the public — the Puritan ethic is hardly dead yet — and similar requirements have been built into Unemployment Insurance for many years and into the 1967 amendments to the public assistance laws without being misused as a device of compulsion to force those who cannot or should not work into the labor force. Yet too much stress on the show-a-willingness-to-work-or-your-kids-will-starve aspect could either lead the Congress to build a real compulsion into any law actually passed or allow state employment officials in some places to produce cheap labor by refusing to certify a lack of available suitable employment for the payment applicant. The potential for misuse is certainly there, but this harmful potential need not be fulfilled, and the political concession may well be necessary.

It should be emphasized, however, that the President's proposal is still just a proposal. The bill submitted to the Congress in October looked less attractive than the proposal made in the August speech in some respects (e.g., a certain ambiguity about changing the administration from state to federal, adding an assets test to the simple income test for eligibility, stress on the work requirements). And this bill still had to go through the Congress. In November 1969 the Heineman Commission made its proposal for a Negative Income Tax for all families, with or without children, at a higher payment level than the Administration's, and without the Administration's work stress. Heineman's proposal was more attractive than Nixon's, but the striking fact remained that the Republican Administration *had* proposed a Negative Income Tax.

The undoubtedly long and tortuous congressional process facing the Income Maintenance proposals, however, means that this best part of the Nixon antipoverty program will inevitably go into effect much later than the worst parts because, as these things go, the worst parts are likely to have the easiest going with legislators and the public. One of the worst proposals was in the field of Manpower, second in importance only to Income Maintenance. By midsummer of 1969, a crucial battle had been lost within the Administration by the advocates of a strong antipoverty training and employment program.

Headed by Secretary of Labor George Shultz, those who favored a "comprehensive" and "coordinated" approach to Manpower programs seemed to have carried the day within the Administration. Instead of the complex-seeming system of delegation of major antipoverty manpower programs from OEO to the Department of Labor — a system in which

249

administrative neatness was traded off for political pressure from OEO to keep the federal and state manpower bureaucracies in line — the Administration proposed a Comprehensive Manpower Act. This would put all manpower programs directly under the Labor Department, thus removing OEO's political and bureaucratic pressure on the old-line agencies. Furthermore, the proposed law encouraged the Labor Department to shift responsibility to the states, the State Employment Services having been the most reactionary portion of the federal-state manpower bureaucracy. Finally, it proposed to remove the mandatory antipoverty focus from the manpower programs, thus ensuring that in the key field of manpower, the situation would return to the pre-1964 days of leaving the untrained out and behind. In the case of the JOBS program in particular, it would mean that business pressure to avoid the hard-core poor would no longer be resisted, and the federal dollar would go heavily to training those whom business would have trained anyhow.

It has been suggested throughout this book that, with a decent income maintenance program, the pressure should be off to confine manpower and other programs to the low-income poor, and the new manpower proposal is contemporaneous with the Administration's income maintenance proposal. But the issue here is not hard-core low-income poor versus easier-to-train members of unequal opportunity groups. Giving the power in manpower programs to the most conservative of the conservative and old-line bureaucracies while simultaneously removing the antipoverty mandate from the law makes it likely that the federal training dollar will go once again to the educated, the white, and the middle-class. And that is not where it is most needed.

If the Administration clearly moved one way in regard to Income Maintenance and the other in the area of Manpower, its policy in regard to the third category — Community Betterment — remained highly ambiguous. The future of community action is tied to the future of OEO itself, and the story of OEO in the first Nixon year illustrates many of the uncertainties and ambiguities of the new Administration.

In the first instance, OEO looked well off, at least as compared with what might have been. To the surprise of those who had expected Nixon to throw the whole thing out and start all over again, the Office of Economic Opportunity, without even a name change, was to retain an important role in the War on Poverty. And to the directorship of OEO too the President appointed a man from the liberal side of the Republican Party, Donald M. Rumsfeld, an Illinois Congressman. Rumsfeld, who had followed the "constructive alternative" lead of Congressmen Goodell and Quie in regard to the War on Poverty, which means that he occasionally voted against it, proved to be remarkably liberal and tough. He clearly came from Senator Percy's progressive wing of Illinois Republicanism, and his initial moves within the Administration showed strong backing for even some of the most controversial aspects of the OEO program. Publicly and privately he backed the independence of Community Action from elected city governments; he also attempted to strengthen the OEO role in the delegated programs run by other agencies.

Yet the slowness with which the Administration, including Rumsfeld, moved with regard to OEO showed an unexpected indecisiveness that ran the risk of undoing much of the good. President Nixon appointed Rumsfeld on April 21, 1969, three months after the inauguration, and his appointment was not confirmed by the Senate until May 23. This delay was hardly Rumsfeld's fault, but even though he had devoted the intervening five weeks to studying OEO, he was sworn in on May 26 without being ready to move in any direction. By July 20, six months after the inauguration and nearly three months after Rumsfeld's appointment and two months after his taking office, he had announced the appointment of only two new subordinate officials, neither of whom was at a high enough level to require presidential appointment or Senate confirmation. Rumsfeld had come into office with no background as an administrator and with the kind of suspicions of existing OEO personnel and structure that had once led Congressman Goodell to characterize the organization as a "fuddle factory." The new Director had apparently discovered that the OEO cadre included a number of effective bureaucrats and that the problems of operating the program were real ones not stemming primarily from internal organization or personalities. But the delay led to inaction, and inaction in turn carried some threat of leading to far more future fuddling than was necessary.

In the personnel search in particular, good men are always hard to find, and good men who are also Republicans are harder because the typical highly competent Republican wants the financial rewards of business whereas the typical highly competent Democrat prefers the power perquisites of government. And Rumsfeld compounded his difficulties by waiting until late summer after the field had been picked over. In many cases, summer was just too late.

Finally, in August 1969, Rumsfeld announced his OEO reorganization and seemed ready to move. First, CAP was to be abolished. Since Job Corps had been moved out of OEO by the Administration, CAP was almost the whole of OEO operations, and it made obvious good sense to merge the hierarchies of OEO and CAP, essentially giving the parent organization the functions for which the subordinate one, CAP, had been responsible. Instead of an OEO with three subordinate organizations, CAP, Job Corps, and VISTA, Rumsfeld retained an independent VISTA and set up Health Services and Legal Services programs on the same level. He then divided the "mainstream" of OEO among directors of Operations and Program Development, with Planning, Research and Evaluation retaining a strong staff role. The new organization was undoubtedly not perfect, but it seemed about as adequate as any other for promoting the role of innovation that Rumsfeld hoped to retain for OEO.

In any case, so far as OEO as an organizational entity was concerned, the period of history that began on January 20, 1969, was marked by continuation of the uncertainty and suspense of the 1968 period although things looked as though perhaps they might begin to settle down by the middle of the summer of 1969. The pattern of settlement looked far better for OEO and the War on Poverty than might have been expected at the time of the Republican election victory. President Nixon initially proposed a continuation of the Economic Opportunity Act unchanged for two years (although, his manpower proposals made subsequently would in effect amend the Act, and much for the worse). In any case, the initial OEO proposal was for a renewed Act with a first-year appropriation of $2 billion. This looked no worse than might have been expected from a continuation of the old Administration although the fate of the bill was uncertain as a bipartisan group of Representatives, led by Mrs. Green and Mr. Quie attempted to turn most of the program over to the states.

The effect of the delay, uncertainty, and ambiguity on Community Action, the key operating program remaining with OEO after the delegation of Job Corps and Head Start, was not clear but presumably not good. As noted, Community Action with capital letters merged into the overall OEO structure and disappeared as a separate entity, but the principle of community action remained. Rumsfeld remained in favor of independent community action, but OEO had not yet won the battle over independence from elected city governments. Secretary of Housing and Urban Development Romney continued to try to bring local Community Action under the final authority of the mayors, but the parallel delay, uncertainty, and ambiguity in his department meant that by the summer of 1969 the battle was a standoff resembling the war between El Salvador and Honduras. But local Community Action was certain to be weakened by the Manpower bill and the Green-Quie attack, and the delay and uncertainty was likely to move the local authorities away from Sundquist's middle-way model of agencies that were "respected . . . aggressive, even militant, but with a quality of leadership and administrative competence to match." Instead the tendency was toward the less effective extremes of "innocuous" agencies or "outcasts — those that had not been able to match their militancy with a leadership and competence that compelled respect." Since Community Action is the third leg of the Income Maintenance–Manpower–Community Action triad, the deterioration would be a serious one.

And in the final crucial area related to the antipoverty effort, the fight against discrimination, the Nixon Administration seemed also to be backing off. The first sign came in the early days of the Administration, when the Department of Defense refused to carry through on the Johnson administration's effort to withhold contracts from certain textile firms until their Southern mills carried out far more effective antidiscrimination programs. The Nixon Department of Defense acted so hastily that it forgot even to notify the Department of Labor, with which it shared responsibility. Throughout the first year of the Administration there seemed apparent further retreats in such fields as school discrimination and voting rights. It may be that these retreats were more apparent than real. But it may also be that Senator Strom Thurmond, to whom these movements were thought to be a response, would not easily be put off by mere motions in the direction of Yankee retreat.

In any case, the picture presented was one of withdrawal in the fight against racial discrimination. Together with the attempted withdrawal in the manpower area of the War on Poverty, this could mean virtual abandonment of the equal opportunity objective of the antipoverty effort, and as suggested previously the social consequences of such reversal could be extremely serious. The Negative Income Tax proposal is a breakthrough, but it is a breakthrough against low-income poverty. The real social dynamite is within the portion of the minority groups already above the poverty line, who will not be helped by the proposed income maintenance program. If they find the political and social progress of the last few years reversed by weakening of the antidiscrimination effort at the same time that the manpower program is redirected away from them once more, trouble is on the way.

Nonetheless, the prevailing and final note of this chapter and book must be optimistic. With its income maintenance proposals, the Nixon administration has made a major move in the War on Poverty. As the Administration gains bureaucratic wisdom with experience in office, those moves that now appear to be in the wrong direction perhaps may be reversed. Or perhaps even they are in the right direction, and I am not yet far enough removed from the fray to comprehend the subtleties of this new phase of the old struggle.

List of Acronyms
and
Abbreviations

AFDC	Aid to Families with Dependent Children
AFDC-UP	Aid to Families with Dependent Children — Unemployed Parents
CAA	Community Action Agency
CAP	Community Action Program
CCC	Civilian Conservation Corps
CDGM	Child Development Group of Mississippi
CEP	Concentrated Employment Program
GAO	General Accounting Office
GNP	Gross National Product
HEW	Department of Health, Education and Welfare
HUD	Department of Housing and Urban Development
IRS	Internal Revenue Service
JOBS	Job Opportunities in the Business Sector
JOPS	Job Opportunities in the Public Sector
MAP	Mississippi Action for Progress
MDTA	Manpower Development and Training Act
MES	More Effective Schools (New York City)
NAB	National Alliance of Businessmen
NYC	Neighborhood Youth Corps
OAA	Old Age Assistance
OEO	Office of Economic Opportunity

R&D	Research and Demonstration
RMC	Resource Management Corporation
RPP&E	Research, Plans, Program and Evaluation (OEO)
SBA	Small Business Administration
SMSA	Standard Metropolitan Statistical Area
SWAFCA	Southwest Alabama Farmers Cooperative Association
VISTA	Volunteers in Service to America

Index